The Little Mac Book

FOURTH EDITION

Robin Williams

Peachpit Press
Berkeley ▾ California

The Little Mac Book fourth edition
© 1990, 1991, 1993, 1995 by Robin Williams
Interior illustrations © 1995 by John Grimes
Photo-illustration by John Tollett; original photo by Alan Bartl.

Peachpit Press
2414 Sixth Street
Berkeley, California 94710
510.548.4393
510.548.5991 fax

Peachpit Press is a division of Addison-Wesley Publishing Company.

ISBN 1-56609-149-7

0 9 8 7 6 5 4 3
Printed and bound in the United States of America

To my mother, Patricia Williams,
who made it possible,
and to my father, Gerald Williams,
who would have been proud.

Acknowledgments

So many thanks to **John Grimes** for his delightful illustrations; to **Jenifer Blakemore** for her outstanding work in editing and proofing up against such a deadline; to **John Tollett** for his thoughtful deeds that helped me get through to the deadline; and to my kids, **Ryan, Jimmy,** and **Scarlett,** for putting up with it all ("but," they say, "did we have a choice?").

John Grimes, who illustrated this edition, wishes to thank **Robin Williams** for her inspiration, and **Robin Chin** for her art direction, patience, love, and encouragement.

**We are confronted
with insurmountable
opportunities.**

Pogo
— Walt Kelly

CONTENTS

Part One   the basics

Part Two   beyond the basics

Part Three   extras

Part Four   what does it all mean?

READ ME FIRST

I hope you were warned that this little computer is addictive. It pulls you in. It has you inventing work for yourself just so you can use it. It creates an attitude that makes you feel like you're having fun while being productive—what a concept.

This book is a direct path to the essentials of operating the computer so you can get straight to the fun, I mean *work,* without wasting too much time diddling around trying to figure it out. There's not much technical information here because most of us don't need it or want it; you don't have to know how to fly the plane to take a vacation in Rio.

This book used to be very little. It's gotten bigger because the Macintosh has gotten more complex. The Mac is still the easiest and most empowering computer to use, but it is a fact that there are some things that are now a little more confusing than they used to be. And in these days everyone is in a rush and no one has time to do anything luxurious like spend time learning how to use a new computer, so these confusing features can be very frustrating. I know—you want to get straight to work.

My Suggestion

I suggest you start with the Tutorial. It will walk you through just what you need to know to get up and running and on your way, telling you specifically which parts of the book to read. The rest of the book you can read another time—pick up the book while you're waiting for a document to come out the printer, open it when you realize there is something specific you don't quite understand, browse through it while waiting for the coffee to drip. You see, if you read this book all the way through, many of the tidbits of information won't get absorbed the first time around. You need to let a certain amount of information sink in before you can absorb other bits. And many solutions just won't make sense until you've had the problem.

Skip over anything that doesn't make sense right away. That's one of the most wonderful things about the Mac—you can bumble along for a long time on a surprisingly small amount of information. When your brain is ready to absorb more, come back to the parts that didn't make sense the first time around.

Whenever you come across a term you are not familiar with, check the index. It will refer you to the page where that term is defined. Really—I spent an inordinate amount of time on the index so you would be able to find an explanation for every term in this book.

After all, I do want you to have fun and take advantage of this new concept in productivity as you, too, become addicted.

Quizzes There are quizzes at the end of each chapter. As a teacher, I always give "open book, open mouth" quizzes. I do believe you are more likely to remember the right answer *if you write down the right answer,* no matter how you discovered it. And you're more likely to have fun discovering the answer if there is less stress involved in the taking of the quiz. So lighten up, relax, enjoy your new computer!

p.s. *In this edition I assume you are using some version of System 7 (see right). If you are still using System 6, check with Peachpit Press for a copy of the second edition of* The Little Mac Book, *which includes information on both System 6 and System 7.*

 If you see this symbol in the upper right of your menu bar, you are using, also called "running," System 7 or 7.1.

 If you see this symbol in the upper right of your menu bar, plus the time, you are running System 7.5.

These three characters are giving you clues! Watch for them.

Important or interesting tip.

Technical info. You might want to come back later.

Serious technical info! You can probably ignore this forever!

TUTORIAL

If you're new to your Mac, I suggest you start here. This tutorial follows a logical pattern that I have found to be successful in my classes (but it's not meant to be completed in one day!). These steps skip all over the book—I apologize for the hopping around you'll have to do, but you really shouldn't read everything about windows or the mouse or whatever at once. You need to know just enough to feel comfortable, then come back later for more. When you get overloaded, turn off the computer and go to bed.

After you've finished the brief tutorial, spend a few weeks working on your Mac. Then come back to the book and read the rest of it. You'll not only find a great number of tips and tricks, but you'll find that you can actually absorb the rest of the information.

Don't Be Limited You might think, in your eagerness to get right into a program and start creating something, that you want to skip all these dumb little exercises at the Desktop, like making windows smaller and larger, copying blank folders onto disks. But trust me. It's too easy to turn on the computer, find the button for your program, and go right into it. But then you're limited. You won't have complete control over your computer. Some things will always confuse you. You'll never be a Power User (your Goal in Life, right?).

Quick Start But for the person who wants to instantly create, save, print, and quit, the steps are quite easy:

- ▾ **Open** your word processing program (or other program of your choice): double-click on its icon.
- ▾ **Save** the new document: from the File menu, choose "Save As...." Name the file and click "Save."
- ▾ **Create** something: start typing.
- ▾ **Print** the document: go up to the File menu and choose "Print...." Click "OK" in all the boxes.
- ▾ **Quit:** go back to the File menu and choose "Quit."

This is the same basic process you will go through in any application—it's truly that easy. But to be powerful—ahhh, that takes a little more time.

System 7 or 7.5? You might need to know whether you are "running" System 7 or 7.1, as opposed to System 7.5. Look in the upper right corner of your screen. Which of these pictures do you see?

If you see this symbol in the upper right of your screen, you are using, also called "running," System 7 or 7.1.

This is called the Help menu.

If you see this symbol in the upper right of your screen, plus the time, you are running System 7.5.

This is called the Guide menu.

System 7.5 has a great *online* tutorial, "online" meaning it is right there inside your computer. I strongly recommend you spend some time walking through it—besides being informative, it is a wonderful example of the kind of animated, interactive presentation the Mac is capable of. To get to the tutorial, you have to use the mouse and menus, which you might not know how to do yet! Ask someone to help you, if necessary!

System 7.5 Online Tutorial

▼ Use the mouse to position the pointer directly on top of the question mark in the upper right corner of your screen. Press the mouse button down. Keep holding it down and slide the mouse down the screen until the command "Macintosh Tutorial" turns black (as shown in the example to the right). When it is black, let go of the mouse button. The tutorial will appear.

▼ **On a Performa,** the first part of the tutorial is in the Launcher (shown below). Use the mouse to position the pointer directly on the "Learning" button, then click the mouse button. Next click on the "Performa Tutorial" button.

When you're done with the first part, you can choose "Tutorial Part 2" from the Guide menu, or click its button on the Launcher.

If you already put away the Launcher, go get it: From the Apple menu, slide down to the Control Panels item, then out to "Launcher." (The Guide menu only has Part 2 of the Tutorial.)

Click here when you want to put the Launcher away.   *Click here to view the tutorial buttons.*

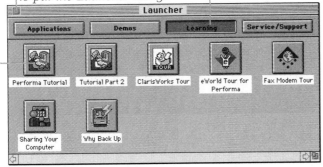

Click once on this button to "launch" (start) the tutorial. Notice the button to its right is Part 2 of the tutorial.

At Ease — If you are using At Ease, this tutorial won't make any sense to you—the Quick Start steps are about all you can do because At Ease puts a "shell" over the regular Macintosh interface. I suggest you disable it (if you're not in a school lab) while you work through the tutorial.

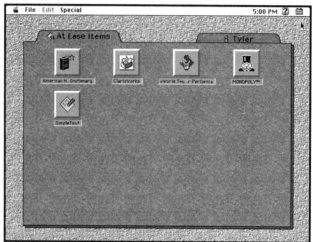

This is the At Ease "shell" that prevents you (or your children or a lab full of students) from getting to the rest of the Mac.

If you are using System 7.5 and you want to disable At Ease temporarily, do this:

▼ From the Special menu, choose "Go To At Ease Setup."

▼ Click the "Off" button, next to the little picture of a Mac.

▼ From the File menu, choose "Quit," *or* press Command Q.

▼ From the Special menu, choose "Restart."

▼ **To turn At Ease back on:** from the Apple menu, choose Control Panels. Choose "At Ease Setup." Click the "On" button. Quit. Restart.

If you are using System 7.0 or 7.1 and you want to disable At Ease temporarily, you must first get to the Finder. To get there, you have to know the password. If you don't know the password, find someone who does. If you can't find someone, you can't get there.

▼ From the File menu, choose "Go To Finder." Type the password. Click "OK."

▼ Once you are at the Finder, use the Apple menu and choose "Control Panels."

▼ Double-click on the control panel called "At Ease Setup." Click the "Off" button. Quit. Restart.

So here are my recommendations on what you should spend time doing if your time is very limited. Actually, this is a good way to start even if you have lots of time; there is so much information to be absorbed that it works best to absorb a little now, then come back for more later. It also helps to run into a few problems, because then when you discover the solution, the solution makes much more sense.

I'll explain a task you need to know and tell you which pages have detailed information.

❖ Read the first chapter on Ks, megs, and disks. C'mon—it will only take a couple of minutes and it will make everything else much clearer. And people will be impressed when you start tossing around terms like "500 meg hard disk."

❖ You've probably already done this, but just in case you haven't, learn how to turn on your computer. Read the first several paragraphs of Chapter 2, page 26.

❖ What you see when you turn on the Macintosh is called the Desktop. It is also called the Finder because the software program that runs the Desktop is the Finder. The Desktop is kind of like home base. It would be a good idea to read Chapter 4, but **skip** the section on "Hierarchy and the Desktop Level" for now, and come back later for the section "Clean Up the Desktop."

❖ If you have never used a mouse before, read Chapter 3. Particularly take note of the hot spot of the pointer, and don't forget the part about how my terminology for "press" and "press-and-drag" differs from what you will commonly read in other documentation. (My terms are more accurate, of course.) If you don't have a trackball, **skip** that section, and you can come back later to figure out how to clean the mouse.

Start Here

If you're using a Performa, close the Launcher before you start this tutorial. Just click in the little close box, shown on page 3.

**Read a
few things first**

Using the mouse Practice using your **mouse:**

- Click **once** on items (icons) you see on the screen, such as the trash can and the hard disk icon at the top right. Notice the icons change color when you click once on them. (If you are using a Performa, don't click once on anything in the "Launcher" window, which you should have closed.)

Hard Disk

Your hard disk icon may look a little different.

- **Double-click** on the hard disk icon or the trash can. Notice you must position the very tip of the pointer on the picture itself, not on the name. Notice also that it takes a very quick click-click or the computer thinks it is two single clicks. And you must hold the mouse very still between the clicks.

- Point to the menu bar across the top of the screen. **Press** (press and hold the button down) on any name in the menu to see the list of menu commands. There are eight items in the menu bar—check out all of them! (Yes, the apple has a menu, as well as the two tiny icons on the far right.) Don't choose any menu commands at this moment.

Menus and commands Read the first two-and-a-half pages in Chapter 5 about **menus** and **how to choose commands.** You can read the rest of the chapter next week. Practice using your mouse to check out the menus, but be careful what you choose!

- Press on any menu and slide down the list—this is a **press-and-drag**. Notice that some menu commands are black and some are grey. As you slide across the black items, the entire line highlights.

  When choosing one of these menu commands, don't click! Just let go! Really. This is not just a suggestion, it is a rule that will prevent trouble later. Be conscious about it—make sure you are not *clicking* in any menu.

Use some of the **desk accessories.** Read the pages mentioned and follow the directions. This will help you feel more comfortable with the mouse, with choosing menu items, and with customizing your computer. If you press on the *name* of the open desk accessory you can drag it around the screen. To put it away, click in the little box in the upper left of the accessory.

- **Alarm clock** (page 204). System 7.0 or 7.1 only. Change the time. Set the alarm for about ten minutes from now. After it goes off, turn off the alarm.

- **Calculator** (page 206). Click the mouse to do the numbers, and use the numeric keypad also.

- Take a look at **Chooser** (page 206). If your computer is brand new, you'll come back here before you print for the first time. If someone has already printed from this Mac, don't choose another printer (don't click on any icons)!

- Come back to the **Control Panels** another day.

- **Key Caps** (page 208). This is a very important feature to know and understand, but don't worry about getting the whole concept now—just take a look at it, perhaps choose new fonts from the Key Caps menu. You will use it again later when you work in the word processor.

- **Note Pad** (page 210). Make some notes to yourself.

- **Puzzle** (page 210). This is really fun. Don't bother right now about customizing the puzzle.

- **Scrapbook** (page 212). For now, just read about it and take a look at it.

Viewing windows

Check out the different ways to **view a window.** Read page 61 about what *is* a window, and pages 63–65 about viewing windows. If you do not see a window on your screen at the moment, double-click on the icon (the picture) of your hard disk, the top picture on the upper right of your screen. Check out each of the views you have in your View menu.

Return the window view to "By Icon" so you can follow the next few steps. When you are done, you can turn the view into whatever method you prefer to work in. Everything you learned while the window was showing icons will still apply when you view as a list.

Icons

Read about icons on pages 79–87. Even if you don't see too many icons at the moment, keep the general concept in mind of what they are telling you, of how rich they are in visual clues. Don't double-click on anything except folder icons at the moment. You can open the System Folder on your hard disk and open other folders in there. Keep these things in mind:

- Folder icons always open to show you their contents in a window.

- Document icons always open the application they were created within and then display the document.

- Application icons always open to a clean, blank page. *or* to an *option* of opening a clean, blank page.

Taxes

It's always safe to double-click on folders.

Where's Chico?

If you double-click on a document, you will open the application it was created in.

(If you accidentally find yourself in an application, go up to the File menu and choose "Quit.")

PageMaker 5.0

Double-click on an application to open a new, blank page.

Learn all about the windows. *Every application you will ever use will have windows in it,* so it's good to get to know them now. Read Chapter 7. Pick out all those parts to a window. Go through the list and use each part:

- Resize the window.
- Move the window.
- Zoom the window large and small. Hold down the Option key (near the Spacebar) and click the zoom box. What's the difference?
- Open another folder; now you should see at least two windows. Which window is active (very important!)? How do you make another window active? What's the point of active windows anyway? *Be sure you can answer these questions!*
- Try all three methods of using the scroll bars when the window is sized small.
- Close the window using the close box.
- Open the folder again, using the menu command this time (*select* the folder first). Then close it using the menu. (Which menu is it in? You will always find the "Open" command in the same menu in every application).

Use the keyboard commands to do some of those tasks you just used the mouse for. Read page 49, "Keyboard Command Shortcuts." Using the keyboard shortcuts is a sign of growing up. The trick to making a keyboard shortcut work is that you must **first** select the item you want to affect. For instance, if you want to open a folder, first click once on the folder to select it, *then* press Command O.

Do each of these things using a keyboard shortcut:

- Open a window.
- Close a window.
- Select every item in a window. (To deselect them, click in any white space.)

**Folders,
backing up,
and the trash**

This is a list of several basic Desktop tasks you need to learn because you will be doing them everyday.

- Read pages 93–94 about folders. Make a new folder. (What is the keyboard shortcut?!) Name your new folder.

- Make a duplicate of this new folder: click once on the folder to select it, then find the command. Which menu is it in, and what is the keyboard shortcut? Change the name of this folder (page 95).

- Read pages 95–96. Put the second folder into the first folder. Take the second folder *out* of the first folder. You will be doing a lot of putting things into and taking things out of folders. It's exactly the same as putting items into manila folders in your office.

- If you have a new floppy disk, insert it. (If you don't have a new one, insert any one). If the floppy is new, initialize it (page 20).

- Backup your work! You should do this to every document you want to keep. Read page 102. Copy the first folder you created onto the floppy disk. *Now this floppy is your backup of that important file!* In case the file on your hard disk gets lost or trashed or your hard disk dies, you have this extra copy.

- Use the trash can (read page 111). Throw away the first folder you made. Empty the trash (page 113).

- Put your second practice folder in the trash. Oh no! That was a mistake! Open the trash can and put the folder back (read the last paragraph on page 112). Be cool—use the "Put Away" keyboard shortcut.

- Change your window view to one of the lists, such as "By Name." Read page 97 about the *outline mode.* Practice expanding and compressing folders. This is just another way to look at the contents of folders, instead of opening each one to a window.

- In icon view, move the icons around: just press on them and drag. Rearrange the icons in a window.

Open a **word-processing** application (double-click on its icon). You surely have at least TeachText or preferably SimpleText on your hard disk. Everything you learn in a word processor will apply to every other program you ever use. Any word processor is a great place to practice the most basic and valuable skills; once you feel comfortable here, you can bumble your way through any other sort of program.

Word processing

- Read pages 121–127 in the Typing chapter. Type several paragraphs and practice using the menus, moving the insertion point, fixing typos (read "Delete" on page 122), selecting text and changing its font and style and size. *Remember, all typing and backspacing starts wherever the **insertion point** is flashing, not where the I-beam or the pointer is pointing!*

- After you've finished several paragraphs and feel comfortable with the features you've been practicing, read pages 128–130 about the **Clipboard. Cut** some of your text. **Copy** some of your text. **Paste** the text somewhere else. Paste it in again. Make sure you can predict *what* will be pasted and *where* it will appear. Use the keyboard shortcuts for Cut, Copy, Paste, and Undo.

- If you are feeling very confident, try using some of the **special characters,** such a ¢ and • and ©. Read page 131 and also page 208 (both pages talk about Key Caps). If you're really feeling sassy, try typing "résumé" with the accent marks (see page 133).

- **Save** your witty and intelligent report. Read pages 135–137. Eventually you should return to pages 140 and 141 and study them, but right now just go ahead and save your document: From the File menu, choose "Save As...," type a title for your document, then click the Save button. (After you lose a few documents you will appreciate pages 140 and 141.)

  If you are working on a *Performa* with the Launcher running, your document will automatically be saved into the Documents folder; see page 342. If you are working on any Mac with *At Ease* running, you will probably be forced to save onto a floppy disk.

Printing

Now you need **to print your document.**

You should just be able to get the Chooser from the Apple menu, click on the picture of your printer on the left, click on either the name of your printer or the printer port icon on the right, then close the Chooser and print. If it doesn't go this smooth, you might want to have someone help you through this because it can be quite confusing.

- **If no one has ever printed from this computer before,** you need to read pages 144–145 and use the Chooser to tell your Mac which printer to use. Once the Mac has printed to a printer, you never need to go back to the Chooser again unless you need to switch printers.

- Read pages 150–153 and just follow the steps 1–5. Basically all you're doing is choosing "Print" from the File menu and clicking the "OK" buttons.

- You need to quit the application if you are done for the day. Save the document again before you quit: just use the keyboard shortcut Command S. Then from the File menu, choose "Quit." The Quit command is always the very last item, and the keyboard shortcut is always Command Q. You really should read Chapter 17 on Closing and Quitting so you understand the difference between closing and quitting.

Other Very Important Features

After you quit an application, you will usually end up back at the Desktop. There are several **very important features** you can learn that will make you the life of any party. Here are suggestions for specific things you need to be in control of:

- Learn how to use Find File. Read pages 261–264 and experiment with it. Later, another day, read the rest of the chapter and learn how to do more complex searches (when you know what you're searching for).

Control Panels

- Learn how to use your control panels. Read Chapter 24. Check out each control panel. Most of the ones you have will be explained in Chapter 24.

Aliases

- Learn how to use aliases. Read pages 253–255. I guarantee you will find aliases to be one of the greatest features of organization and convenience on the Mac.

- Learn how to take advantage of your **Apple menu.** Read the entire Chapter 23, even if customizing the menu doesn't quite make sense yet.

Apple Menu

- Read the the chapter on **visual clues.** Absorb that information and keep your eyes open for other visual clues. Teach them to others. Find at least five more visual clues yourself.

Visual clues

- So you don't have to use Find File twenty times a day, learn how to **save** a document directly **into the folder** of your choice. It is critical that you have power over where your documents go when you save them. After you start to feel pretty competent, study the dialog boxes an pages 140–141, and read Chapter 29 on **Navigating,** page 285. Learning to navigate (getting yourself where you want to go and finding files through the dialog boxes) is one of the most important things to know, and seems to be one of the most difficult concepts to grasp.

Saving and navigating
Also read Chapter 29 on Navigating.

- After you've gotten several "out of memory" messages or had applications "unexpectedly quit" or suddenly disappear, read Chapter 30, called Very Important Information. It discusses the difference between hard disk space and memory and virtual memory, how to avoid running out of memory, and where to find those lost applications.

Very important information

- Read *The Mac is not a typewriter.*

p.s.

User Groups!

One of the best things you can do for yourself is join your local user group! Macintosh users have a history of joyfully sharing information, and a user group is an incredible source of help and support. To find the user group in your area, call this Apple number: **800-538-9696, press 3, then press 1.** *You will be asked to enter your zip code, and you will get the phone number of your user group's Apple Ambassador.*

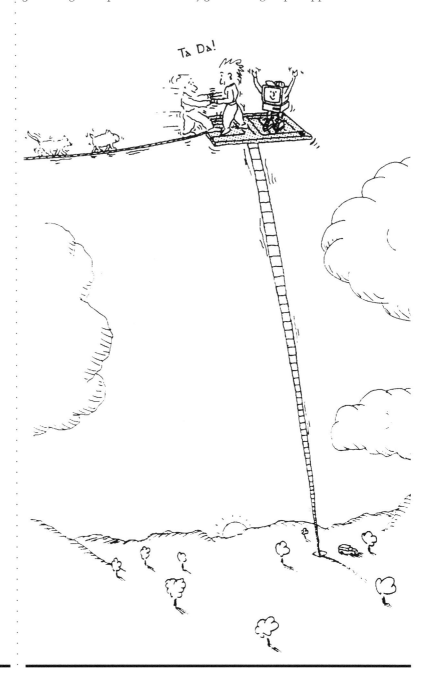

PART ONE

This section describes the things you need to know to get up and running on your Macintosh, from starting up to shutting down. This section actually tells you more than you *need* to know—there are lots of little tips and tricks embedded in these chapters, tips and tricks that may even impress your power user friends.

Remember, though, if you're in a hurry, start with the Tutorial. The Tutorial gets you up and running in the least amount of time. Then you can come back later and read all the parts you missed. If you come across terms you don't understand, look them up in the index!

Ks, MEGS, AND DISKS

People who've been working with the Mac for a while start tossing around jargon like, "It's a small file, only 230K," or "Hey, *my* Mac has a 550 meg hard disk," and people who are not familiar with the Mac feel dumb because it all sounds so esoteric and we're sure we'll never be able to understand all this sophisticated computer stuff and besides we don't want to know all that technical stuff anyway, we just want to learn how to run the darn thing. Well, as far as technical stuff goes, all most of us need to know is the machine is magic. Pure, simple, magic. Like an airplane.

Knowing the difference between a bit and a byte and a K and a meg, though, will help you understand your computer, computer advertising, your applications and documents, memory and hard disk, and your friends.

IF YOU CRACK OPEN A FLOPPY DISK YOU'LL RUIN IT.

INSIDE IS A FLOPPY PLASTIC SHEET THAT RECORDS THE ELECTRONIC IMPULSES THAT COMPRISE YOUR DOCUMENTS.

Bits

0 1

Each one of these electronic messages is one bit.

Actually, the computer isn't that smart; it can only count to one. Remember in school when we learned the binary system, which we have now completely forgotten, except that for some reason we could only count from zero to one and we had to use exponential notation? Well, the Mac uses a binary system: it counts zero and one—zero means Off and one means On. It sends these little electronic messages, each a series of Off and On. And each one of those little messages is a **bit.**

Bytes

01000001

This byte represents the letter A.

Now, one little bit doesn't tell the computer a whole lot, so it strings together a bunch of bits to create a more important message: eight bits, such as **01000001,** make one **byte.** As you can see in the column to the left, one byte of information is still rather limited—it takes a lot of bytes to create a document.

Kilobytes

Approximately 1000 Bytes equals 1 Kilobyte.

So a bunch of bytes is grouped together and called a **kilobyte.** You would think that a kilobyte would be a thousand bytes, yes? No. Since the computer can only count to one, the closest it can get to 1000 in its binary system with exponential notation is 1024. But we generally round it off and say there are about 1000 bytes in a kilobyte. And kilobytes are the **K**s everyone talks about.

How do Ks figure in real life? Kilobytes are what disk space and file/document size are measured in; the larger and more sophisticated the document or the software program, the greater the number of K it will occupy on the disk. (Don't worry—we're getting to *megabytes.*)

You've probably seen the nice little 3.5″ **floppy disks** that the Mac uses. A disk can store information for running the computer, for operating the programs, for saving the documents you create. Originally the Mac could only deal with a single-sided disk (one that took information on only one side of itself), but unless you have a very old machine with only a single-sided floppy drive, you won't be using single-sided disks.

Floppy Disks

A **double-sided disk** holds about **800K** (kilobytes) of data. Four pages of double-spaced typewritten text takes about 6K of disk space; therefore, you can get about *500 pages* of text on one disk (leaving some room for the messages the disk has to send to the computer). Spreadsheets, graphics, and other complex info take up a lot more space, of course.

Disk Capacity

More common now, though, are the **high-density double-sided disks,** which hold about **1.4MB** (megabytes, which are bigger than kilobytes; we'll get to megabytes in a minute) of data. These disks look just like regular double-sided disks, except they usually have the letters HD somewhere on them, and they have an extra hole with no tab to close it. That extra hole tells the Macintosh that the disk is high-density. Only Macs with an "FD-HD" drive (floppy disk, high density), also known as a "SuperDrive" (which includes any Mac since the SE30, including Classics and Performas) can read these high-density disks. Some people may suggest putting a piece of tape over the extra hole to trick older Macs into reading the disk, but that almost always eventually ends in a disk failure. Don't risk your valuable work.

High-density disks have an extra hole on the right side of the disk.

Why is the disk called a floppy disk when it's not floppy? Actually, it *is* floppy. If you slide over that metal end you'll see the floppy disk inside. Don't touch it! It's full of tiny messages that your oily fingers or sharp nails can destroy. Keep your disks away from heat: they'll warp just like a record album when left in your hot car. And keep them away from magnets—a magnet will destroy all the data on the disk. So don't attach them to your refrigerator; don't store them near your telephone or stereo or any other electronic device; don't keep them in your purse with your automatic camera; and don't pile them on top of your magnetic paper clip holder.

Caring for Floppy Disks

I also recommend you don't keep disks in those little plastic bags they often come in; the plastic can build up static electricity which has the potential to destroy your precious data.

Initializing a New Disk

When you buy your floppy disks, they might be **initialized,** or *formatted,* already. That means the disks have already been prepared so a Macintosh computer can "read" them. If they are already formatted, make sure the box says they are formatted for a Macintosh!

Some disks are **unformatted** because other kinds of computers also use these handy little things, and they can be initialized for several types. So when you first insert an uninitialized, or unformatted disk, the Mac will ask you to name the disk. You may see a warning that you are about to erase all the information on the disk, but since it's blank, so what. When you finally click OK, the Mac will lay down the formatting it needs to store all the valuable info you will be giving it.

Locking a Disk

This disk is unlocked.

It is possible to **lock** a floppy disk. When a disk is locked, whoever is using it cannot change anything on it, nor can other files be saved onto it. To lock a disk, find the little black tab in the corner. You'll notice you can slide it up or down.

▼ When the tab covers the hole, the disk is unlocked.

▼ When you can see through the hole, the disk is locked.

Some disks have two holes, but only one has a tab that can be moved. The second hole indicates that the disk is a high-density disk (see the previous page) and has nothing to do with locking.

Hard Disks

A **hard disk** is actually a large, *hard disk,* a platter rather than a floppy piece of film. (Actually, it is several platters.) In principle it works the same as a floppy disk, but it can hold much more data. The hard disk itself may be installed inside your Mac, or it may be a separate unit encased in a sturdy plastic box. Or you might have both.

There are also hard disks on *cartridges* that you can insert into a "removable" disk drive (meaning you can take the hard disk out whenever you want), sort of like how you insert a video into your VCR, so you can have a collection of cartridge hard disks.

In any form, a hard disk is a storage container, like a filing cabinet, that holds all your software programs and documents, and holds the *System Folder* that starts your machine. Hard disks allow you to store your files all on one disk instead of on a lot of separate floppies, which makes it *much* easier and faster to work.

All Macintoshes are now built with hard disks because they are essential. The bigger your hard disk, the more information you can store on it.

In fact, a hard disk holds so much data that it's not even measured in kilobytes; it's measured in **megabytes,** also known as **megs** or **MB.** You've already figured out that one megabyte is 1024 kilobytes, right? Right.

Megabytes
Approximately 1000K equals one megabyte (1MB).

Now, 1024 kilobytes (one megabyte) is more than what *one* normal floppy disk can hold. Hard disks come in various sizes, able to store from 80 megs to 250 to 500 to 880 megs of information, and they're getting bigger all the time. So a small hard disk, say 80 megs, has as much storage space as *100-plus floppy disks!* You can load all kinds of applications onto your hard disk and create all kinds of documents. As the software applications get more and more sophisticated, they take up more and more space, and already there are applications that just can't be used without a hard disk.

In fact, **gigabytes** are becoming commonplace—gigabyte hard disks, gigabyte graphic files. A gigabyte, as you might guess by now, is approximately 1,000 megabytes.

Gigabytes!

You often see advertisements for Macs that describe the computer with numbers like these: **8/250** or **12/500.** The second number in these **specifications** indicates the size of the *hard disk,* in megabytes. The first number indicates how much *memory* is in the computer (see page 298 for an explanation of memory).

Specifications

So if you see a Mac advertised as "Mac 12/500," it means there are 12 megabytes of RAM (memory) and a 500 megabyte hard disk. The bigger, the better.

Making Backup Disks

Always **backup** your software applications. As soon as you buy a new application, make a copy of all the disks (see pages 101–105) and **use the copy** (the *copy* is your backup); keep the original disks safe in a clean, dust-free place. That way if a catastrophe happens to befall your application that you paid so much money for, you always have an extra copy. Software companies, you know, won't give you a new copy if you destroy yours.

Backup any document that is important to you

Also and even more important, always make sure you have a current backup of *everything* on your hard disk—all your documents you have so laboriously created. A hard disk can "crash" and leave no survivors. Now, I know that in everything you ever read about the Mac you will be warned to backup regularly, but you won't really do it until you have experienced your own catastrophe of considerable dimension. As you know, "Experience is what you get when you don't get what you want," and "Experience teaches us to recognize a mistake when we've made it again."

At the end of each working day, *or more often if it is really important,* make copies (page 102) onto disks of everything you created or modified that day. Then label those disks! Never work longer without backing up than you could stand to re-do the work. That is, if you're working on a catalog and the last time you created a backup copy was three hours ago, would you mind re-creating those three hours? Could you? Then back it up.

A hard disk comes with a backup application—be sure to check it out. If you are in a situation where there are massive amounts of information to backup regularly, check into those applications designed specifically for large-scale, automatic backing up.

Rule Number 3

Backup Often. Like everyday. *(No, you didn't miss Rules 1 and 2— Rule 1 is on page 137; Rule 2 is on page 126.)*

Below is a diagram for putting the **label on your disk.** At first it may seem as if this diagram is telling you to write the information upside down, but once you start storing disks in a box of some sort, you will realize that writing on them as shown below makes the words upside right when they are stored.

Be sure to name every file that is stored on this disk, with the date it was last updated. And give the files names you will recognize later!

Labeling Your Disks

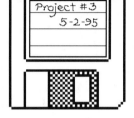

If your label has a colored tab, fold that tab over the top of the disk. You can use the tabs to color-code your filing system (ha — do your organizational skills really go beyond good intentions?). Write the most important information across the top where you will see it easily when the disks are stored in a box.

Write the name of every file on this disk! Always date each file. Really. This will save you much time and occasionally grief.

1. An off-on signal, a 1 or 0, is an electronic signal called a:

. . . .

2. Arrange these in order from smallest to largest:
   megabytes · bits · gigabytes · kilobytes · bytes

. . . .

3. How much storage space is on a high-density floppy disk?

. . . .

4. What is the most important item to keep away from
   floppy disks?

. . . .

5. If you can see through both little holes on a high-density
   floppy disk, is the disk locked or unlocked?

. . . .

6. The initial K stands for:

. . . .

7. The initials MB stand for:

. . . .

8. If you see an ad that states "Macintosh for sale, 16/500,"
   what does the 500 indicate?

. . . .

9. What two things (at least) should go on every disk label?

. . . .

10. Are you going to backup all your important files every day?

. . . .

Answers on page 369.

STARTING UP

This is easy to do—so easy you will be tempted to skip this chapter. At least skim through it, though. The more information you can absorb about the Macintosh, the more power you will have over it.

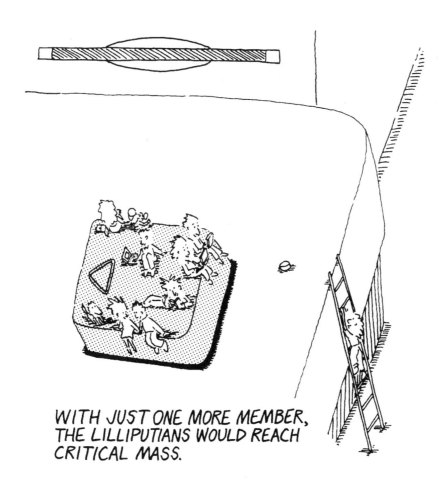

WITH JUST ONE MORE MEMBER,
THE LILLIPUTIANS WOULD REACH
CRITICAL MASS.

Turning It On Depending on what kind of Macintosh you have, the on switch is located in various places. The smaller Macs turn on with a little switch on the back left of the machine (*back,* yes, as in behind the monitor)—admittedly a very inconvenient place. Most of the larger, modular Macs are turned on with the big key with the triangle on it. This key is at the top of the standard keyboard (and it is useless for everybody else), or in the upper far right corner on the extended keyboard. On some models, like the LC, you may have to press two buttons on the back of the monitor. Don't let all this confuse you, though. Even though you'll forget half the other stuff in this book, once you figure out how to turn on your computer you probably won't forget it.

Internal hard disk If you have an *internal hard disk* for your machine (which you most surely do if you bought a new Macintosh in the past five years), as soon as you turn it on it will **boot up** from the System on the hard disk. (The term "boot up" or "boot" comes from the idea of pulling itself up by its bootstraps, as the Mac is going into its own System and turning itself on.)

External hard disk If you have an *external hard disk,* that piece of hardware should be turned on first, and then turn on your Mac.

Other switches If your computer has *any other switches* for turning it on, either on top of the monitor or on the keyboard, the switch on the back of the Macintosh must always be turned on as well.

You must have a **System Folder** on your hard disk. The System Folder must have at least two icons in it: the **System** icon and the **Finder** icon (shown to the right). Without those two items in the machine, the Mac can't start itself up; it will spit out any other disks you try to insert and will give you the Sad Mac face.

All Macintoshes now come with the System Folder already installed on your computer, ready to run. This System Folder is such an extremely important item that there is an entire chapter dedicated to it (Chapter 20, page 177). Although you *can* rename the folder, I strongly suggest you don't, just to keep the concept clear. And don't go sticking things in it if you are not absolutely positive they belong there.

The **System** runs the computer, and the **Finder** runs the *Desktop,* which is the first thing you see when you boot your Mac; (see Chapter 4, page 41).

The disk icon that appears on your Desktop in the upper right corner is the **startup disk,** the disk that holds the System Folder that booted (started) the Mac. It is sometimes called the *boot disk.* The icon for the startup disk, or boot disk, will always be the first icon in the upper right corner of your Desktop.

The term **floppy drive** refers to the little slot on the front of your machine where you **insert a floppy disk.** Disks go in the slot with the label-side up (the side that does *not* have the *round* metal piece on it), and the metal end goes in first. (If the box portion of your computer is on its side, then "up" refers to what *would* be up if the box was not sideways. The Macintosh logo on the front gives you a clue as to which side should be up.)

You might have two internal drives, and you might also have an **external floppy drive** (a little box that sits on the side of the computer). You can have a floppy disk in each of these floppy drives, and you can save data onto any disk in any drive.

System Folder

System Folder

System   Finder

Startup disk

Macintosh HD

Inserting a Disk into a Floppy Drive

Installing Your New Software

You may have had your software installed before you brought your computer home, in which case it is already on your hard disk waiting for you. But if not, or if you bought some new software, you may need to **install it yourself.** Piece o' cake. These instructions here, though, are very generic and thus very limited. I can't cover every piece of software, so really the best advice is: **RTFM.** That stands for "Read The Manual." Always make sure the software disk is locked (page 20) before you insert it so you can't change anything.

One-disk software

DeskPaint®

This is a normal-looking, kind-of-pretty, and a-little-fancy application icon.

If your software arrived on **one disk** and there are only one or two "normal-looking" icons on it, you can create a new folder on your hard disk (see page 94) and just copy those files into the new folder (see page 102). What do I mean by "normal-looking"? Well, that's hard to say, isn't it. If the icon is kind of pretty and a little fancy, it is probably normal. If it looks like a monkey wrench or like exploding arrows or if it has an abbreviation after the name like "sea" or "sit" (see below) then the program has probably been **compressed** (squished, to put it crudely) so it could fit onto one disk.

Compressed software

MAD

PlayBall.sea

These are examples of commonly seen "compressed" files.

If you have any clue that the software has been *compressed,* then you need to first copy that compressed file into a new folder on your hard disk (see pages 94–95; the new folder actually has nothing to do with it except to provide a contained place for the related files). Once the compressed file is on your hard disk, double-click on it. It will either open itself up and put files where they belong, or first ask you where you want to store the files. After you un-compress the software, you can throw away the compressed file, if it still exists. You still have the original on the disk.

If your software arrived on **more than one disk,** the disks are probably labeled and one of the labels says something like "Program disk" or "Installer disk" or "Disk 1." Find the one that looks like the first in the series and insert it into the floppy drive. There is probably an icon called "Installer." Double-click that icon and it will install the program for you. It will spit out the disks when ready and tell you which one to put in next. If there is an installer, *use it.* Many installers put various files in various folders in and around the System Folder, besides the main program where you can see it. If there is an installer, chances are great that the program won't even work if you try to just copy the files onto your disk.

Multi-disk software

You will often see a file called **ReadMe** on new software disks. Guess what you should do with that file? Yes, Read It. Just double-click on the icon. The word processing utility called TeachText or SimpleText is often on the disk also, and the ReadMe file opens in one of those. If you have no version at all of TeachText or SimpleText (which would be very surprising), you can open ReadMe files in almost any other word processor. This file contains important information that was discovered too late to put into the manual. Yes, you should also read the manual.

ReadMe files

ReadMe

Often this file is called "Read Me First." Do it.

Installing new fonts (typefaces) is different from installing a software application. Please see the chapter on Fonts, page 185.

Installing new fonts

System and Software Versions

All computer software is constantly being upgraded and updated, making it more efficient, powerful, magical. And sometimes they update software just to fix a *bug* (a minor problem that is not supposed to be there but supposedly they didn't know it was there when they sent it to you). The developers let you know which upgrade you have by labeling it with a **version number.**

How to pronounce version numbers

There is usually a period in the version number, which is pronounced "point." Thus the version 4.2 is pronounced "four point two." The version 5.0 is pronounced "five point oh"; 5.01 is "five point oh one." And 7.0.1 is "seven point oh point one."

How to pronounce document names

But when a file name for a *document* includes a period, the period is pronounced "dot." For instance, a compressed file may be labeled "Brochure.sit" (the "sit" is a common file name *extension* that gives you a clue that the file is compressed). This is pronounced "brochure dot sit." You might name your file "Newsletter.March," which you would pronounce as "Newsletter dot March." The word "March" is an "extension" to the name; the extension makes the document name more precise.

Aside: this "dot" is also true in Internet addresses. When someone tells you their address is "AOL dot com," the dot means "period" and it would be typed like this: aol.com.

Upgrade your System regularly!

As the System upgrades, the software programs are created to work with the particular nuances of the newer System, so it's a good idea (often it's critical) to keep up on both System upgrades and software application upgrades. If you never upgrade the System, eventually you will be severely limited as to the software you can use with your Mac.

You should never have more than one System in the computer. This will invariably end in a "crash." It's not as easy to have more than one System anymore, because the System itself is so big. But until recently many programs and especially game disks arrived on your desk with a System Folder also on the disk. Many people (not you, of course) copied the entire disk onto their hard disk, which means they copied the extra System Folder also. It is still possible to do this if you get older software.

Only One System per Computer!

If you have any suspicion at all that there may be more than one System in your computer, use Find File (Chapter 26) to find it. Remove any extra Systems besides the one that is running your machine (don't worry—you won't be able to trash the one that is running your machine). You should, in fact, remove any extra System Folders, not just the System file itself. You may want to have your power user friend help you do this.

What is a **power user**? A power user is a person who knows more about computers than you do. Well, real power users know a lot. They can throw around terms like "32-bit addressing" and "clean ROMs" and "CPU" and actually have a clue as to what they mean. Power users use all the keyboard shortcuts instead of the mouse, and they load up their computers with all the INITs and cdevs they can find. They get a thrill out of the speed of the SCSI-2 port and debate the advantages of RISC vs. CISC processing. Power users can even use ResEdit without quivering. Everyone should have a power user as a friend.

Power User

CAROL, SORRY TO KEEP CALLING BUT..... REALLY, 3 A.M? SORRY. HEY, WHILE YOU'RE ON THE LINE.... .....CAROL?

1. What is the "boot disk," or "startup disk"?

2. How do you know which icon belongs to the startup disk?

3. Which two files (represented by icons, of course) must be on your hard disk so you can start your Mac?

4. What should you put into the System Folder?

5. Where do you insert a floppy disk?

6. What does RTFM stand for?

7. What should you do with ReadMe files?

8. How would you pronounce this system version: 7.5.1

9. How would you pronounce this file name: LoveLetters.sit

10. How many Systems should there be in your computer?

Answers on page 369.

THE MOUSE

The **mouse,** of course, is that handy little piece of hardware that controls the movement of the cursor on the screen. As you move the mouse across the desk, a pointer moves across the screen in the same direction. In most Macintosh applications, you cannot fully utilize the program without the mouse. A few programs give you the option of doing absolutely everything from the keyboard if you choose; but why learn 450 keyboard commands—isn't that just what we're trying to avoid?

This chapter helps you get familiar with the various ways of using the mouse.

Using the Mouse You'll use the mouse in several different ways. Always, the mouse sits on a flat surface and you roll it around with your hand on top of it, your index finger resting on the *mouse button* (the part that clicks). Do not hold the mouse in the palm of your hand, and don't pick it up and point it at the screen.

Single Click A **single click** is a quick, light touch on the button of the mouse, with the "cursor" (a pointer, an I-beam [page 122] or other shape) located at the spot of your choice on the screen.

> Single-click with the *arrow* on an icon at your Desktop to *select* an icon; single-click with the *I-beam* to *set down an insertion point;* single-click to press a button.

Double Click A **double click** is a quick click-click on the button, again with the cursor located at the appropriate spot on the screen. A double click has to be quick and the mouse must be still, or it will be interpreted as two single clicks.

> Double-click on a file to *open* that file; double-click on a folder to *open* the window for that folder; double-click on a word to *select* that word for editing.

Press A **press** is simply pointing to something and *holding* the mouse button down.

> Press with the pointer on the *menu* to see the commands under that item; press on the arrows in a scroll bar to *scroll* through that window.

This is often misleadingly referred to as "click." You may see directions that tell you to "click" on the menu. They really mean "press" on the menu.

Press-and-Drag **Press-and-drag** means to point to the object or the area of your
(also known, choice, *hold/press the mouse button down, keep it down,* and *drag*
misleadingly, across, then *let go* when you reach your goal.
as click-and-drag)
> Press-and-drag to *choose menu commands;* press-and-drag *to move icons* across the screen; press-and-drag to *select text.*

When you're using the **pointer,** remember that the only part of the pointer that does the trick is the *very* tip, called the "hot spot." So be sure that the extreme point of the arrow is in the area you want to affect.

Pointer

The hot spot . . . . *The tip of the pointer does the trick.*

Some people prefer to use a different "pointing device," such as a joy stick or a **trackball.** The Macintosh **PowerBooks,** the beautiful little laptop Macs, use a trackball. A trackball is like an upside-down mouse—instead of moving the little mouse box around to make the ball roll underneath, you use your fingers to roll the little ball on top around as it sits in the box. Trackballs have buttons to press that act like the button on the mouse. Depending on what kind of trackball you have, you may click the button with a finger or, as seems to be easier on the PowerBook, with your thumb.

Trackballs, PowerBooks

Trackballs are particularly convenient for those people who have to use the mouse backwards. Yes, I have met several people who have to turn the mouse with the tail facing themselves. When they push the mouse to the right, the pointer on the screen moves to the left. If more than one person uses this computer, each person has to turn the mouse around. With a trackball, your idiosyncrasies don't matter.

DON'T TRY THIS AT HOME.

TRACKBALL

Mouse Pad

You've probably seen a **mouse pad,** a small pad to put on your desk to roll the mouse across. The pad has nothing to do with the operation of the mouse, really—the mouse will work just fine without a pad. The purpose of a mouse pad is simply to provide better traction and a clear spot on your desk for the mouse. You can use a book, illustration board, a coaster, or even a piece of smooth paper.

Moving the Mouse *when you've run out of space*

Sometimes you may be **moving the mouse** across the mouse pad or the desk and **run out of space** before the pointer or the I-beam gets where you want it to go. Just do this: Keep your finger on the mouse button, pressing it down. Pick up the mouse, keeping the button down, and move the mouse over to where you have more room. Then just continue on your path.

Mouse Control Panel

Mouse

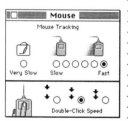

The Mouse *control panel* is the first control panel you should change. You will read about control panels in Chapter 24, but this one is so important I think you should take a look at it as soon as you feel comfortable using the mouse and pulling down menus. *If you are brand-new to your Mac, come back to this page in a couple of days.*

▾ From the Apple menu, choose "Control Panels."
· If you are on System 7.5 and the menu pops out to the side when you choose "Control Panels," slide out and down to "Mouse" to open the Mouse control panel.
· If you are on System 7.0 or 7.1, you will get the Control Panels folder when you choose it from the Apple menu. Double-click on the Mouse control panel to open it.

▾ When the "Mouse Tracking" is set on or near "Slow," you have to move the mouse a long way on your desk to move the pointer across the screen. If you click in the button above "Fast," you only need to move the mouse a short distance to move the pointer across the screen. You can notice the effects immediately.

▾ After you have selected the "Fast" button, click in the *close box* (upper left corner) to put the control panel away. If the Control Panels folder is still open, click in its close box.

The mouse can be **plugged** into any of the ports (plugs) that they fit into, which are all called ADB ports (ADB for Apple Desktop Bus). You'll find a port on the back of the computer (you can't miss it—it's the only one that fits) with a funny little symbol on it (shown to the right). There is also an ADB port on either side of your keyboard. If your computer is too far from your mouse pad, you might want to plug the mouse into the keyboard. The keyboard cable itself can be connected into either side, so if you are left-handed, plug the mouse into the port on the left-hand side of the keyboard.

Connecting the Mouse

Left-handed mousing

Some monitors also have ADB ports around the bottom, making things even easier to connect keyboards and mice.

> Before plugging and unplugging *anything* from your computer, including the mouse or the keyboard, always shut down completely and turn off the power.

Why is it called a mouse? Well, if you grab the cord about four inches from the mouse and hold it at arm's length, squint your eyes and wrinkle your nose, it looks like a dead mouse.

Did You Ask *Why?*

NICE POINT, POP, BUT LIGHTEN UP ON YOUR CLICK.

Cleaning the Mouse

It's important and easy to **keep your mouse clean.** As you're rolling it around you can feel if any cat hairs or dustballs have gotten inside. Take it apart regularly and clean it, following these steps:

1. Take the mouse in your right hand and turn it upside-down.

2. With your thumbs, slide the round wheel to the left. (You may see little symbols on the back of the mouse—an "O" and an "L" for Open and Lock). Sliding the wheel around will open the lid.

3. Flip the mouse back over into your left hand so the lid and the ball fall out into your palm.

4. You can clean the ball with a soft, dry cloth; clean the rollers inside with a cotton swab dipped in rubbing alcohol.

5. When clean, put the ball in your left hand; with your right hand place the mouse on top of the ball and flop your hands over. This places the ball safely into its little cubby.

6. Put the lid back on and twist it to the right, lining up the marker with the "L" for Lock (if you see one).

That's it!

MOUSE WASH

HEALTH TIPS

ROOM LIGHTING BALANCED WITH BRIGHTNESS OF MONITOR

REDUCE REFLECTIONS ON MONITOR BY: 1) CHANGING YOUR POSITION; 2) CHANGING ROOM LIGHTING; AND 3) USING GLARE FILTER

DOWNWARD GAZE ANGLE

MONITOR & KEYBOARD DIRECTLY IN FRONT OF YOU

WRISTS LEVEL WITH FOREARMS

RIGHT HEIGHT

GOOD POSTURE

BACK SUPPORT (ESP. LUMBAR)

FOREARMS USUALLY LEVEL

WRIST RESTS (BUT DON'T "PLANT" WRISTS WHILE TYPING)

COMFORTABLE, SUPPORTIVE, CORRECTLY-ADJUSTED CHAIR

CYBER DUDE

TAKE BREAKS! (USE THESE)

LISTEN TO YOUR BODY, ESPECIALLY THESE AREAS

RECOMMENDED READING: "ZAP! HOW YOUR COMPUTER CAN HURT YOU— AND WHAT YOU CAN DO ABOUT IT" BY DON SELLERS (PEACHPIT PRESS; $12.95)

Would you single-click (**S**), double-click (**D**), press (**P**), or press-and-drag (**P&D**) to accomplish each of the following tasks? Circle the appropriate abbreviation in the margin for each task.

S   D   P   P & D

1. Select an icon (you always select something before you do something to it).

S   D   P   P & D

2. Open a file, such as your word processing document so you can type in it.

S   D   P   P & D

3. Activate a button.

S   D   P   P & D

4. Select a whole word for editing (to change it).

S   D   P   P & D

5. Open a folder to see what's in it.

S   D   P   P & D

6. See what's in a menu.

S   D   P   P & D

7. Choose something from a menu.

Answers on page 369.

DESKTOP AND FINDER

The **Desktop** is what you see on the screen when you first start up your Macintosh. Consistent with the Mac environment that analogizes everything to parts of our real lives, this Desktop works much the same as your desktop at home or in your office: You have desk accessories (under the Apple menu) such as a calculator, a clock, and a note pad. You have a filing cabinet (the disk) that stores all your folders full of information. You have as many file folders as you could possibly want to organize it all. You can put folders inside of folders inside of folders almost *ad infinitum* just like you would organize your hanging files. You even have a trash can. This chapter helps you understand your Desktop, which is critical since you will be seeing it often.

Finder

The **Finder** is the system software that manages the Desktop. The Finder keeps track of all the files you have stored on your Desktop, as well as where you keep your applications and which disk you have stuck in the floppy drive, among other tasks. When you upgrade to a higher System (such as from System 7.0.1 to 7.5.1), you also get a new, upgraded Finder.

Well, What's It Called— the *Desktop* or the *Finder*?

The **Desktop** is the actual place you see, and the **Finder** is what controls and keeps track of the Desktop. But because the two are so closely related and you can't have one without the other, you will hear people interchange the terms as if they were the same thing. That's okay (it has to be okay because that's the way it is). When you hear someone say, "Are you at the Finder?" you will understand that they mean, "Are you at the Desktop?" and vice versa.

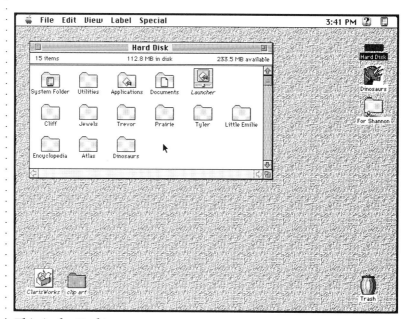

This is the Desktop.

Whenever you "Quit" working in an application, the Mac automatically takes you back to the **Desktop level,** which is kind of like home base. If you don't see "Special" in the menu, *then you are not at the Desktop.*

(Perhaps you didn't actually "Quit," but just "Closed" and you are still in the application, or perhaps you're in some other application that is still open.) To actually get to your Desktop/ Finder, click once on what you see of the Desktop. As soon as you click, you'll notice that your menu will include "Special." If this does not make complete sense to you (this is a test), then you really, really should read the chapter called "Very Important Information." It will make you a happier, more powerful person.

The Desktop as Home Base

It's a good idea to keep your Mac **Desktop organized,** just like you would your office desktop. Create new folders (from the File menu; also see page 94) for each category of information, and store all applicable files in it. If you create a new folder on the hard disk before you begin work in an application, then you can put your new document right into that folder when you *Save* (see page 140). This way, when you come back to the Desktop after working, everything is organized and in its folder so nothing gets misplaced.

Organizing Your Desktop

This is an example of a neatly organized hard disk, using folders-inside-of-folders.

Each category of software or information has its own place, and inside these folders may be other folders, each storing other files. It's much easier to keep things organized on a Macintosh Desktop than on an oak desktop.

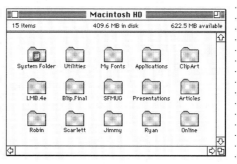

Hide Others
Sometimes when you are working on the Desktop, you can see windows from other applications in the background. This can be very annoying, but it is easy to fix. Simply go up to the *Application menu,* which is the icon on the far right corner of the menu bar (see the illustration), and choose "Hide Others."

*Notice the checkmark on the bottom half, next to "Finder." That is a **visual clue** that I am at the Finder, or Desktop.*

The other applications listed in the bottom half are also open at this time. If I don't want to see any of their windows while working at the Finder/Desktop, I can choose "Hide Others."

While you are working in your application, hold down the Option key when you go to the Application menu to choose "Finder," and the windows for the application will automatically hide. Also, if you hold down the Option key while you click on any part of the visible Desktop, you will go to the Finder and the windows of the application will automatically hide.

Clean Up Desktop
You can store files on the Desktop, outside any window. Really. Just drag 'em outside the window and stick 'em on the patterned background. When you're working in an application, you can choose to save a document onto the Desktop level. Sometimes, though, with all the stuff hanging around the Desktop, like the disks and maybe a few *aliases* (icons representing files) and a document or two and some e-mail, the place starts looking a little messy. It's easy to **clean up the Desktop,** though.

When the Desktop level is selected, the Special menu displays "Clean Up Desktop."

- ▾ Click once on any *icon* on the Desktop, like your hard disk icon or on the trash can.

- ▾ Press on the Special menu. The first item is now "Clean Up Desktop." This will make all the *icons* (not open *windows*) snap to the nearest spot on an underlying invisible grid.

- ▾ If you press the Option key before you choose "Clean Up Desktop," then all the icons on the Desktop will snap over to the far right and will line up in alphabetical order (but the disk that is running your computer, sometimes called the "startup disk" or "boot disk" is always first and the trash can is always last).

Desktop Pattern

You can change the pattern of your Desktop. In System 7.0 or 7.1, you don't have a lot of options—see page 229 for details on how to use the General Control Panel to change the pattern.

In System 7.5, though, you have from 56 to 64, depending on your computer (see page 235). The patterns range from pleasant to utterly obnoxious, plus you can make your own. From the Apple menu, slide down to "Control Panels," then slide out to "Desktop Patterns." Simply press on the left or right arrows to see a slide show of patterns. When you like one, click on the button "Set Desktop Pattern." You will see the Desktop change instantly. The last one you choose is the one you will keep until next time you decide to change it. Remember, there are more details (like how to create your own patterns) on page 229.

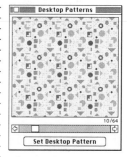

This is the Desktop Pattern control panel in System 7.5.

1. The Desktop level can be compared to:
   a) home base
   b) outer space
   c) the icing on the cake

2. What's the difference between the Desktop and the Finder?

3. What kind of icons do you use to organize your Desktop?

4. Can you store files directly on the Desktop, instead of all in the windows?

5. Describe how to clean up your Desktop, with all the icons in alphabetical order.

6. In System 7.0 or 7.1, which "control panel" do you use to change the pattern of the Desktop?
   In System 7.5, which one do you use?

7. How can you tell if you are actually at the Desktop (or Finder), just by looking at the screen?

8. How can you temporarily get rid of (hide) the windows of the open applications you are not currently using?

9. What is the secret, advanced tip by which you can click to get to the Desktop and have the windows of your current application disappear?

10. Are you going to keep your Desktop organized?

Answers on page 369.

MENUS

Almost every program you'll ever use on the Mac has a **menu** across the top of the screen. This is called a **pull-down menu,** because when you point to a menu item and *press* the mouse button down, a list of menu commands drops down. This chapter discusses the various sorts of menus, the commands, and how to use them.

| 🍎 | **File** | **Edit** | **View** | **Label** | **Special** | **Wed 10:15 AM** | ② | ▯ |

The Desktop, or Finder, Menu

This day and time feature shows up automatically if you are using System 7.5.

MENUS OFFER...

...A BANQUET OF CHOICES!

Choosing a Menu Command

To **choose** a command in the menu, simply keep the mouse button pressed and slide the pointer down; you'll notice that certain commands become *selected,* or *highlighted,* as you pass over them. When the command you want is highlighted, *just **let go*** *of the mouse button—don't click!*

The command "Close" is highlighted—
just let go to choose it!

Pop-Out and Pop-Up Menus

In some programs the pull-down menu itself contains a **pop-out menu** where you not only slide *down,* but also *out to the side,* usually (but not always!) in the direction of the arrow. These are also known as **hierarchical menus,** or **h-menus**.

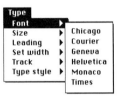

Pop-out menus don't always pop
out in the direction of the arrow!

You will also find **pop-up menus** where you press on an item toward the bottom of the screen and the list pops upward.

Gray *vs.* Black Commands

In the list of menu commands, you can see that some **commands** are in **black** letters and some commands are in **gray.** When a command is gray, it means *that particular command is not available at that moment.*

The most common reason that a command is unavailable is that you did not *select* something before you went to the menu. For instance, you cannot choose "Open" from the File menu if you haven't first selected a disk or file as the item to be opened. You cannot "Copy" text unless you have first selected the text you want to copy. To select an *object,* click *once* on it; to select *text,* press-and-drag over it.

Some commands are gray;
some are black.
Rule #2 states:
Select first, then do it to it.

To the right of the commands in the pull-down menus you often see a little code, such as ⌘N. This is a **keyboard shortcut** you can use *instead* of using the menu. Memorize it from the menu, then use it *instead* of picking up your mouse.

To use a keyboard shortcut, hold down the Command key (the one with the apple and the cloverleaf symbol on it: ⌘). While this key is down, type the letter associated with it. The computer reacts just as if you had chosen that command from the menu. For instance, if you click once on a file to select it and then press ⌘O, the selected file will open just as if you had chosen that command from the File menu with the mouse. Thoughtfully, most of the keyboard shortcuts are alliterative: **⌘O O**pens files; **⌘P P**rints; **⌘E E**jects; **⌘W** closes **W**indows; etc.

In written documentation you will see keyboard shortcuts spelled out with a hyphen, a plus sign, or perhaps a comma between the keys. *Don't type the hyphen, the plus sign, or the comma!* Just press the keys! For instance, if you see a shortcut spelled out as "Command + Shift + B" ignore the plus signs—just hold down the Command and Shift keys, then tap the letter B.

Sometimes the keyboard shortcut on the right of the menu will include other symbols; see the following chapter.

Anytime you see an **ellipsis** (the three dots: **...**) after a menu command (such as "Open**...**" or "Save as**...**"), it means you will get a **dialog box** when you choose that command. There are different varieties of dialog boxes, such as alert boxes or message boxes, but basically they all are meant to communicate with you.

Dialog boxes always give you an option to **Cancel,** so it is quite safe to go exploring menu commands this way. Just choose a command that is followed by an ellipsis, check out the dialog box, then click Cancel. Even if you click around on buttons or type in the dialog box, clicking the Cancel button will make sure none of your changes are put into effect.

*There is always a Cancel button. And you can almost always use the keyboard shortcut **Command Period** instead of clicking the Cancel button.*

Keep an eye out for menus in odd places!

You'll find other menus in all kinds of odd places. Well, they won't seem so odd once you become accustomed to the **visual clue** that indicates a menu is hiding. In the dialog box below, can you guess which boxes have menus hidden beneath them? Also, what do you think will happen if you click on either the "Rules…" or "Spacing…" buttons?

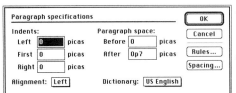

Both the "Rules…" and the "Spacing…" buttons have ellipses, indicating that if you click either button you will get another dialog box.

Watch for shadows

Notice that the boxes for "Alignment" and "Dictionary" (above) have a little **shadow** behind them. That little shadow is your **visual clue** that if you press on the word, you will get a pop-up menu, as shown below. Look for that shadow!

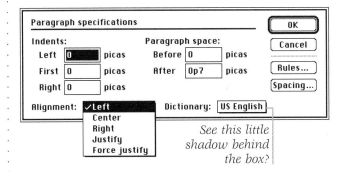

See this little shadow behind the box?

Edit boxes

The boxes that do *not* have a shadow behind them (look in the dialog box above) are called **edit boxes.** You can type into these edit boxes to change the specifications.

Here is a closer look—in the example below, the **edit box** for "Bottom" has no shadow behind it; "Grid size" has a shadow, plus it has an **arrow,** which is another **visual clue** indicating a hidden menu.

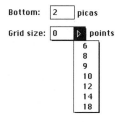

*When you see a sideways arrow in its own box (as in "Grid size"), you can press on the arrow to get the menu, **or** you can type right in the edit box to change the information.*

When you see a **downward-pointing arrow,** generally above a *list box,* you can press anywhere in that label to view and choose from the menu. Notice in the example below there is both a shadow and an arrow!

Save publication as

[☐ Memory Analogy ▼] ◄——*Press anywhere on this* **label.** *As you press, you will get the* **menu** *shown to the right. Try it!*

☐ 1.closeBox (pntg)
☐ 1a.File.close (pntg)
☐ 2.File.quit (pntg)
☐ 3.ap menubar (pntg)
☐ 4.ap menu (pntg)
☐ 5.UM control panel (pntg)

6.Virtual Memory

Save publication as

☐ Memory Analogy
☐ MacHomeJournal
☐ Publications
☐ Hard Disk
☐ Desktop
☐ 4.ap menu (pntg)
☐ 5.UM control panel (pntg)

6.Virtual Memory

*Watch for those
visual clues!*

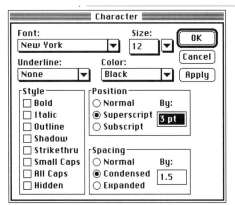

1. Which menu command is selected?

2. How many of these commands have *h-menus (hierarchical menus that will pop-out to the side)?*

3. How many of these commands will give you a dialog box when you choose them?

4. How many of these commands are not available at the moment?

5. How many of these commands have keyboard shortcuts?

6. Which keyboard shortcut could you use to get this menu item *instead* of choosing it from the menu?

7. When you choose this item, what are you going to get?

8. How many menus are there inside this dialog box?

9. How many edit boxes are there inside this dialog box?

10. What keyboard shortcut could you press to Cancel this dialog box?

Answers on page 369.

IMPORTANT KEYS

There are several **keys** on the Macintosh keyboard that are particularly important and useful. They come in handy for shortcuts, manipulating images, accessing alternate characters, and any number of things in specific applications.

Speaking of **keyboards,** there are basically two kinds for the Mac. There is the *standard* keyboard with the keypad at the end (like a ten-key adding machine)—one version for the Mac Plus and older models, and one for SEs, Classics, and similar models. And there is the *extended* keyboard that has all the function keys and other little arcane sets of keys. Often people think the *standard* keyboard is the *extended* one because it has the numeric keypad (that calculator pad on the right) that we didn't have on our typewriters. It isn't. Both keyboards have standard characters, although they may be in different placements on different models. No matter where they are placed, though, all the keys perform the same function (although the function of some keys varies from program to program).

WONDER WHAT THIS DOES?

Modifier Keys

The symbols shown in the outer column under each of the following headings are the symbols that will appear in menus to indicate pressing that key.

Some of the keys on the keyboard are called **modifier keys** because they don't do anything all by themselves, but they are used in combination with regular keys to make something happen, like keyboard shortcuts (see "Keyboard Command Shortcuts" on page 49). The Shift key, for instance, is a modifier key you are already familiar with. The Shift key doesn't do anything all by itself, but if you hold it down while you type an alphabetic character, you get the capital letter instead of the lowercase one.

Sometimes a keyboard shortcut uses more than one modifier. Always *hold down all the modifier keys together* (Command, Shift, Option, etc.) while you give *one quick tap on the associated letter key.* For instance, to *paste* an item, the shortcut is ⌘ **V**: hold down the Command key and type a quick V. If you *hold* the character key down instead of tapping it once, you will usually end up repeating the command.

Any Key

There really is no **Any key.** When a direction tells you to "PRESS ANY KEY," it means to press any key you want on the whole keyboard.

Caps Lock

The **Caps Lock key** does *not* act just like the Shift Lock on a typewriter. In Caps Lock you get capital letters, yes, but you do *not* get the characters above the numbers or above the punctuation. If you want the Shift-characters you must still press the Shift key to get them. (Some keyboard shortcuts will not work if the Caps Lock key is down, so check its position if you're having problems.)

Command Key
⌘

The **Command key** is on the bottom row, the key with the California freeway cloverleaf symbol on it: ⌘. On most keyboards it also has an apple on it, and you may hear it referred to as the "Apple key" or "Open Apple."

Most keyboard shortcuts use the Command key. Do not confuse it with the Control key!

The **Control key,** found only on the bigger, "extended" keyboards, doesn't do much yet in many applications. Often it's just a dead key, although more programs are using it in keyboard shortcuts and commands. And it's important for people who are running DOS programs on the Macintosh.

Control Key
ctrl
Λ

The **Delete key** (labeled the **Backspace key** on older keyboards), is located on the upper right. The name was changed to Delete because that's really what it does—whateveris *selected* will be removed when the Delete key is hit; whatever letter is to the *left* of the "insertion point" will be deleted as it is backspaced over.

Delete Key/
Backspace Key

The **Enter key** on the *numeric keypad* (the set of number keys on the right side of the keyboard) will also activate buttons with the double border, just the same as the Return key (see following page), and it will usually start a new paragraph as well. Different programs use the Enter key in many different ways.

Enter Key

The **Escape key** (labeled **esc**) on the upper left of the larger keyboards is another key that we will grow into. It's used in a few programs (like SuperPaint, to undo the latest action), but at the moment not too many programs make use of it. If your screen freezes (that's when neither the keyboard nor the mouse have any effect), you can try holding down Command Option and then pressing the Escape key. This will often, but not always, unfreeze the screen.

Escape Key
esc

This is a "force Quit." See page 329.

Next to the Command Key is the **Option key.** It's often used in combination with the Command key and/or the Shift key. It's through the Option key that you access the special characters, such as ¢ and ®, as well as accent marks, as in résumé and piñata (see page 133).

Option Key

Return Key
¶

The **Return key** is often used for other procedures than simply starting a new paragraph. For instance, any button in any dialog box that has the double border around it can be activated with the Return key instead of the mouse. Different programs use it in different ways.

Whenever you see a button with a double border, such as "OK" and "Print" to the right, you can always press the Return key to make it happen, instead of clicking on it with the mouse.

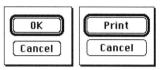

Spacebar
⎵

The **Spacebar** is represented in menus by the symbol shown to the left, *or as a blank space.* That blank space can really throw you. How long does it take to figure out that "⇧ ⌘ ⎵" means to press the Shift key, the Command key, and the Spacebar?

Shift Key
⇧

The **Shift key** is one of the most commonly used keys in keyboard shortcuts, symbolized by an upward arrow.

Tilde
~

The **Tilde** (~) is located on the upper left of some keyboards and next to the Spacebar on others. It's often called the Undo key, because in certain applications it will undo the action immediately preceding (such as in SuperPaint or the paint portion of HyperCard). Although on some keyboards the upper left key now says esc (*escape*) and the tilde has been placed next to the Spacebar, in many applications *esc* can still be considered the Undo key because it usually does the same thing.

Asterisk
★
(star)

The **asterisk** (*, which is Greek for "little star") is used as a multiplication symbol in calculators, spreadsheets, databases, etc. You can use the asterisk on the numeric keypad or you can press Shift 8 to get the asterisk above the number 8 on the keyboard. Thank goodness this key is also known as the star key, because so few people can spell or pronounce "asterisk."

Forward Slash
/

The **forward slash** (/) is used as a division symbol, in calculators, spreadsheets, databases, etc. You can use the slash on the numeric keypad or the one on the regular keyboard. Don't use the straight slash (|) or the backward slash (\, backslash) when you mean to divide.

The **Tab key** (upper left) acts like a Tab key on a typewriter in that when you press the Tab key you'll start typing at the next tab stop you have set. In most word processing programs, you simply click in the ruler you see across the top of the screen to create a tab stop (press-and-drag the tab down off the ruler to remove it).

An aside: Electronic tabs in word processing and page layout can be tricky to work with until you understand their electronic logic (yes, there is logic). Keep in mind, as you scream and yell at tabs and indents, that tabs and indents are extremely consistent and dependable and *they do exactly what you tell them.* But *you* need to know what you are telling them. [Commercial: If you do much word processing or page layout, I suggest you get another of my books, one cleverly titled *Tabs and Indents on the Macintosh.* I guarantee it will give you the power you need over those rascals.]

In spreadsheet and database programs, the Tab key will move the selection to the next cell or field *to the right,* just as it would move your typing to the right (the Return key will move the selection to the next cell or field *down*). Hold the Shift key down as you press Tab to move the selection backwards to the left (or Shift Return to move up).

When you are in a dialog box, you can press the Tab key to select edit boxes. Just try it: open a dialog box, then press the Tab key to cycle you through the edit boxes. If there is something in an edit box already, the box will highlight; *anything you type will replace what is highlighted.* If it is empty, the insertion point will flash, indicating you can now type something in it.

The **Fkeys** are at the top of the *extended* keyboards, that row of keys labeled F1, F2, F3, etc. If you don't see Fkeys, you don't have an extended keyboard, (that's okay if you don't—you can live without it). But those Fkeys are handy for shortcuts. In most programs you can press F1 to *undo* your last action; you can press F2 to *cut* an item, F3 to *copy,* and F4 to *paste* (see pages 129–130) for information on what it means to undo, cut, copy, and paste). Some programs use the other Fkeys for other shortcuts particular to the application (check your manual). You can program the extra ones yourself if you buy a special little program for doing so. But generally, they are extra and not indispensable keys.

Tab Key

➡ |

The Tab key is not usually used in conjunction with other keys. You may see this symbol in word processing to indicate that a Tab has been pressed.

This is a little more advanced tip. Come back later.

Fkeys
F1–F15

Arrow Keys

Depending on your keyboard, you may have **arrow keys** (keys with nothing but an arrow on each of them) tucked in with your letter keys, or you may have a separate little set of four arrow keys. Arrow keys are used in different ways in different programs.

In word processing programs you can use the arrow keys to move the insertion point.

> Usually if you hold down the Shift key as you hit the arrow key, the text will be selected as the insertion point moves along. Try it.

Other programs, such as page layout or graphics programs, may use the arrow keys to nudge graphic images around on the screen. In spreadsheets and databases, they might be used to move the insertion point or they might be used to select other cells or fields.

In dialog boxes, the arrow keys will move the insertion point in the edit boxes.

RightArrow
LeftArrow
UpArrow
DownArrow

In the documentation I write I use what might seem like an odd convention for naming the **arrow keys,** as shown in the left column. I do this because I have seen beginners follow a command such as "Press Command + right arrow" by pressing the Command key and then looking for the key that says "right," plus an arrow key. (And many new users also try to press the + key.) So even though it may seem odd at first, combining the two words makes it clearer that there is just one key.

On the far right of the keyboard is a **numeric keypad** that looks like calculator keys. These keys will sometimes type numbers and sometimes move the insertion point. Sometimes they do both, depending on whether you have pressed the "Clear" key (sometimes called "Num Lock" because it locks the keypad into typing numbers).

In the Calculator desk accessory, these keys can operate the calculator. The asterisk (*) is the multiplication key, and the slash (/) is the division key.

Numeric Keypad

If you have an extended keyboard, you have an extra little set of keys between the alphabet keyboard and the numeric keypad called the **edit keys.** These keys are primarily there to make the Macintosh compatible with IBM PC programs. Not many Mac programs use these keys, although if you read your manual you may be surprised. Try them in your word processor. Or select a file in a Desktop window and try the PageUp and Down keys, as well as Home and End. The **del key** often deletes the character it is in *front* of (opposite of the Delete key we usually use).

Edit Keys
Help
Home
End
PageUp
PageDown
Del
Ins

The **PowerOn key** is the big key embossed with a left-pointing triangle, found at the top of some keyboards and at the upper right in others. This key turns on some models of Macintosh. On the other models, it's a useless key. The PowerOn key makes it very easy for your cat or your small child to turn on your Mac when you least expect it.

PowerOn Key

In System 7.5.1, this key will also **Shut Down** your Mac. With cats and kids swarming around my house, I don't know if I like this feature.

PowerOff key

1. If you want to activate the OK button in this dialog box, but don't want to pick up the mouse, which key would you press?

2. If you want to select another edit box in this dialog box, which key would move the selection from box to box?

3. Which keys would you press to:

Check the grammar?

Do a word count?

Renumber?   Insert a page break?

Get the list of Commands?   Insert a section break?

4. Connect the name of the key with its symbol:

Escape key	a)	➡|
Option key	b)	⇧
Control key	c)	**esc**
Command key	d)	~
Tilde key	e)	/
Asterisk, or star	f)	∧
Shift key	g)	⌃
Forward slash	h)	⌘
Backslash	i)	★
Tab key	j)	\
Enter key	k)	⬊ ⌁

Answers on page 369.

ALL WINDOWS

A **window** is a basic, fundamental element of the Macintosh. The first windows you'll use on the Mac will be those at the Desktop (or *Finder*). In this chapter I explain the details you will find in just about *every* window on the Mac, whether it is in your word processor, spreadsheet, database, or whatever application you love to work with, *as well as* the windows at the Desktop. But because Desktop windows have many more features than the windows you will use in your applications, I've devoted the entire Chapter 8 exclusively to the features of Desktop windows.

Windows

Below is a window. You will find each of the items labeled below in just about every window on the Mac *(icons are only found at the Desktop).*

Explanations for each one of these items are found on the following pages.

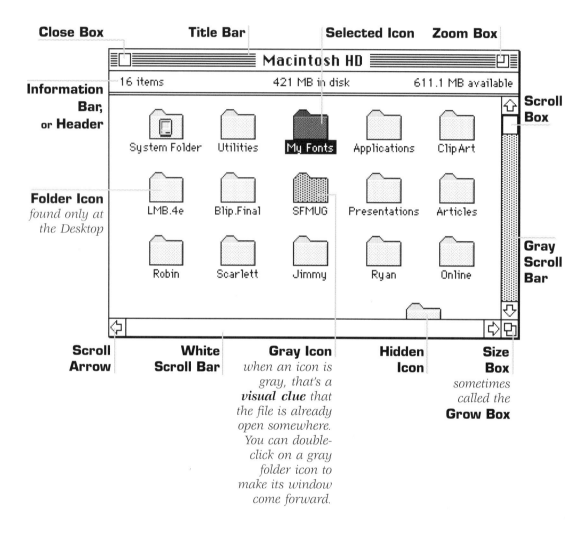

Close Box   **Title Bar**   **Selected Icon**   **Zoom Box**

Information Bar, or **Header**

Scroll Box

Folder Icon
found only at the Desktop

Gray Scroll Bar

Scroll Arrow   **White Scroll Bar**   **Gray Icon**
when an icon is gray, that's a **visual clue** *that the file is already open somewhere. You can double-click on a gray folder icon to make its window come forward.*

Hidden Icon

Size Box
sometimes called the **Grow Box**

The **title bar** is the striped area at the top of the window in which, logically, the title appears. This title is the name of the disk, folder, or document you have opened.

Title Bar

Position the pointer in the title bar, then press-and-drag to **move** any window around the screen. As you drag, you will see the *outline* of the window. Just let go when you have the outline placed where you want, and the window will appear in that position.

Moving the Window

If you have more than one window open, only one will have lines, or stripes, in its title bar; this means it is the **active window.** If the windows are overlapping, the active window is the one that is in front.

Active Window

The active window is the window that the commands from the keyboard or the menu will affect. For instance, if you go to the File menu and choose "Close," it will close the active window. If you choose "New Folder," a new folder will appear in the active window. It's very important to be conscious of this!

To make a window **active,** simply click on any visible part of it; this will also bring that window to the front of any others. You may have to move other windows around in order to see the window you want to make active.

To make the window active

> To move a window *without* making it active, hold down the Command key while you press-and-drag in its title bar.

On the bottom right corner is the **size box,** sometimes called the "grow box" (which I personally think is a very dumb term). Press-and-drag in the size box to make the window larger or smaller. If you have several windows open, you can resize and rearrange them so they all fit on your screen without overlapping. You can have two word processing documents on the screen, or perhaps a database file and a spreadsheet worksheet and a word processing letter, and view them all at the same time.

Size Box

On the upper right corner is the **zoom box.** If you click in the zoom box it will enlarge just big enough to display everything inside. If you click in it when it's large, the window will zoom back down to the size it was *just before* you zoomed it larger.

Zoom Box

Scroll Bars

Along the right and bottom edges of the window are the **scroll bars.** The scroll bars allow you to view everything in the window, even if it cannot all fit on the screen at once or if the window is sized too small. You'll notice in the example on page 62 that the scroll bar along the right side is *gray,* while the one on the bottom is *white.* These are **visual clues!**

Gray Scroll Bar

When a **scroll bar is gray,** it is a **visual clue** that *there are other items in the window you can't see.* In the example on page 62, you can see a folder along the bottom edge that is barely visible, so the scroll bar is gray, telling you something more is beyond its borders. When you see a gray scroll bar in a list of items, as in an "Open" dialog box, it means there are more items in the list than can be displayed. You need to scroll to see the others.

White Scroll Bar

When the **scroll bar is white,** it indicates *there is nothing more in the direction of the arrows* (the horizontal direction in the example) than what you can see.

Scroll Arrows

At either end of the scroll bars are the **scroll arrows.** When the scroll bar is *gray* you can press on a scroll arrow, making the contents of the window glide past you, like the scenery outside a train window. Try it.

Scroll Box

Scroll Box

Notice the little **scroll box** in the gray scroll bar (you will *only* see a scroll box if the scroll bar is gray). As you press on the arrows, this box moves so you can tell what portion of the window you are viewing. When the scroll box is all the way at one end, that's the end of the list or of the window. Some people call the scroll box an *elevator* because it goes up and down like one.

Press-and-Drag the Scroll Box

Press-and-drag this scroll box

Another useful technique using the scroll box is this: **press-and-drag the scroll box** to move it to any position on the scroll bar, let go, and the window will immediately jump to that particular place rather than scroll through everything. This is very handy inside an application like a word processor where you have a long document and scrolling with the arrows would take too long. For instance, if your document is 50 pages long, dragging the scroll box to the middle of the scroll bar would take you to page 25. In some applications a number appears within the scroll box to indicate what page you're on.

There's yet another way to use the scroll bars: simply **click** the pointer in any *gray* area of the bar, and the window will move up, down, or across, usually a full window view—what was at the bottom of the view will then be at the top or vice-versa.

And, of course, in the upper left is the **close box.** Click once in that little box to close the window, which sends the document it was displaying back to the disk or folder it came from. Many programs use the keyboard shortcut Command W to close the *active window.* That is, instead of clicking in the close box, you can press Command W to put the window away.

Close Box

The example on page 62 shows an **information bar,** or **header,** that provides information about the window and the disk. At the Desktop/Finder, this tells you how many items are in the window, how much space on your disk is already used for storing your files, and how much disk space is left.

Information Bar, or Header

| 4 items | 596K in disk | 175K available |

You will only see this kind of information bar when you're looking at windows at the Desktop. Within your various applications, this area in the window may vary. For instance, in a word processing program, you'll see a "ruler" at the top of the window instead of this information bar.

If you are running System 7.5 (see page 2 if you aren't sure), you can **"roll up" your window shades:** simply double-click in a title bar. The entire window rolls up so all you see is the title bar (see below). To **unroll the window,** double-click in the title bar again. This is a great way to reduce the clutter on your Desktop or in any application.

Rolling up your WindowShades

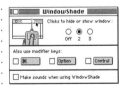

There is a WindowShade control panel that allows you some controls over this feature—see page 248 for details, although it's quite self-explanatory.

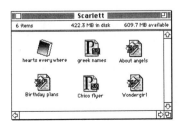

If you double-click on the title bar of any window (as shown to the left), it will "roll up" (as shown above).

1. Label the window below with the following parts:

   Close box   **Size box**
   Zoom box   **Title bar**
   Scroll box   **Gray scroll bar**
   White scroll bar   **Folder icon**
   Information bar, or header   **Scroll arrows (4 of them)**

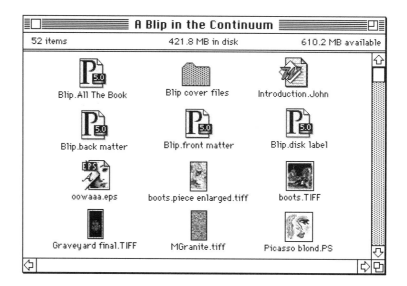

2. Which icon in the above window is *selected*?

   ·

3. Which file is already open?

   ·

4. How many files are stored in this window (folder)?

   ·

5. What is the other instant visual clue that tells you there are more files than what you see?

   ·

Answers on page 369.

DESKTOP WINDOWS

8

The Macintosh allows you a great deal of control over the look and the feel of your computer and the options available so you can arrange your work in a way that is most effective for *you*. The **Desktop windows** are a good example—you can choose to see what's in your window in a variety of ways, all appropriate for different purposes or styles; you can organize them any way you like, you can create new icons for the files. The techniques in this chapter apply only to the windows at the *Finder* (also called the *Desktop*).

Views of the Window

This is the View menu. Yours may not look exactly like this because your Views control panel has different options checked.

You can change how you **view** the items in a Desktop window. Some people like the items to appear as icons; other prefer to have a list of the items as text. These different views are found, of course, in the View menu when you're at your Desktop.

To change the view of a window, first click anywhere in the window to make it *active* (because when you choose a view it applies to the *active window,* the one that has the lines in its title bar). The window will stay in the display you choose until you change it.

The options you see in the View menu depend on what you have chosen in the Views control panel. So if one of these views in the illustration to the left (and described in the following pages) interests you but you don't see it in *your* menu, read the details on page 71 for customizing your window and menu.

View by Icon

View by Icon is what you typically see—icons are the pictures representing the files. Visually oriented people (like me) tend to prefer to view by icon. When viewed by icon, the files are in no specific order, although there *is* a little trick by which you can organize the icons by name or size or date, etc. See page 251.

View by Small Icon

View by Small Icon retains that feeling of looking at pictures, if that's what you prefer, but the icons are tiny so you can fit more in the window. The icons are not automatically arranged in any specific order.

This is a View By Icon.

This is a View By Small Icon.

The rest of the view options do not show icons—the files are arranged in a **list.** When you view the files as a list, you can still manipulate any item in the list just as if it were an icon; that is, you can pick it up and put it in the trash or in another folder, rename it, copy it, open it, etc. (see Chapter 9 on Icons). For information on what those little triangles are doing in your window, see Chapter 10 on Folders.

If you are viewing the window by one of the lists (Name, Size, Label, etc.), you can switch views simply by clicking once on another column header in the information bar, instead of having to choose it from the menu. You'll see an underline below the header that indicates how the list is currently organized.

Click on one of these column headers to switch to that view.

View by Name turns the icons into an alphabetical list for those who prefer looking at words rather than pictures. A tiny, generic icon is still present so you can see what sort of file it is.

View by Name

If you would like to view your list by name yet still see the individual icons that belong to the files, use the Views control panel to make the icon bigger. See page 250, "List View Icons."

View by Size lists the files in order of size, beginning with the largest. It tells you how much space, in K (kilobytes), each particular file is taking up on your disk. This is handy if you need to remove something to make more room on a disk; you can see which files you would need to remove to clear enough space. Or you might organize a window full of graphic files by size so you can keep tabs on reality.

View by Size

Unfortunately, View by Size won't show the size of *folders;* to find their size you need to select the folder and choose "Get Info" from the File menu (see page 90). *Or* you can customize the view so it *will* display the sizes of folders (see the Views control panel, page 250), but then it takes much too long to display the list.

View by Kind · **View by Kind** lists the files in groups of applications, documents, or folders. This is handy if you want to see a list of all your applications, or all the documents you've stored in your budget folder, etc.

View by Kind is particularly useful for a folder that holds an application (or a game) plus all of its accessories—the dictionaries, tutorials, technical files, samples, etc. This view will always put the application (or game) at the *top* of the list so it's easy to find.

View by Label · **View by Label** groups the files according to their "label." A label is something you make up and apply to a file (see page 236), Labels control panel). For instance, you can create a label called Love Letters and apply it appropriately. Then when you View by Label, all the love letters in that window will be grouped together.

View by Date · **View by Date** lists the files in chronological order backwards from the date they were last *modified,* not the date they were originally created. This is handy when you have, for instance, several budget documents and you want to see the most recent edition.

View by Version · **View by Version** lists the files in alphabetical order, with applications being listed first. Each application has its version number displayed. Have you ever noticed how many copies of TeachText you have in your computer? Well, you can use Find File (Chapter 26) to find and gather them all into one folder, then view that folder By Version. Throw out all but the newest version, the one with the highest number.

View by Comments · **View by Comments** will display in the window the first 31 characters of the text you typed into the Comments box in the Get Info window (see page 90).

When you're viewing *icons* in your window, they often get all scrambled and the place looks like a mess. To align all your icons nicely, simply choose **Clean Up Window** from the Special menu—all the icons will fly to the nearest little cubby available on the underlying invisible grid. If the name of an icon is too long, though, there will be an empty spot next to that icon so its name doesn't bump into the next icon. That's a good reason to give your files short names, and to *never use all capitals letters* because they take up twice as much room (besides being more difficult to read).

▼ If you want to **force an icon** into one of those empty spaces, hold the Command key down while you drag the icon near the space. The Mac will tuck it right into the invisible cubby.

▼ To **organize the icons,** here's a good trick: Hold the Option key down before you choose "Clean Up Window"—the Mac will arrange the icons according to the last list view you chose! For instance, first choose "By Size" and you will get a list in order of largest to smallest. Then choose "By Icon" again. Now hold the Option key down while you press on the Special menu, and you'll notice the menu command has changed to "Clean Up by Size." Choose it. Cool.

▼ To **clean up *selected* icons,** press the Shift key as you choose "Clean Up" from the Special menu. Icons you had previously selected will snap to the nearest spot on the invisible grid.

▼ Click on one of the items on your Desktop, such as your hard disk icon or the trash can (*or* press Command UpArrow), and the Special menu will show **Clean Up Desktop** instead of "Clean Up Window." When you choose this command, all the *icons* (not the open windows) on your Desktop snap to the nearest spot on the underlying invisible grid. If you press the Shift key first, then only the selected items will snap to the grid.

▼ Press the Option key before you choose "Clean Up Desktop," and all the icons on the Desktop will snap over to the far right and line up in alphabetical order (your hard disk always being first and the trash can always being last, though).

Clean Up Window

This is the button I want in my house—to make the dishes jump onto their shelves, the laundry to put itself away in the drawers, and all the toys to fly back into the toybox.

Clean Up Desktop

Also check out the information on the Views control panel (page 250) for even more ways to customize your windows.

Gray Icons

Sometimes you can't see the window itself but you *can* see the **gray icon** of a folder or disk, which indicates *its window is open somewhere, you just can't see it.* In that case, double-click on the gray icon to bring its window forward and make it active. (Also see pages 83 and 166 regarding gray icons; gray disks can sometimes mean something else.)

Close *all* the Windows

To simultaneously **close every window** that is open on your Desktop, hold down the Option key while you click in the active window's close box; all the windows will go away one after another!

and other tricks

▼ You'll notice in the File menu a keyboard command to close the active window: Command W. **To close all the windows at once,** press Command Option W and *all* the windows will fly home. You don't need to click anywhere.

▼ Another fancy trick to **automatically close any Desktop windows when you quit an application** is to hold down the Option key when you choose "Quit." *Keep holding the Option key down until you see your Desktop.* When you arrive, there won't be a single window open.

▼ Often the file you want to open is buried within several folders. Hold the Option key down while you double-click to open those folders to get to your file. The windows will **close up behind you** as you go along.

▼ When you eject a disk or turn off the computer, the Mac remembers which windows were open when you left. When you insert the same disk or when you turn the computer back on, those windows will re-open in the same position in which you left them. You can take advantage of this fact, *or* you might find it irritating sometimes to open a disk and have windows pop up all over the place. But if you hold down the Option key when you insert a disk or start the computer, **any windows that had been left open will be closed** when you get to the Desktop.

To view the hierarchy of a nested folder (that means to *see the folders that this particular folder is contained within*), hold the Command key down and press on the title of the window (not the stripes in the title bar, but on the actual title or word itself). This displays a pull-down menu, as shown below.

You can choose any other folder in that drop-down menu to open its window and bring it to the front.

Hold down the Command key and press right here.

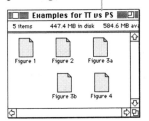

You will see the list of folders that contain this window.

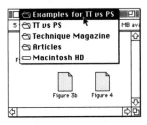

For example, we can see that this folder, "Examples for TT vs PS" is inside a folder called TT vs PS, which is inside the Technique Magazine folder, which is inside the Articles folder, which is in the hard disk window, meaning it is stored on my hard disk.

Minor Differences

The following three items are notes on how several of the common features of windows act a little **differently on the Desktop** than they do in applications. Don't bother to read this page unless you are feeling very comfortable with the windows and want to know some subtle features. If you're new to your Mac, skip this section; come back next month.

Zoom box

▼ When you click in the zoom box (upper right of the window, see page 62), the window will zoom open only as large as it needs to be to display all the files. If you want to open the window as large as possible (yet still see the trash can), hold the Option key down as you click in the zoom box.

Drag an icon to scroll

▼ The window will scroll as you drag an icon within it. When you let go of the mouse button, the icon will pop into the nearest space in the window. You can also press the arrow keys to select icons, which will in turn scroll the window as well. Or in a list view, you can press in a blank area and drag the mouse up or down to scroll. Also see the chapter on Selecting (page 101), because selecting icons can make the window scroll, plus there are some great tricks.

Active windows

▼ When you click on a window, that **window** becomes **active** and comes to the front, obscuring the other windows. Sometimes you don't want it to do that.

Remember, you can *move* a window without making it active by holding down the Command key and dragging its title bar.

Also, keep in mind that when you click on an item in a window that is *not* active, the window doesn't become active until you *release* the mouse button while the pointer's still in the window. This subtle bit of information makes it easier to move and copy items that are in different windows; that is, you can grab a file from an inactive window and drag it into another window without the first window popping up to the top. (Make sure you press on an icon or a file name, though; if you just click in any *blank* space in the window, that window will immediately become active and pop to the top.)

More Cool Tricks

There are a great number of **cool tricks** you can use to manipulate the windows at the Desktop (Finder). In fact, there are so many that Apple has provided several Help screens describing them. All of these shortcuts are embedded somewhere in this book in their appropriate places, but using the "Finder Shortcuts" information is probably handier than having to look them up, or worse yet, having to memorize them. But, y'know, if you *do* memorize and use them, you will really impress people.

To view these Help screens, press on the Help menu (the question mark in the far right of the menu bar, see right). Choose "Finder Shortcuts" (System 7 or 7.1) or "Shortcuts" (System 7.5).

To get to the Shortcuts.

> If you don't see the "Finder Shortcuts" or "Shortcuts" command, it is because you are not at the Finder (Desktop). To get to the Finder, press on the icon in the top far right of the menu bar, next to the question mark (see right), and choose "Finder." Or, if your trash can is showing, click once on it.

To get to the Finder.

Here's an **example** of a Finder (Desktop) shortcut:

To make the desktop active	⌘-Shift-Up Arrow

This means that if you are looking at windows on the Desktop and you want to make the *Desktop level active* (perhaps you want to make a new folder on the Desktop itself, not in a window, or perhaps you want to clean up the Desktop), then you can press Command Shift UpArrow. (You could also click on any icon on the Desktop, but this shortcut lets you do it without having to pick up the mouse.)

**Printing
the Window**

Occasionally you may have a need to **print** the information you find in a particular **window.** For instance, you might want to make a list of all the documents that are on that floppy disk, or all the dated budget files that are in the Budget folder.

This only works with the windows on the Desktop. If you want to print a window or a screen within an application, or any dialog box, see the next page, "Print Other Windows."

To print the info in the active window:

▾ Turn on your printer.

▾ Make sure the window that contains the data you want is the active window (click once on it).

▾ From the File menu, choose **Print Window...** (it's the very last item).

▾ In the Print dialog box, change any of the options to suit your fancy, then click "OK" (or hit the Return key).

**Printing
the Screen**

The above procedure prints only the *visible* contents of the *active window.* While you are at the *Desktop* (this will only work at the Desktop level), if you want to **print everything on the screen,** the whole screen and nothing but the screen, follow these steps:

▾ Turn on your printer.

▾ Make sure the Desktop is active (click on any icon on the Desktop, like the trash can or your disk, *or* press Command Shift UpArrow).

▾ From the File menu, choose **Print Desktop...** (it's the very last item; if the command you see is "Print Window...," then you are not at the Desktop level).

▾ In the Print dialog box, change any of the options to suit your fancy, then click "OK" (or hit the Return key).

If you want to print a picture of a window in an *application,* see if there is a command called "Print Window" in one of the menus. If not, then you can create and print a *screen shot,* or *screen dump,* of the entire screen.

Printing Other Windows or the Screen

Picture 1

▼ While the image you want to print is on the screen, press Command Shift 3. You will hear a nerve-wracking little sound as if a tiny fuse is breaking inside your computer and your screen will freeze for a moment. Don't worry—it's okay. The computer is taking a picture of the screen. *(Jimmy, one of my sons, tells me that the disturbing sound is the sound of a picture being taken. That one went right over my head.)*

▼ Now go to your Desktop and look in the window belonging to the hard disk. You will see a new item called "Picture 1."

▼ Double-click on "Picture 1" and it will open in the application called TeachText or SimpleText, a tiny word processor.

▼ From the File menu, choose "Print…," then click OK.

▼ After it prints, choose "Quit" from the File menu, *or* press Command Q.

If you are wondering about those little triangles to the left of folders in a list view, please see Chapter 10 on Folders, page 97 in particular. The triangles in this **outline view** collapse and expand the folders so you can see what is inside each one without having to open a new window. There are some great tricks to working with these, all of which are explained in that chapter.

Outline View

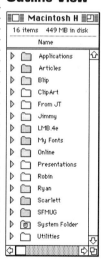

1. Which view of a Desktop window would you choose to see how large your files are?

. . . .

2. Which view would you choose to alphabetize your files?

. . . .

3. What is the shortcut for changing views from one list to another?

. . . .

4. How do you print a picture of the active window?

. . . .

5. Look up the Finder Shortcuts and name two other shortcuts dealing with Desktop windows.

. . . .

6. What is the shortcut that makes a window enlarge (zoom open) to fill almost the entire screen?

. . . .

7. How can you move a window without making it active?

. . . .

8. How can you close all the Desktop windows at once without touching the mouse?

. . . .

9. How can you view a list of *all* the folders in which a folder/window is nested within?

. . . .

10. If a folder icon is gray, what does it mean? What will happen if you double-click on a gray folder icon?

. . . .

Answers on page 370.

ICONS

Icons—the little pictures you see on the screen—are an intrinsic part of the look and feel of the Macintosh. Instead of having to type a code to get into an application or document, you simply click on the icon representing it.

The icons offer rich **visual clues.** At first they may look like an odd collection of junk, and many people instantly change their view to a word list so they're not overwhelmed by all the pictures. But once you really look at them, you will see how much information icons instantly provide. This information is valuable to you, and that's the purpose of this chapter—to help you take advantage of these clues. I suggest you leave your windows in the icon view for a while in the beginning. After you start seeing the patterns and noticing the clues, after you are comfortable with copying and moving and organizing your icons, go ahead and view your windows in whatever sort of list is useful to you (pages 68–70).

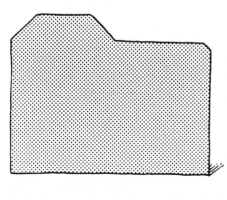

ICON

TINA TURNER

Disk Icons

Hard disk

Floppy disk

When you initially turn on your machine and get to the Desktop (as on page 41), you'll always see an icon of any **disk** you're using, whether it's a hard disk or a floppy (your hard disk icon may look different from this one shown, depending on where it is and what kind it is).

▼ Single-click on a disk icon to select it.

▼ Double-click on a disk icon to open it to show you a window displaying all the files.

Note: If a *disk* icon is gray, it is either already open (page 84 or has been left in RAM after being ejected (page 166).

Folder Icons

Whenever you have a window open, most likely you'll see **folder icons.** They act just like folders in your filing cabinet in that you store items in them for organization, and you can open them to see what's inside. Be sure to read the following chapter on Folders, as they are an important tool.

▼ Single-click on a folder to select it.

▼ Double-click to open the folder to show you a window with all the files that are stored in that folder.

This folder icon means I will share its contents with another computer.

***Skip** the rest of this page unless you see one of these odd folder icons on your computer!*

If a folder icon has a little dark bar across its tab, or if it has wires coming out the bottom, or if it has happy little faces on it, these are all **visual clues** indicating that this folder is being or is capable of being shared.

*When the **other** computer turns on file sharing, **my** folder gets happy faces.*

The icon that looks like a platter of items being served (shown below), indicates a "file server," which is the computer that holds files that other people want to use. When a folder on one computer is being shared through a "network" (cables that connect several computers to each other), that folder appears on the *other* person's computer as this file server icon. This icon is like a folder in that you can double-click on it and there are things stored inside; the things inside are actually on the other computer, the file server, but you can copy them to your own hard disk.

*On the **other** computer, my happy face folder is seen on **their** computer as this file server icon.*

For details on simple networking and sharing folders with other people in your home or office, see Chapter 27 on Sharing Files.

Application (or **program**) **icons** are the fancy ones. These belong to the actual applications (the software programs that you work in). Each application has its own design, so they all look different, but what they have in common is that they all try to give some sort of **visual clue** as to what they do. For instance, in the icons to the right you can see that MacWrite is a word processing program; SuperPaint is an art program.

▾ Single-click on an application icon to select it.

▾ Double-click to open to either a new, blank page within that program, or at least to a dialog box where you can choose to *create* a new, blank page.

Document icons represent documents, or files, that *you* (or someone like you) have created in any particular application. Whenever you are working in an application and you save your document with a title, a document icon is created for you on your Desktop.

Document icons almost always look like a piece of paper with the top right corner folded down, or perhaps a sheaf of papers or a stack of cards. Typically they have some resemblance to the application they were created in, as you can see by the MacWrite and the SuperPaint icons on the right, which match their corresponding programs as shown above.

▾ Single-click on a document icon to *select* it.

▾ Double-click to open the application *in which the document was created,* with that particular document on the screen. (If you get an error message, check page 330, "Can't open a file.")

Application Icons

MacWrite II

SuperPaint

Application icons are typically rather fancy.

Document Icons

Article

Zamoura

Document icons almost always have the top right corner turned down.

Blank Document Icons

Zamoura

*This is the same file as on the previous page. The fact that it is blank is a **visual clue** that the program it was created in is not installed in the computer.*

Occasionally you will see a **blank document icon.** This usually means that the application in which this document was created is not in the computer. For instance, the blank document shown to the left is the same as the SuperPaint file on the previous page. When this file is in a computer that has SuperPaint installed, it looks like it belongs to SuperPaint. But if I copy the same file to a computer that does *not* have the application SuperPaint installed, the icon is blank.

Letters

(If the blank document icon has a *bottom* corner turned up, that's a visual clue that the document is actually a *stationery pad;* see page 91.)

If you double-click a blank document icon, you will usually see this message:

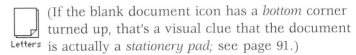

The document "Zamoura" could not be opened, because the application program that created it could not be found.

OK

Advanced tip!

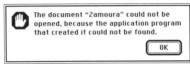

You can try dragging the *document* icon on top of various *application* icons. If an application can open a file of this type (Microsoft Word, for instance, can open almost any text file), the application icon will become highlighted (as shown below). This is your clue that this application can open this file; let go of the document and it will open in that program.

It's difficult to find the source of a blank document icon without special utilities that tell you those sorts of things. If this is something you need to do often, ask for help at your local user group.

Microsoft Word

Drag the icon on top of various applications and see if any of the others will open the file.

Inside the folder named System Folder are **system icons** that help run the Macintosh, as well as a variety of icons that are for extra or fancy options. System icons represent programming that performs essential operations. You'll see a variety of types of system icons. You'll see one called System and one called Finder—if those two are not inside the System Folder, you won't even be able to use your machine.

▼ Single-click on a system icon to select it.

▼ Double-clicking on most system icons will give you a message that "This file is used by the system software. It cannot be opened." That's because most system icons are just visual representations of the data on your disk that makes them work—there's really nothing to look at besides the cute little icon. (Although you *can* open the System file itself and the control panels.)

Your System Folder has quite a grand collection of icons, doesn't it? The System Folder is so important that it earns its own special chapter, page 177, and you should probably actually read it. And I'll remind you once again—don't go stickin' things in the System Folder unless you *know* they are really supposed to be there.

When an **icon is dark,** like the one on the right, that means it is *highlighted,* or *selected*—it got selected because someone clicked once on it. Once an icon is selected, you can press-and-drag it somewhere. Menu commands, such as Open or Put Away, will affect highlighted (selected) icons.

▼ Single-clicking is what selected this icon in the first place.

▼ Double-clicking a selected icon will open it just like any other icon.

System Icons

System   Finder

Icons that are part of the operating system appear in several sizes and shapes.

Mouse   Sound

Apple CD-ROM   Finder Help

Control panels (such as Mouse and Sound) and extensions (such as the CD-ROM and Finder extensions), each have a consistent look.

Highlighted, or Selected, (dark) Icons

Scarlett

Gray Icons

When an **icon is gray,** like the ones shown on the left, it is a **visual clue** that means it's *already open.* Maybe you don't see the icon's window because it's hidden behind another open window, but you know it's open somewhere.

An open folder icon.

Jargon

▼ Single-click on a gray **folder icon** to select it.

▼ Double-click on a gray *folder* icon to bring its window to the front as the *active* window.

An open disk icon.

Fonts

Now, if the icon is not a folder, but a **disk icon,** one of two things is causing it to be gray: If the disk is still in the computer, its window is open somewhere, in which case you can just double-click on the gray icon to bring the window forward.

But if the disk *is not even in the computer,* it means you have ejected the disk but the computer is holding information about the disk in *memory.* See pages 166–167 for details on why this happened, what to do about it, and how to prevent it from happening.

Microsoft Word

An open application icon.

If the icon is an **application icon,** it means the application is still open. If you double-click on its gray icon, the application will become active. So you double-click on it, and you say nothing happened? It did. Look at your menu bar. When you are at the Finder (Desktop), your menu bar will have the item "Special" in it, and the File menu does not have "Quit" at the bottom. Read Chapter 30 (pages 297–306) called Very Important Information. You need that information to have control over your Mac. And that control will make you happy and powerful.

Putting Away Wayward Icons

Have you ever dragged a file out of its folder, left it on the Desktop, then forgot where it came from? Or perhaps someone else pulled it out and forgot to put it away and you don't know where it belongs. Or maybe you're just too lazy to do it yourself. Simply select the icon (click once on it), then from the File menu, choose **Put Away** (or press Command Y). A little invisible person grabs the file and puts it right back where it last came from.

You can also ask this little guy to put away a file that you stuck in the trash can and then changed your mind about. Double-click the trash can to open it, select one or more files (hold down the Shift key to click on one or more), then press Command Y.

To move icons, simply press-and-drag them. You can put any icon into or drag any icon out of any *folder* icon. For details, see Chapter 11 on Copying and Selecting.

To rename any icon—a folder, a document, a program, a disk—just click once on the icon's *name* (not on the icon's *graphic*); then simply type the new name. A box appears around the name so you know you're changing it. Or instead of clicking on the name, you can select the icon and press Return to get that box around it. (The box and the insertion point do seem annoyingly slow to appear; be patient.)

Use standard word processing procedures, as detailed in Chapter 14 on Typing, to set an "insertion point" (the flashing bar that is your **visual clue** that you are in typing mode). Double-click a *word* to select it, backspace to delete, etc. You can use your arrow keys to move the insertion point. In fact, press the UpArrow or DownArrow to move the insertion point to the very beginning or the very end of the name. As soon as you click somewhere else, or hit the Return or Enter keys, the name is set.

Renaming Icons

When an icon is ready to be renamed, you'll see a border around the name.

If you do **accidentally change the name** of an icon (which is very easy to do—files have been known to mysteriously change their names to \\\\\\\\\\\ or `````` while you weren't doing anything but leaning on the keyboard), you do have one chance to restore the name to its original form: **Undo.** As soon as you see the mistake has been made, from the Edit menu choose "Undo." *If you haven't done anything* since this minor catastrophe (and things could be worse), Undo will restore the original name, even if you forgot it. If you are too late to catch Undo, you'll just have to rename it yourself (if you know what it was). Remember, the keyboard shortcut for Undo is Command Z.

Undoing a Name Change

If the computer does not let you change the name, see the following page.

If You Can't Change the Name

For Shannon

The little black bar on the tab indicates that this folder is being shared.

You **cannot change the name** of a folder, disk, or application that is being **shared** (see the chapter on Sharing Files, page 271) or that is **locked.** A shared folder is indicated by a little black bar along the top of the tab, as shown to the left. A *disk* has no visual clue that it is being shared; the clue will be the fact that you don't get a border around the name when you click on it. If you really need to change the name of a shared item, you need to first turn off sharing (page 274). Even though a disk or folder may be shared, you can still change the name of any of their *contents* that are not being shared.

To unlock a *file* (folder, application, document, etc.), see page 91. To unlock a *disk,* see page 20.

Coloring Your Icons

Scrapbook of Lovers

Color can be a very effective organizational tool (pretend this icon is a deep red color).

If you have a color monitor, you can **color your icons.** You can do this just for the heck of it, or to make your dull life more colorful, or you can use the color as an organizational tool. For instance, you may want to apply a passionate red color to all the love letters you have written and received. That way no matter what folder they are stored in or what sort of file they are (maybe you keep a database of all your lovers and letters, a stationery pad for multiple copies, a faxable version, and a graphic file of your photograph for sending over the modem), you can instantly recognize any file belonging to the passionate red classification.

To color an icon, use the Label menu:

▾ Select the icon you want to color (click once on it).

▾ From the Label menu, choose a color.
   This will also apply the corresponding "label" to the file, which you can use for "searching." For more details on labels and how to change the color of the labels (and thus the icons), see the chapter on Control Panels, page 227.

You can **create your own icons** and apply them to any existing icons. This is too cool.

▼ Open a graphic program like SuperPaint or MacPaint. Or instead you can also use any clip art or Scrapbook image.

▼ In the graphic program, create the little picture that you want as your icon. No matter what size you make the art, the Mac will reduce it to an appropriate size as it becomes the new icon. (If you create it too large, though, it will be unrecognizable when reduced.)

▼ Select the image you just created or found; copy it (from the Edit menu).

▼ Quit the graphics program.

▼ Go back to the Finder (press the Application menu in the far right corner of the menu bar; choose "Finder").

▼ Click once on the icon you want to replace. From the File menu, choose "Get Info" (or press Command I).

▼ Click once on the icon that appears in the upper left of the Get Info window (see below).

▼ From the Edit menu, choose "Paste" (or press Command V).

▼ Close the Get Info window (press Command W).

To change an icon back to the original, select its tiny icon in the Get Info window and choose "Clear" or "Cut" (Command X).

Scarlett   Robin

Really, although this can be a wonderful trick, I don't like to encourage beginners to run around changing all their icons, because that original icon tells you so much information. If you start changing icons, how do you know what will happen when you double-click? Is this object a folder that will open to a window, or is it an application, or a document, or a system icon, or what? Just be sensible.

Click here to select the icon's image.

Screen Shot

Picture 1   Picture 2

These icons represent screen shots. These are in the PICT format.

TeachText

You can open a screen shot in TeachText or SimpleText.

How to take a screen shot

Occasionally you will see or create an icon named Picture 1 or Picture 2, etc.; this is a **screen shot,** also known as a "screen dump" or "screen capture." A screen shot is a picture of the computer screen at the time you pressed the special key combination.

For instance, in the original edition of this book in 1988, I created all the graphics using screen shots. With the image on the screen in its natural habitat, I pressed Command Shift 3. Then I opened MacPaint and opened the Picture 1 file (it was called Screen 0 at that time) that had been created. Since the screen shot took a picture of the entire screen, I had to erase all the excess stuff around the image. Then I could change, resize, rotate, flop, etc., the graphic. I put the images in the Scrapbook (page 212) and later pasted them onto these pages. Now I use a "screen capture utility" so I can selectively choose which portion of the screen I want to make a copy of, but screen shots still come in handy for many things, like when you want to capture the image of a dialog box or a warning message for later reference, or when you want to print an image or a window that you see on the screen.

To **take a screen shot,** press Command Shift 3. You will hear an unsettling noise, like a tiny fuse shattering, and your screen may freeze for a moment. Don't worry—the computer is just taking a picture of the screen. In the window for your hard disk you will see the Picture 1 icon as shown above. Every time you take a shot, the icon will have another number. You should rename the icons so you'll know what they are.

You can open a screen shot to see what it looks like in TeachText in SimpleText; in fact, simply double-click on the Picture 1 icon and it will open TeachText or SimpleText and put itself there.

You can also open it in just about any paint or draw program and do whatever you want to it (see following page).

You can open the Picture 1 screen shot in most paint or draw programs and view/change the image just like you would any other graphic image. You can **print a screen shot** from the paint or draw program, or you can paste it into another document, such as a letter or a newsletter.

To print a screen shot as is:

▾ Double-click on the Picture icon at your Desktop. It will open in the utility called TeachText or SimpleText, which is a tiny, limited word processor that you probably have a dozen copies of.

(A screen shot in System 7 will only open in TeachText version 7.0 or later; see the next entry for how to tell which version you have.)

▾ To print the screen shot, from the File menu, choose "Print...," *or* press Command P. Click "OK" when you see the print dialog box.

If you get a message when you double-click on a Picture icon that "TeachText cannot open this kind of file" or that you should "try opening the document within the application," then:

▾ First open TeachText (find it and double-click on it).

▾ An open window automatically appears; close it by pressing Command W.

▾ From the File menu, choose "Open...," *or* press Command O.

▾ Find the name of the Picture icon you want to open and double-click on its name. Now it should open and you should be able to print the image.

Get Info

This is the box into which you can type your own notes.

Get Info is not an icon, but a menu item that can give you important information about any file represented by an icon on your Desktop, be it application, document, system, folder, or any kind at all.

Select an icon, any icon (or of course any file name in a list) by clicking once on it; then from the File menu choose "Get Info." You'll get a little information window that tells you interesting things about the file, such as how big it is, when it was made, which software program it was created in, which software version you have.

Another nice thing about this window is you can type your own information in the Comments box at the bottom (the "insertion point" flashes, waiting for you to type). This comes in very handy: you can write notes to yourself about that particular file and what it contains, briefly detail this budget file from that budget file, make note of further changes you want to employ, leave notes for your lover, etc. The information is automatically saved.

Use Find File to search comments

You can also take advantage of the fact that Find File can search through these comments. Perhaps you have a great habit of making notes in this box about which files need to be updated. You can then search for all the files that need to be updated. See Chapter 26 on Find File.

View comments in your Desktop windows

You can also choose to view your Desktop window with these comments displayed (as shown below). Use the Views control panel to set this up (details on page 250).

The comments appear here.

Note!!!

If at some point you choose to rebuild your Desktop (see page 325), the rebuilding process will unfortunately destroy any Get Info notes. Darn it. I wish they'd get that fixed.

There is a **Locked** checkbox in the lower left corner of the **Get Info** window. If you check this box (click once on it), this file cannot be renamed or inadvertently thrown away—as soon as it hits the trash, a dialog box comes up telling you a locked file cannot be thrown away. It also becomes a *read-only* file: anyone can open and read the file, but no one can save any changes to it. This is handy for sending around copies of a document and ensuring no one accidentally changes anything. You can't even change the Get Info notes.

> If you hold down the Option key, you *can* throw away a locked file. Uh oh.

To **unlock the file,** click in the checkbox again. If there is no X, it is unlocked. (To unlock a *disk,* see page 20.)

Also through the **Get Info** box you can make a "template," out of any document, which is called a **stationery pad.** This is like a reusable "pattern" of a document. For instance, you could create your blank stationery by setting up and arranging your typefaces, margins, indents, graphics, etc. Then make a template of the document. When you next open the template, you'll actually open an *untitled copy* of the file (you may get a little dialog box telling you to name it before it opens). You can write the body of the letter, save it, and print it. The *original* template, or stationery pad, remains unchanged so you always have a clean master copy. The icon for a stationery pad looks like a sheaf of papers, as shown to the upper right.

To make a stationery pad, be at the Desktop:
- ▾ Select a *document* icon by clicking once on it (this doesn't work on any sort of file except a *document*).
- ▾ Press Command I to get the Get Info box.
- ▾ Click the checkbox at the bottom called "Stationery pad." If you don't see that checkbox, it's your **clue** that you can't make a template out of that file.

Christmas Letter   Christmas Letter .template

*On the left is the original document. On the right is the stationery pad created from the document. The **visual clue** is the turned up corner on the **bottom** right instead of the top right. Sometimes a stationery pad icon is **plain white,** as shown above right.*

Locking the File

 Locked

This file is now locked.

☐ **Locked**

This file is now unlocked.

Stationery Pad

Letters

⊠ **Stationery pad**

Document   Stationery

*This little button will eventually appear in most software—it will **also** make a stationery pad, or template. It creates the same kind of file as the Get Info box does.*

Draw lines to match the description with the icon! Carefully read through the list first—although there are several similar icons, each has a different visual clue.

application

hard disk

folder

document

open file

floppy disk

stationery pad

unknown document

selected icon

trash can

control panel

Picture file

System file

ready to rename

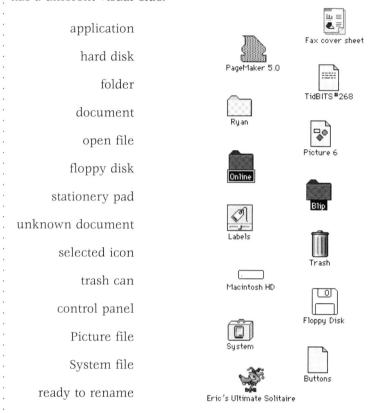

Match the application with a document created in that application:

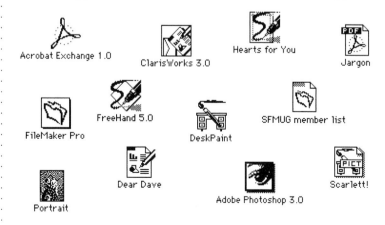

Answers on page 370.

FOLDERS 10

Folders are essential to the organization of your work on the Mac. They are, of course, visual representations of our office and home environment, and they function in much the same way.

You can consider your disk to be the main filing cabinet. When you store items in a filing cabinet, you don't just toss them in the drawer, do you? Can you imagine what a mess your filing cabinet would be without folders? Many Macintoshes become just as messy and just as difficult to find work in. It's very important to learn to take advantage of the folders.

**Creating a
New Folder**

It's easy **to create your own** new, empty folders.

▾ Make sure the window in which you want a new
folder is *active* (click on it).

▾ From the File menu, choose "New Folder," or use the
keyboard shortcut, Command N. A new, "untitled
folder" will appear in the active window.

**Naming the
New Folder**

*If you view your
window "By Icon,"
this is what a new
folder looks like.*

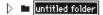

*If you view your
window as a list,
this is what a new
folder looks like.*

When the new folder appears in the active window it is already
highlighted, or *selected* (the **visual clue** is that it's dark), with the
name "untitled folder." The Mac assumes you want to **change
the name,** so while the folder is black with a white border around
the title, **just type the name you want it to have and the new
name will appear.** Yes, really, all you do is type. If you type an
error, just backspace over the error (use the Delete key
[Backspace] in the upper right of the keyboard) and continue
typing. (See the next page if you blew it already.)

You can use up to 31 characters, but you can't use a colon. If
you *try* to type a colon, the Mac will substitute a hyphen. And
don't ever start a folder name (or any file name) with a period.

After you name the new folder, the border disappears as soon as
you click anywhere else or hit the Return or Enter key. When
the border disappears, you are no longer in the naming mode.

**Where did your
new folder go?**

If you are viewing your window in a "list view," such as By Name
or By Size, the new, *untitled* folder will appear in the list *according
to your view.* For instance, if you are viewing your window By
Name, the untitled folder will appear near the bottom of the list,
alphabetized as "untitled." If you are viewing your window By
Date, the untitled folder will appear first in the list because it is
the most recent. After you name the untitled folder and click
somewhere or hit the Enter key, *the new folder gets arranged in
the list according to the view you have chosen.* That is, if you are
viewing By Name, the folder will instantly get alphabetized into
the existing list, *which means it may disappear from your sight.*
You can use the scroll bars to go find it, or just type the first
letter or two of its name and it will pop up again right in front of
your face.

If you accidentally un-highlighted the new folder before you changed its name, or if you want to change the name of any other folder (or any icon of any sort, actually), it is still very easy to do: simply click on the *name* and the icon will turn dark with a border around the name. The border is a **visual clue** that whatever you type now will replace the title that is already there. So go ahead and type the new name while you see the border.

> Once you click on the name, it seems to take a long time for the border to appear. It's a bit faster to click on the icon, then hit the Return key to get the border.

> Use standard word processing procedures (Chapter 14) to type the new name: press-and-drag to select text; click to insert an insertion point; backspace to delete characters, etc. Hit the UpArrow key to move the insertion point to the beginning of the name, and the DownArrow key to move it to the end of the name.

Changing the Name of a Folder

To put something inside the folder, press-and-drag any icon over to it; when the folder turns black or changes color, let go and the icon will drop inside. Remember, it is the tip of the pointer that selects the folder, *not* the shadow of the icon that goes inside.

You can have folders inside of folders inside of folders, which is technically called the *Hierarchical File System* (HFS). You can drag an item from one window and put it into a folder in another window.

The folder does not have to be open to place an item inside of it, and the folder can be gray. Your window does not have to be in Icon View; you can use the same technique in any list of files in the window. The only trick to putting something inside a folder is that you have to be able to see both the item you want to drop in *and* the folder you want to drop into. Sometimes this requires moving your windows around the screen so you can see both items at once.

Putting Something inside a Folder

Double-click on any folder to **open** it to a window that displays all the valuable files you have stored inside. You can also, of course, select a folder (click once on it) and then choose "Open" from the File menu. Or select the folder and press Command O as a shortcut.

Opening a Folder

Removing Something from a Folder

To **remove** something from a folder, you must *open* the folder first (see previous page) so you see its window and the icons inside. Then simply press-and-drag the icon(s) out, either to the Desktop or to another folder or window.

Note: Moving as opposed to Copying

If you are moving the file to someplace else on the *same* disk, the file will just pop out of that one folder and into the other.

BUT if you are moving the file to a *different* disk, the original icon will stay put in the original folder and a *copy* of the file will be placed on the other disk. (See the tips on pages 102–103.)

Organizing Your Disk Using Folders

Below is an example of a well-organized hard disk; there isn't a bunch of junk lying around making it difficult to find things. (*I wish it was this easy to keep a house organized.*) It's basically arranged the same way a filing cabinet would be. Some folders have folders inside of folders.

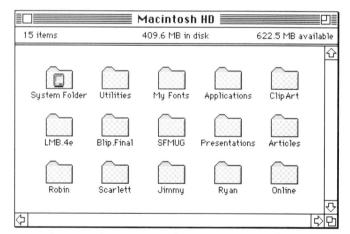

Everything on the hard disk (the "filing cabinet") is tucked into a folder. The folders may each contain more folders to further organize their contents.

You may prefer to view your window as some sort of list, as described in the chapter on Desktop Windows (pages 68–70). When you choose any sort of list (by Name, Kind, Size, etc.) your folders are displayed in what is known as **outline mode.** There's a tiny triangle next to each folder's name, and if you click on that triangle you will see what's in that folder without opening another window—as in the folders "Scarlett" and "Online" to the right. The items contained within a folder are indented just a little from the left, which is your **visual clue** that they are inside.

You can keep opening folders within folders until you are all the way to the bottom level of your filing system, *with everything displayed in the same window.*

Using the outline view, you can see at a glance exactly how your files are organized and what's in them. You can move items from one folder to another, even if the folders are several levels apart. You can Shift-click (page 106) to select items from any number of different folders. (These techniques are explained in detail in Chapter 11 on Copying and Selecting.)

▼ To **expand,** or *open* a folder, single-click on the little sideways-pointing triangle (or select the icon and press Command RightArrow).

▼ To **compress,** or *close* a folder, single-click on the downward-pointing triangle (or select the icon and press Command LeftArrow).

▼ To simultaneously **compress all the folders** that are expanded, press Command A to select everything in the window. Then press Command LeftArrow.

▼ *Or* you can choose "By Icon" from the View menu. Then go back to the View menu and choose your preferred list view again—all the folders will be closed.

Outline Mode

Expanding a folder

Compressing a folder

Compressing all folders

Creating a New Folder for a Specific Project

One of the best ways to keep windows tidy is to **create a specific new folder** for a new project *before* you create the documents for the project, and then *save the documents right into their own folder*. For instance, if you are about to create a budget report with seven variations, or a newsletter in which there will be ten to twelve separate stories, it is best to store all these files in one folder with a recognizable name, right?

Don't read this yet!
Don't read it until you are comfortable with your Mac, and until you have experienced frustration over losing files through disorganization.

The solution makes more sense if you've had the problem first.

▼ **At your Desktop, before you open the application** to start creating the reports, make your new folder and name it (let's name this one *Budget News*). This new folder can be inside of another folder, of course.

This is the new folder in the hard disk window, waiting for you to save new stories inside.

▼ Open your application and create the first report.

▼ Choose "Save As..." and name the story. Find the folder *Budget News* in the Save As dialog box (as shown below).

If you have trouble finding the folder, read the details in Chapter 15 on Saving, page 135.

▼ In the *list box*, or *directory*, you'll see the name of the folder you created earlier. Double-click the name ("Budget News" in this example) to open the folder in the directory.

In this example, here in the list box is the folder Budget News; double-click the name to open it.

If you don't see the folder listed here, perhaps you have it tucked inside of another folder, in which case you will need to open that other folder first. Or click the Desktop button to see if the folder is on another disk.

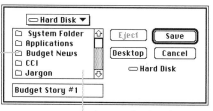

This is the list box, or directory.

▼ After you double-click on the name of the folder, you will see its name and an open folder icon in the label above the list box, as shown below. If you choose to Save right now, it will be saved into *that* folder.

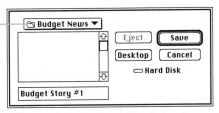

*Make sure this **label** shows the name of your folder.*

If you see the name of your folder in the directory beneath the label, double-click on that name to open the folder and make its name appear in the label.

Whenever you save a file, it is always saved into whichever folder or onto whichever disk appears in the label!!!

▼ When you go back to your Desktop you'll find that everything is tucked away right where it belongs, right into its own folder, and nothing will have been misplaced.

If you refuse to read and follow these directions and have lost files because *you don't know where you saved them,* do read about Find File in Chapter 26. And when you really get frustrated with losing files all the time, read the special chapter on Navigating (finding your way around these dialog boxes), Chapter 29.

For more details

1. What is the purpose of a folder?

   . . . .

2. When you go to the File menu and choose "New Folder," how do you know where that new folder will appear?

   . . . .

3. What is the keyboard shortcut to create a new folder?

   . . . .

4. How do you rename a folder, and what is the **visual clue** that tells you a folder is ready to be renamed?

   . . . .

5. How do you open a folder?

   . . . .

6. What happens when you open a folder, and what do you see?

   . . . .

7. What are the keyboard shortcuts for expanding and compressing folders in outline mode?

   . . . .

8. How can you close all the expanded folders at once?

   . . . .

9. What are two big advantages to outline mode?

   . . . .

10. Are you going to create folders to organize your Macintosh work, just like you would make folders for your filing cabinet?

   . . . .

Answers on page 370.

COPYING AND SELECTING

Copying files is an everyday task. You may need to copy an application from its original disk onto your hard disk; copy a report to give to a co-worker; copy a document to take to a service bureau for high-resolution printing; create the ever-necessary backup copy; etc., etc., etc. Before you copy any file, though, you must first **select** it.

Apple has made it as easy as possible to copy files on the Mac (which is why *pirating,* or copying software without paying for it, has always been such a problem). Copying files has no effect on the *original file,* nor is there any loss of quality in the new version—there is absolutely no difference between the original and the copy.

SOFTWARE PUBLISHERS

Copying from the Hard Disk to a Floppy Disk

Actually, the copying process only works when you copy a file *from one disk to another disk.* When you drag an icon into another position on the same disk, such as into another folder on the same disk, you are simply *moving* the file, not *copying* it.

To copy a file from your hard disk to a floppy disk:

▾ Click on the icon representing the file you want to copy.

▾ Press-and-drag the selected file to the icon of the disk you want to copy it onto. A little message comes up telling you it's being copied.

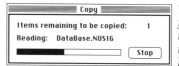

*This message will appear when you copy. Notice there are lines in the title bar; this is a **visual clue** that you can drag this message box around on the screen.*

Copying from a Floppy Disk to the Hard Disk

There are a couple of ways to copy files from your floppy disk to your hard disk. Read the rest of this page before you copy.

Copy from a floppy disk to your hard disk (one way):

▾ Press on the icon of the floppy disk and drag it onto the icon of your hard disk. The Mac will make a new folder on the hard disk, name it with the name of the floppy disk, and copy all the contents of the floppy disk into the new folder. Too cool.

But unless you are absolutely sure that you want to copy *every single item* from the floppy disk, don't do it this way! More often, you want to *selectively* copy files from the floppy.

Copy from a floppy disk to your hard disk (another way):

▾ Double-click on the disk icon to open its window.

▾ Take a look at the files on the disk, *then selectively* choose the ones you need to copy. Press-and-drag the chosen files to the hard disk icon, or drag them directly into a folder on the hard disk.

Don't ever copy another System Folder onto your hard disk!

You can copy from your hard disk onto a floppy disk, or from a floppy disk onto your hard disk, or into a folder on any other disk. In every case, make sure that the icon of the disk or folder you are copying *into* turns *black,* which is your **visual clue** that it is *selected* as the place to copy to. When the icon is black, that means it's ready to accept the file/s. If the icon is not black, you'll just be placing it *next* to the icon, not *inside* of it. The *tip of the pointer* is what turns any icon black.

Make sure the disk or folder you are copying to is selected!

When you copy straight into an open *window,* though, the window will not turn black. If you look closely in System 7.5, you will see an extra border line appear around the inside of the window, your **visual clue** that the window is selected.

The *copying* process, remember, only takes place if you drag the file to another *disk.*

Duplicate/Copy a File on the Same Disk

To make a copy of the file on the *same* disk:

- ▾ First click *once* on the file icon to select it.
- ▾ From the File menu choose "Duplicate" (*or* press Command D). This creates a second version in the same folder named "_____ copy." If you make more copies of the same file, they will be named "_____ copy 1," "_____ copy 2," etc.

When you duplicate or copy *folders,* every item contained within that folder is also copied.

> If you want to *put a **copy** of a file into another folder **on the same disk,*** hold down the Option key while moving the file. This does *not* rename the file "_____ copy."

Important tip you will like!

If you have a large file to copy, you can **go back to work** on something else while the computer is going through its copying process. The trick is that you must have the document you want to work on *already open* before you choose to copy. If it is open, then while the Mac is copying go to the Application menu (far right on menu bar) and choose the application you were previously working in.

Go back to work while computer is copying

Copying from Floppy to Floppy with Only One Floppy Drive

Ejected Disk

*When you eject a disk using the menu, the icon turns gray. This is a **visual clue** that the computer still knows about this disk.*

Sometimes you need to copy information from one floppy disk onto another floppy disk. If you have two floppy disk drives, this is no problem, right? You stick a disk in each drive and do it. But most people do not have two floppy drives. There is a little trick **to copy from floppy to floppy with one floppy drive:**

▼ Insert the floppy disk you want to copy *onto*. While the disk is selected (click once on its icon if it isn't), choose "Eject Disk" from the Special menu (*or* you can press Command E). This will eject the disk but leave a gray icon on the Desktop.

▼ Insert the disk to be copied *from*. Open this disk (double-click on the icon) and select the files to copy. Press-and-drag the files over to the gray icon of the ejected disk.

▼ As the Mac reads info from one disk and copies it onto the other, it will spit out each disk and tell you which one to insert next. Just follow the directions; this is called *disk swapping*. It will eventually end.

▼ If you end up with a gray disk icon on the screen, just drag it out through the trash can.

Disk-to-disk copying

Ejected Disk

Inserted Disk

*If you drag the icon of one floppy disk on top of another floppy disk (as shown by the shadow under the pointer), you will replace **the entire contents** of the other disk. Be careful! Be sure that's what you want to do!*

Instead of copying selected files, you can just drag the icon of the inserted disk itself onto the gray disk, which will **replace** everything that was ever on the gray disk with the entire contents of the inserted disk. When you replace the contents of one disk with the contents of another, it's called a **disk-to-disk copy.**

If you *want* to replace the contents of the disk, this is a tidy way to do it. Fortunately, the Mac knows that sometimes you do things you didn't really mean to, so when you drag the inserted disk icon and drop it onto the ejected disk icon, you get a thoughtful message:

Notice that the dark border is around the *Cancel* button. The dark border is a **visual clue** indicating you can press the Return or the Enter key to activate that button; that button is *usually* the safest thing to do (Cancel, in this case).

To copy more than one file at a time, *select* more than one file (detailed in the next paragraph). When more than one file is selected, dragging *one* file will drag them *all together,* either to the trash can, into another folder, onto another disk, or simply to clean up the joint. Just make sure when you drag that you press on one of the *black* items; if you click anywhere else, all the items will be deselected!

You may have noticed in the Desktop that when you *press in an empty space and drag the pointer,* a dotted rectangle comes out of the tip—this is the **selection marquee** (sometimes known as *marching ants*), common in many Mac programs. On the Desktop, any file that is partially enclosed in this marquee will be selected.

 *The selection marquee — just press-and-drag with the pointer tool.*

Selecting all the icons this way will of course turn them all black.

  ▾ When you press-and-drag on the *black* area of one of the selected items, they will all drag together.

  ▾ Click in any *white* space or on any unselected icon or on the Desktop to *deselect* all the files.

You can also drag to select files that are next to each other while viewing a window in one of the list views (by Name, Date, Size, etc.). Press in a white space in the window next to a file name and start to drag. The selection marquee will appear when you drag, and any item that is even partially enclosed within the marquee will be added to the selection.

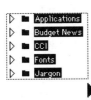 *Press-and-drag to select adjacent items in a list view. Click anywhere else to deselect all the items in the group.*

Copying More Than One File at a Time

Selecting more than one file in a list view

Shift-Click to Select More Than One File

Another method of selecting more than one item is to **Shift-click.** You may have noticed that once a file is selected, it gets deselected the instant you click somewhere else.

> *But, hold down the Shift key while clicking* and every one of the files you click will be selected. You can select several files in different corners of your window.

Shift-Click to Deselect

In the same manner, you can **deselect** one file at a time. For instance, if you group a bunch of files within the selection marquee but you don't want the one in the middle, simply hold down the Shift key and click once on that one—it will be the only one deselected.

Hold the Shift key down and click once on a selected file to deselect it.

Selection Shortcuts

To select any single file (no matter how you are viewing the window), just **type the first letter** of the name of the file and you'll be taken right to it. If there are several files with the same first letter, quickly type the first couple of letters. This makes it a lot easier to find your folder named Waldo in an alphabetized list, for instance, or a file that starts with Z, or any icon in a crowded folder. *This technique also works in any dialog box with a list of files, such as in an "Open" dialog box.*

Arrow keys

You can also use the **arrow keys** to select files. Once you have a file selected, either by clicking on it or typing its first letter, the arrow keys will select the next icon or file name in the window. In a list, the UpArrow and the DownArrow select, of course, the next file in the list. In an icon view, all four of the arrows will select the icon to the left, right, up, or down, unless there is nothing else in that direction.

Select the next file alphabetically

▼ To select the icon that would be alphabetically *after* the currently selected icon, whether you are in an icon view or a list view that is not alphabetized, press the **Tab key.**

▼ To select the icon that would be alphabetically *before* the currently selected icon, press **Shift Tab.**

You can also use the **edit keys** on an extended keyboard to scroll through a window, although this does not *select* anything. The edit keys (that little set between the alphabet keys and the numeric keypad) come in handy, though, if you want to get to the top or the bottom of a list instantly, where you might want to select something, or if you want to move the window past in a hurry.

Home rolls the window straight to the top.

End rolls the window straight to the bottom.

PageUp and **PageDown** roll the window one window-sized section up or down.

A common complaint about selecting a file name in a list by typing the first letter or two is that the name appears at the *bottom* of the window. It is much more convenient (really—you'll soon discover this) if the file name shows up at the *top* of the window. You can take advantage of the edit keys to solve this problem:

If you have an extended keyboard, press the **End** key before you type the first letter or two of the file name. This will make your selected file appear at the *top* of the window!

Edit keys

Selected file name at the top of the list

You really must have had the problem first before you can appreciate this solution. If you haven't had the problem, ignore this until later.

Selecting from Expanded Views

If you are viewing your window By Icon, you can select items *from only one window at a time.* But if you view the window by any kind of list (Name, Date, Size, etc.), then you can **expand** the folders and **select** *any number of files from any number of expanded folders.*

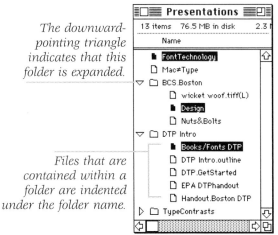

The downward-pointing triangle indicates that this folder is expanded.

The three high-lighted files you see in this window are selected. Press on any one of them to drag them all together, to open them all at once, to print them, etc.

Files that are contained within a folder are indented under the folder name.

Notice there are two files in the above window that are not in any folder. Then there are three folders, two of which have been *expanded* (I clicked on their triangles) to show the contents. By Shift-clicking I selected three separate items from three separate places. If I press-and-drag on any one of these three items, all three of them will move. I can copy them, trash them, print them, move them, etc., etc., etc.

You can also **use Find File to select files** from all over your hard disk (see Chapter 26 on Find File for all the intimate details). Even if there are so many files that Find File cannot display all of them at once on the screen, they are all selected. Dragging one of the selected icons to the Desktop will actually drag all of the found files to the Desktop, even if you can't see them.

I often use Find File to select a file even when I know where it is because it is so much faster than digging through layers of folders. If I need a document, I hit Command F, type in a few letters, hit the Return key, then lo and behold there is my file in front of my face. I hit Command O to open it (since Find File *selects* it for me) and off I go.

System 7.5 has a new, improved version of this Find feature. All the found files will be shown in one window, and you can select them from there and drag them to the trash (remember, press on one selected item and all selected items will follow; the tip of the pointer will turn the trash can black).

No matter which system you are running, make it a point to learn to use the Find feature (Chapter 26)—you'll discover uses for it quite often.

Using "Find File" to Select Files

Circle the correct choice in the following multiple choice and true/false questions.

1. When you drag a file from your hard disk to a floppy disk, you are:
   a. making a copy of the file onto the floppy disk.
   b. making a copy of the file onto the hard disk.
   c. simply moving the file from one place to another.

2. When you drag a file from one window on your hard disk to another window on your hard disk, you are:
   a. making a copy of the file onto the floppy disk.
   b. making a copy of the file onto the hard disk.
   c. simply moving the file from one place to another.

3. When you drag a file from a floppy disk to your hard disk, you are:
   a. making a copy of the file onto the floppy disk.
   b. making a copy of the file onto the hard disk.
   c. simply moving the file from one place to another.

4. If you want to make a copy of a file on the same disk, the best way is to:
   a. make a copy onto a floppy disk, then drag that copy back onto the hard disk.
   b. select the file, then from the File menu, choose "Duplicate." *Or* press Command D.
   c. hold down the Option key as you drag the file into another folder or window.

5. In outline mode, you can select multiple files:
   a. by dragging around them with the pointer tool.
   b. that are in different folders.
   c. both a and b.

T F 6. It's always okay to drag the icon of the floppy disk onto the icon of the hard disk when you want to copy something onto your hard disk.

T F 7. To select more than one file at a time, hold down the Option key as you click each one.

T F 8. You can press-and-drag the pointer around any number of files to select them all.

T F 9. The quickest (and coolest) way to select a file is to type the first letter or couple of letters of its name.

T F 10. Once a file is selected, the Tab key will select the next largest file.

Answers on page 370.

TRASH CAN

The **trash can icon** works just like the trash can in your yard—you put things in it you don't want anymore and the garbage collector comes and takes it away and you never see it again. You can move the trash can around on your Desktop and it will stay where you last left it.

Trash

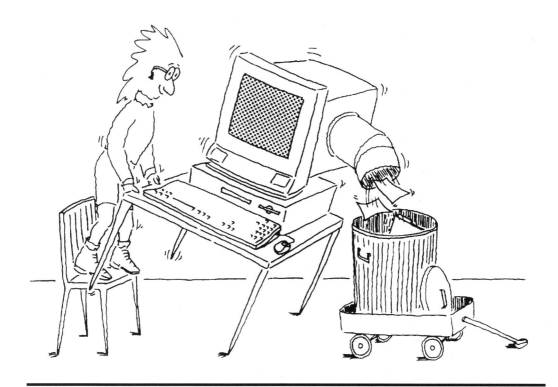

Putting Something in the Trash

Trash

The bulging trash can is an obvious **visual clue** *that there is something in the garbage.*

To put something in the trash, press-and-drag an icon over to the can. *When the can becomes black,* let go and the icon will drop inside. Don't let go of the icon before the can turns black! If you find a bunch of garbage hanging around outside the trash, *it's because you didn't wait for the can to turn black*—you just set the trash down next to the can. Try again.

The trick here is that the *tip of the pointer* must touch the can! Whether you are putting one icon in the trash or whether you have selected fifteen icons and are dragging them all together to the trash, **the tip of the pointer** is the thing that opens the lid (figuratively, of course). The shadows of the objects *have nothing to do with it*—forget those shadows trailing along behind; just make sure the tip of the pointer touches the can and turns it black. *Then* let go.

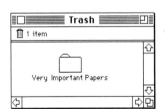

It's the tip of the pointer, not the shadow of the icon, that opens the trash.

Taking Something out of the Trash

To remove something from the trash, double-click on the trash can and you'll find that it opens up to a window, just like any other window. So if you decide you want that item you just threw away, you can go get it. Either press-and-drag the icon back to the disk/folder it came from, **or** click once on the file in the trash to select it, then from the File menu choose **Put Away,** and the file will go right back where it came from.

```
┌─────────────────────────┐
│▤□══════ Trash ══════□▤│
├─────────────────────────┤
│ 🗑 1 item              ⇧│
│                         │
│            ┌──┐         │
│            │  │         │
│      Very Important Papers│
│                        ⇩│
│◁               ▷ ◫     │
└─────────────────────────┘
```

The trash can opens to a window.

Anything you put in the trash can will stay there, even if you turn off the computer, until you consciously empty the trash: from the Special menu, choose "Empty Trash." Once you do that, everything in the trash can is gone forever. No amount of crying or pleading or screaming or kicking will bring it back. Believe me. *(Well, there is software and there are technicians who can often bring back your information, so if you lose something really important call your local guru or user group. But in general, consider it gone.)*

Emptying the Trash

When you empty the trash, you'll get a **warning box** asking if you really want to throw the files away.

The Warning Box

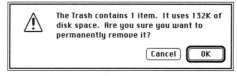

> ⚠ The Trash contains 1 item. It uses 132K of disk space. Are you sure you want to permanently remove it?
>
> [Cancel]   [OK]

- ▾ **If you don't want to see the warning box,** hold down the Option key when you choose "Empty Trash."
- ▾ **If you want to throw away a locked item,** hold down the Option key when you choose "Empty Trash."
- ▾ When trashing items to make more space on the disk, the trash must be emptied before the space will open up; watch the numbers in the information bar of the window when you *empty* the trash.

If you find this warning box to be a nuisance (yes), you can easily **disable it** permanently (permanently until you choose to turn it back on again). Perhaps if you have kids working on your machine, you might want to leave it there.

Disabling the Warning Box

- ▾ Select the trash can icon (click *once* on it).
- ▾ From the File menu, choose "Get Info."
- ▾ Click the checkbox "Warn before emptying" so there is no check in it.
- ▾ Close the Get Info window (click in its close box *or* press Command W.)

Uncheck this box to avoid the warning.

> **Trash Info**
>
> 🗑 Trash
>
> **Where:** On the desktop
>
> **Contents:** 1 file and 1 folder are in the Trash for a total of 33K.
>
> **Modified:** Mon, Apr 10, 1995, 10:38 PM
>
> ☒ **Warn before emptying**

1. What does it indicate when the trash can is bulging?

2. When does the stuff in the trash disappear?

3. What happens if you double-click on the trash can?

4. If you decided a file should *not* be in the trash after all, how do you get it out? What is the keyboard shortcut that makes it easy to put an item in the trash back where it came from?

5. If you have emptied the trash, can you get your file back?

6. How can you throw away a locked item?

7. What key do you hold down to avoid seeing the trash warning?

8. How can you disable the trash warning?

9. Can you think of times when it would be best to maintain that warning instead of disabling it?

10. Does the trash can have to stay in the bottom right corner?

Answers on page 370.

OPENING FILES

What is a **file**? It is a rather generic term referring to just about any icon on your computer. A file might be an "application," which is the program you use to create things, or a "document," which is the thing you created in your application, or a "font," which is a typeface, or a number of other sorts of computerized pieces of information. The files you will work with the most are applications and documents. This chapter just gives you some basic guidelines to understanding and working with these files.

What is an Application?

The term **application** is often used synonymously with **program** (although an *application* is only one form of programming). *Application* refers to the software package you use to create your documents, such as ClarisWorks, Adobe PageMaker, Macromedia FreeHand, etc. They all do something different; they all have a particular function. Sometimes it takes a little research to find the software applications to meet your specific needs.

Opening an Application

PageMaker 5.0

Application icon

To **open an application,** or software program, you will need to find its icon or file name, whether it's on your hard disk or on a floppy. Application icons, as noted in the chapter on icons, typically look fancier than anything else.

If you view your window "By Kind," as shown below, the applications will be at the top of the list. You can click on the title "Kind" in the information bar to change views!

All the files in this folder relate to PageMaker. The window is organized "By Name," so you have to really look for the actual PageMaker application. Do you see it?

*Notice there is an underline below the heading "Kind" in the information bar, which is a **visual clue** that this list is organized "By Kind." Do you see the application listed first?*

▼ From the Desktop, double-click on an application icon or name.

▼ This usually opens to a blank page, ready for you to create a new document. Some applications, however, open to a commercial, and you need to go to the File menu and choose "New" to create a new page, or "Open" to find a document you previously created that you want to open again. Some applications ask you what sort of document you want, or how you want your pages set up.

To **open a document** that has already been created and saved in an application, find its icon or its file name on your Desktop. (A document icon, remember, typically looks like a page with the upper right corner turned down.)

Double-click on a document icon; most of the time this will open the *application,* placing your *document* on the screen as you last saved it.

Now, just because you have an icon representing a document you created in a certain software application *doesn't mean you can open up that document just anywhere.* Double-clicking on a document icon will only open it **IF** *the application itself is also in the computer,* either on the hard disk or on another disk that is inserted into one of the drives. If the application isn't there, then the document doesn't have anywhere to put itself! Generally, you must have the same *version* of the application as the one in which it was created (for info on "versions," see page 30).

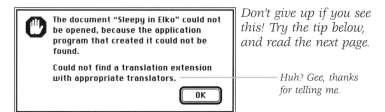

The document "Sleepy in Elko" could not be opened, because the application program that created it could not be found.

Could not find a translation extension with appropriate translators.

OK

Don't give up if you see this! Try the tip below, and read the next page.

Huh? Gee, thanks for telling me.

And then again, some programs won't *allow* you to open their documents from the Desktop. If you know the software program is really installed *in* the computer on the hard disk, and you still get a message telling you an application can't be found, there is a possible solution. Also, if your document was created in an older version of the application, also try this:

▼ *Open the application first.*

▼ From the File menu, choose "Open." This will take you to the Open dialog box—tips for getting around in it are on the next page.

(See the section on the following page for tips on using the Open dialog box and also on opening documents for which you don't have the application.)

Opening a Document from the Desktop

Where's Chico?
Document icon

Important Note!

Drag-and-Drop to Open a Document

You can also open a document by **dragging the icon** and **dropping it** on top of its application icon. You'll notice that the application icon will turn black, which is the **visual clue** that if you let go your document will open.

Now, a cool thing about this trick is that you can open a document in an application other than the one it was created in! For instance, ClarisWorks is able to open documents created in many other applications. If you have a word processing document that someone gave you but you don't have the program they wrote it in, you can drag the foreign document on top of the ClarisWorks application icon. If ClarisWorks turns black, let go of the document and Claris will open it for you.

So if you ever get those blank document icons with no clue where they came from, or even whether they are paint files, or text, or spreadsheets, drag them over every application program you own. Whichever application turns black will open the document.

Check Chapter 25 on Aliases, page 257, for directions on creating an alias of each application you own. You can store these aliases in one folder on your Desktop and thus make them easily accessible for opening all files, strange or not.

New vs. Open

Once an application is up and running, in the File menu you see two choices: **New** and **Open.** This confused me at first because I thought, "Well, I want to *open* a *new* one." The difference is this:

▾ **New** creates a clean, blank page on which you can begin a *new* document.

▾ **Open** takes you to a dialog box (shown on the next page) where you can choose to *open* a document that has been previously created and saved.

Finding your way around an **"Open" dialog box** is called "navigating." It's one of the most important skills you can learn, and you'll need this skill in other dialog boxes, like when you Save documents or when you import or export text. Try to take the time to understand and absorb what each part of the dialog box is telling you. I guarantee you will be a happier person.

An "Open" Dialog Box

See Chapter 29 on Navigating for full details!

*The name in the **label** shown here is the specific folder or disk that contains the files you see in the list below.*

*When the icon in the **title** or **label** here is a **folder** (as opposed to a disk) this is a **menu**. Press on the label to see the hierarchy. As shown here, this menu indicates that the folder **Robin** is on the **Hard Disk,** which is on the **Desktop**.*

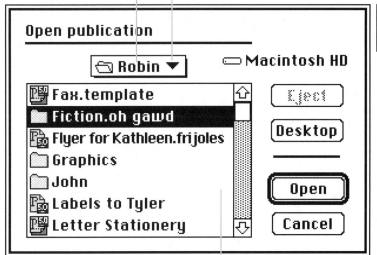

*The only **documents** you will see in this list (directory) are documents that the current application can open.*

*Single-click on any name to **select** that file.*

*Double-click the name to **open** the file.*

*When you **double-click on a folder,** it opens here to show you a list of the files inside that folder.*

*When you **double-click on a document,** it opens that document on your screen.*

*Click **Eject** to eject a disk so you can insert another.*

*Click **Desktop** to see what's on the Desktop level, including disks in other drives.*

*Click **Open** to open the **selected** file; **or** double-click on the file name.*

*Click **Cancel** to take you back to wherever you were without opening anything.*

ClarisWorks 3.0

1. Is this file an application or a document?

. . . .

2. What will happen when you double-click on it?

. . . .

Dear Dave

3. Is this file an application or a document?

. . . .

4. What will happen when you double-click on it?

. . . .

5. What would be the fastest way to view this window "By Kind" so you can tell which icon is the application?

. . . .

6. In the File menu in an application, what is the difference between "New" and "Open"?

. . . .

7. Label these parts on the Open dialog box, below:
   a. the **directory,** or **list** of files and folders you can open.
   b. a **document** that can be opened.
   c. the **name of the folder** that contains the files you see in the list.
   d. the hidden **menu.**

Answers on page 371.

TYPING

In some applications **typing** is the main idea, as in a word processor. In some, it is the way to input the data whose purpose is to be manipulated, as in a database or a spreadsheet. In others, it is a sideline that is occasionally necessary, as in a paint program. And everywhere you find dialog boxes where you type some answer or other, and even on your Desktop you type the names of files and folders. Fortunately, in the consistent Mac environment, typing follows the same patterns and features everywhere.

I-Beam

You may already be familiar with the Macintosh word processing **I-beam** (pronounced eye-beam): ⟙

On the Macintosh, the I-beam is a **visual clue** that you are now in a typing mode, as opposed to having an arrow or a cross-hair or any number of other "cursors" that appear in various programs.

The I-beam is simply another pointer. And just like the pointer, it doesn't do anything until you *click it* or *press-and-drag it.*

Insertion Point

When you move the I-beam pointer to a spot within text and *click,* it sets down a flashing **insertion point** that looks like this:| (but it flashes).

After you click the mouse to set the insertion point, then you can move the I-beam out of the way (using the mouse)—**the insertion point is what you need to begin typing,** *not the I-beam!!*

With the insertion point flashing, anything you type will start at that point and move out to the right. This is true whether the insertion point is at the beginning or the end of a paragraph, in the middle of a word, in a field of a dialog box, under an icon at your Desktop, or anywhere else. (The only time the words will not move to the right is if the text is flush right or centered, or if a tab other than left-aligned has been set.)

At any time you can take the mouse, move the I-beam pointer somewhere else, click it, and start typing from the new insertion point.

Delete (or Backspace)

Also from that insertion point, press the **Delete** key (found in the upper right, called the **Backspace** key on older keyboards) to backspace over text and remove any letters along the way. So you can backspace/delete to **correct typos** as you go, or you can click to set the insertion point down anywhere else in your text and backspace/delete from there.

When you **select text,** it becomes **highlighted.** Once it is selected, you can do things to it, such as change its size, the typeface, delete it, etc.

If you double-click on a word with the I-beam anywhere on the Mac, the entire word is selected, indicated by the highlighting.

This ▉word▉ is highlighted.

If you want to select more than one word, press-and-drag over the entire area you wish to highlight.

▉Part of this line▉ is highlighted.

Once a word is highlighted (selected), anything you type will *entirely replace* the highlighted text. Or you can now change the font (typeface) or style or size of the text using your menu commands. Or you can copy or cut or delete that text. Or you can paste something in to replace it. In fact, you *cannot* do any of these things *unless* the text is first highlighted. (Each of these procedures is explained in this chapter.)

To **un-highlight,** click once anywhere, even in the black or colored space.

FRANK, HOW'S YOUR FIRST DAY ON A MAC?

GREAT! IT'S LIKE TV WITH TYPOS.

When to Use the Return Key

A word wrap is sometimes called a soft Return (although technically it isn't, really).

Word wrap: In a word processor, you should *never* hit the Return key at the end of your line, *unless* it is the end of the paragraph or unless you *really do* want the line to end there, as in an address. This is because word processors *word wrap*—the words just wrap themselves around onto the next line when they get to the right margin. Why is that? Well . . .

Hard Return: When you press the Return key you insert what is called a *hard return* that tells the computer to always stop the line at that point. Then when you change your margins, your line will *always* break at that hard return, even if there are only two words on the line. So, just keep those nimble fingers moving along and only hit the Return key when you really want a new paragraph.

> On the Mac, a **paragraph** is created every time you hit the Return key. So a return address of three lines is really three paragraphs.

Double-Return: Hitting the Return key twice is like pushing the carriage return on a typewriter twice—you get a double space between the lines. This is for extra space between paragraphs (although in most word processors you can ask for an automatic increase of space between paragraphs). If you want the entire document, or even just a piece of it, double-spaced—that's different: there is always an instant way to change your spacing to double-spaced, usually just a button to click *after you select all the text*. Check your manual for the method for your particular application.

Most word processing programs have a command for showing invisible characters such as Returns and spaces, which makes it easier to get rid of them. The command might be something like "Show invisibles" or "Show ¶" or "Display ¶."

Removing a Return: The computer sees a Return as just another character, which means to remove a Return you simply *backspace over it,* just as you would to remove an unwanted character. The problem is, in most programs you can't *see* the Return character. So you must set the insertion point just to the left of the first character on the line and backspace/delete, like so:

> |Set the insertion point at the beginning of the line (as shown here) and backspace to *remove the empty line* above this one. Backspace/delete *again* to *wrap the sentence back up* to the one above.

The computer thinks a **blank space** is just the same as any other character you can see. Every tab, return, Spacebar space, etc., is a character on the Mac. This means you can select blank spaces, blank lines, blank tabbed spaces, or Returns to delete them. Select and delete them just like you would any other character.

Blank Spaces

> **The space between**
> **these▮▮▮▮▮▮words is highlighted.**
>
> **If you hit double Returns,**
> **you can also select the blank space**
> ▮▮▮▮▮▮▮▮▮▮▮▮▮▮▮▮▮▮▮▮▮▮▮▮▮▮
> **between the lines to delete it.**

Also, since these blank spaces are characters, you can actually change the size of them (font size, that is), as well as the *leading* (space between the lines), the style, the paragraph spacing, etc.

And a most important thing: when you **center** a word or line, the Mac takes all those blank spaces into consideration, so any Spacebar spaces or any first-line indents or any tabs you've inserted will be used to calculate the center of the line, making the line not *appear* centered!

Centering Text

> **This line is centered.**
> **This line is also centered** —— *I hit the Tab key before I typed the*
> **but it includes a tab.** *first word in this centered line. Thus*
> *the line appears not to be centered.*
>
> **The invisible tab character**
> **that is disrupting the alignment**
> **must be highlighted**
> **and removed, like so:**
> —— *I selected the tab space and deleted it.*
> ▮▮▮▮**This line is also centered.**
>
> **Then it will be centered just fine:**
>
> **This line is also centered.** —— *After I deleted the invisible space,*
> *the line centered just fine.*

Changing Fonts (typefaces) and Rule #2

Throughout the entire Mac environment, to make any changes to anything you must follow Rule #2:

Select First, Then Do It To It.

For instance, **to change to a different font,** or typeface: first *select* the characters you want to change (press-and-drag over the word[s]), then *choose* the font name you want to change it into. The font list is found in your menu under various labels, depending on your program.

Formatting of the insertion point

Notice that the insertion point picks up whatever font and style and size and alignment *is directly to its left.* No matter where you set the insertion point, you will type in the font, etc., of that character, even if that character is an empty space.

Advanced tip!

Now, let's say you know that the next thing you're going to type is going to be in a different font. Do you need to type the text first and then select those characters and change the font? No!

▾ Make sure your insertion point is positioned where you are going to type with the new font.

▾ *With no text selected,* go up to the menu and choose the font (and style and size, if you like); *when there is no text selected, all the formatting gets poured into the insertion point*—whatever you type next will be in the font you just chose.

As soon as you place the insertion point elsewhere, though, it will again pick up all the formatting of the character to its left.

Changing Style

Style refers to whether the type is plain, **bold,** outline, *italic,* etc. To change the style of the type, you need to follow Rule #2: *select first, then do it to it.* **Select** the type you want to change (highlight it), then **choose** the style you want from the menu. You can choose more than one of these; for instance, you can have a face that is *bold-italic-outlined-shadowed.* Yuk.

To remove all of the style choices at once, simply *select* the text and *choose* Plain or Normal.

As mentioned in that last section about changing *fonts*, you can choose the style you want from the menu *before* you type it (as long as you don't move the insertion point after choosing). But even that's a pain if you just want to italicize the next word and then return to normal text. This is an easier method:

Notice the keyboard shortcuts in the style menu? They are almost always Command **B** for Bold, Command **I** for Italic, etc. (Some programs may use Command Shift B and Command Shift I, etc.).

- ▾ As you're typing along, simply press Command **B** and the next word you type will be **bold!**

- ▾ When you want the next word to be *not* bold, press Command **B** again and it will take *off* the bold (that's called a *toggle switch*—when choosing the same command turns that command off).

- ▾ Logically, you can press Command **B I** to create a word that is (guess!) ***bold italic.***

- ▾ If you want to take all the extra formatting off at once (for instance, you want to remove the shadow, the outline, and the bold), select the text and apply the shortcut for Plain, Normal, or Regular style (whatever your application calls it).

Size in type is measured in *points*. There are 72 points in one inch. In your menu you see different numbers referring to the size of type; logically, the bigger the number, the bigger the type. Again, to change the size of characters: *select first, then do it to it*. Or set your insertion point down and choose the size from the menu *before* you type (see the last two sections on changing fonts and styles). For more information on type sizes, see Chapter 21 on Fonts.

Alignment refers to where the margins are lined up: *align left* has the text lined up on the left margin; *align right* is on the right, obviously; *align center* has everything centered on a vertical axis *between your margins; justified* has both the left *and* right margins lined up. To change your alignment, you know what to do! That's right: *select first, then do it to it*—highlight the text, then choose the alignment from the menu or the buttons, if you see them.

Changing Styles Mid-Sentence— Without Using the Menu

Style	
✓Plain Text	⌘T
Bold	⌘B
Italic	⌘I
<u>Underline</u>	⌘U

Learn these keyboard shortcuts!

Changing Type Size

8 point

48 point

Alignment

Cut, Copy, and the Clipboard

Almost anywhere you can type, you can cut or copy text. When you **cut** text (or graphics), it is *removed* from your document and placed on the "Clipboard." When you **copy** text (or graphics), the original text *is left in your document* and a *copy* of it is placed on the Clipboard. Well, what the heck is a Clipboard?

Clipboard

Clipboard

This is the Clipboard icon that lives in the System Folder. If you double-click on it, you'll see what is currently being stored in it.

The **Clipboard** is an invisible "container" somewhere in the depths of the Mac. It holds whatever you have *cut* or *copied,* be it text, spreadsheet data, graphics, etc. Once something is on the Clipboard, it waits there until you paste it in somewhere (you'll get to that in a minute).

The most important thing to remember about the Clipboard is that it holds *only one thing at a time;* that is, as soon as you cut or copy something else, whatever was in the Clipboard to begin with is *replaced* with the new selection.

In some programs, including the Finder, you'll find a menu command called *Show the Clipboard*, in which case it appears as a window with its contents displayed. In most programs, though, you never see the actual Clipboard—simply trust that it's there.

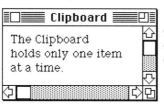

The Clipboard appears as a window (if it's available for looking at in your program).

Items will stay on the Clipboard even when you change applications: you can put something on the Clipboard in a paint program, then open up a word processing program and paste it into a new document.

Items will leave the Clipboard all by themselves if the computer is turned off or if there is a power failure—the contents are stored in RAM, so anytime RAM gets wiped out, so do the contents of the Clipboard. (RAM info on page 136; plus read Chapter 30, Very Important Information.)

How to Cut: Simply select, then do it to it. For instance, select the text you wish to remove from the document (press-and-drag over it). Then from the Edit menu choose "Cut." The text will be *eliminated* from your document and placed on the Clipboard. (Be sure to read about "Delete" further on in this section.)

Cut

How to Copy: Simply select, then do it to it. For instance, select the text you wish to copy (press-and-drag over it), then from the Edit menu choose "Copy." The text will *remain* in your document and a *copy* will be placed on the Clipboard.

Copy

OK, it's on the Clipboard. Now what? Well, the Clipboard holds objects for *pasting*. You can take text or a graphic out of one place and paste it into your document somewhere else, just as if you had a little glue pot.

How to Paste: From the Edit menu choose "Paste." If you are working with text, whatever was on the Clipboard will be inserted in your document *beginning at the flashing insertion point*. If you have a range of text selected, the pasted item will *replace* what was selected. Spreadsheet data, graphics, etc., all can be pasted in also. In some programs, especially graphic programs, the pasted object will just land in the middle of the page.

Paste

As long as something is on the Clipboard, you can paste it in a million times.

Now, the **Delete** key (found on the upper right, called **Backspace** on older keyboards) works a little differently: if you hit this key while something is selected, whatever is selected is *deleted* and is *not* placed on the Clipboard. This means if you are holding something in the Clipboard to paste in again, whatever you *delete* will not replace what is currently being held. But it also means that you don't have that deleted item anymore—whatever you delete is really gone. **Clear,** in the Edit menu, does the same.

Delete *or* Clear and the Clipboard

Undo   **Undo** can sometimes save your boompah (no, that's not computer jargon—it's Grandma's euphemism). When you do something that makes you scream, "Aack! Oh no!" then try Undo. It's always the first command in the Edit menu (or press Command Z).

> What Undo can undo is *only the last action that occurred*. For instance, if you selected two paragraphs of brilliantly witty text that you spent three hours composing and just then the cat walked across your keyboard and obliterated the entire work, Undo could give it back to you **IF** you ask to Undo before you touch *anything.* If you start fiddling around with the keys and the mouse, then what you will undo is that fiddling around. So if something goes wrong, don't scream—**UNDO.** Then scream if necessary.

> (Some applications, such as illustration programs, can Undo multiple times. Check your manual. But most other sorts of programs can't Undo more than one move.)

Command Z X C V   Thoughtfully, the Mac designers have made the keyboard shortcuts for the cut/copy/paste/undo commands very handy. Notice on your keyboard the letters **Z, X, C,** and **V,** all in a row right near the Command key.

- ▾ Command **Z** will Undo (the closest to the ⌘ key).
- ▾ Command **X** will Cut (X like eXiting or Xing it out).
- ▾ Command **C** will Copy (C for Copy, easy mnemonic).
- ▾ Command **V** will Paste (V because it is next to C; it's sort of like the caret symbol ^ for inserting).

It's nice to get familiar with these. Remember, select first (*except to Undo*); then hold down the Command key and lightly tap the other letter.

Special characters are the symbols you have access to on the Macintosh that aren't available on a typewriter, such as upside-down question marks for Spanish (¿), the pound symbol for English money (£), the cents sign (¢), the registration or trademark symbols (® ™), etc. You can view all these with your **Key Caps** desk accessory (greater details are found on pages 208–209).

To get special characters into your document, follow these steps:

▾ While working in your document, pull down the desk accessory Key Caps from the Apple menu (far left; press on the apple).

▾ From the Key Caps menu (a new item that appears in your menu bar!), choose the font you wish to view.

▾ Find the character you want by pressing Shift **or** Option **or** Shift-Option together; press the character key. Notice which combination of keystrokes produces the character you want. For instance, Shift Option K in the font Times will produce an apple.

▾ So *remember* that keystroke combination. Close Key Caps and go back to your document (remember, you can access desk accessories in any program).

▾ In your document, click to set your insertion point. Choose the font Times and press Shift Option K. The apple will appear!

Accessing Special Characters

Accessing Special Characters

Using Key Caps

Some special characters and the keys to access them in any font:

Option 8	•
Option g	©
Option 2	™
Option r	®
Option $	¢
Option Shift 8	°
Option ;	…
Option hyphen	–
Option Shift hyphen	—

There is also a handy chart on the last page of this book.

Using Characters from a Different Font

If the character you need is in a different font than you are using, such as a ❤ in Zapf Dingbats, you can also do this: Through Key Caps, find the keystroke combination for the character (Option 6 in this case). Press Option 6 in whatever font you are currently using; some strange character will appear. Select the strange character and change it into Zapf Dingbats; it will turn into a ❤.

You can also select the character showing in the Key Caps entry bar and paste it into your document. But the Key Caps character will turn into the font already on your page. If the character you need is in a different font, you will still have to select the new characters and change them into the font that holds those characters you wanted. It's easier just to do it the other way.

Remember, the insertion point picks up the *formatting of any character immediately to its left, even if it's a blank space*, so anything else you type will be in that character's font, style, etc. To continue in your *original* font, leave your insertion point right where it is; from the menu just choose the font specifications you were originally using.

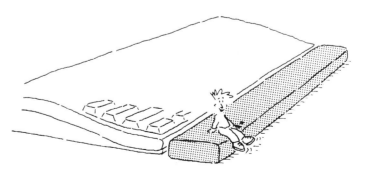

A GOOD "WRIST REST" CAN REDUCE STRESS ON YOUR WRISTS AND HANDS.

Included in the special characters are **accent marks,** as in résumé and piñata. You can find them in Key Caps, but it's easy to remember that you get accent marks by using the Option key, and they are hiding beneath the characters on the keyboard that would usually be under them. For example, the acute accent over the **e** is **Option e;** the tilde over the **n** is **Option n.**

To type accent marks in your document, follow these steps (using the word résumé):

- ▾ Type the word until you come to the letter that will be *under* the accent mark; e.g., **r**
- ▾ *Before* you type that letter (the letter **e** in this case), type the Option combination (**Option e** in this case, which means hold down the Option key and tap the **e** once)—*it will look like nothing happened.*
- ▾ Now type the character that is to be *under* the accent mark, and both the mark and the letter will appear together; e.g., **r é s u m é**
- ▾ That's easy, huh!

What?! One space after a period? If you grew up on a typewriter, this is not an easy habit to change, I know. Or if you were taught keyboarding skills by someone who grew up on a typewriter, they taught you typewriter rules. But characters on a Macintosh are not *monospaced* as they are on a typewriter (except for Monaco and Courier), so there is no need to use two spaces to separate two sentences. Check any book or magazine on your shelf; you will never find two spaces after periods (except publications produced on a computer typed by someone still using typewriter rules). If you find this hard to accept, read the following commercial.

If you are typing on a Macintosh, you must face the fact that it is not a typewriter and that some of the standard conventions developed particularly for that wonderful little mechanical appliance do not apply to the kind of type you are now creating. A very important book to read is The Mac is not a typewriter. *It's small, it's cheap, it's easy to read, and it's true. Well, yes, I did write it myself, but that's beside the point. I didn't make up anything in the book—I just reported the typographic facts.*

Using Real Accent Marks

A list of common accent marks:

′ Option e

` Option ~

¨ Option u

~ Option n

^ Option i

One Space After Periods

A Commercial

1. What is Rule Number Two on the Mac?

. . . .

2. Draw an I-beam, an insertion point, and a pointer.

. . . .

3. Which of the three items above do you use to select text?

. . . .

4. When you press the Delete key, which of the three items above backs up?

. . . .

5. Name the two ways that an insertion point knows what typeface and size and style to type in.

. . . .

6. What is the keyboard shortcut to make selected text bold? Italic? Underlined?

. . . .

7. How can you make the next word you type be in bold, without going to the menu? After you type it in bold, how do you make the next word you type be in plain text?

. . . .

8. If you decide you really want the last paragraph in your document to be the first paragraph, what are the four steps you must take to make that happen?

. . . .

. . . .

Extra Credit:

How many spaces should you type after a period?

. . . .

9. What are the keyboard shortcuts for cut, copy, and paste?

. . . .

10. What is the difference between "cut" and "clear"?

. . . .

Answers on page 371.

SAVING DOCUMENTS

15

While you are in the process of creating a document of any sort within any program, the information you put into that document is floating around in the depths of the computer. If you were to turn off the computer, that document would disappear. In fact, if there is a power flicker, the document would disappear. If your computer crashes, the document would disappear. You probably want to keep a permanent copy of it, right? So you need to **save the document** onto a disk.

GRANDMA, TELL US A REALLY SCARY STORY.

OKAY, HERE'S ONE ABOUT A YOUNG ASTRONAUT WHO TRIES TO SAVE TIME BY NOT BACKING UP MISSION-CRITICAL FILES.

WHOA!

RAM:
Random Access
Memory

Until you actually go through the process of naming a document and saving it, the document hangs around in **RAM,** which stands for **Random Access Memory.** RAM is sort of like the top of the desk in your office, and you can consider your *hard disk* as a filing cabinet where you keep all your folders of information.

When you are working on a project, you don't keep running to the filing cabinet every time you need a little piece of information, do you? No, you take out all the applicable info and put it on your desk, then when you're finished you put it all away again and take out something else. RAM is sort of like that: when you open an application the computer puts a copy of that application into RAM, also called *memory.* When you quit that application and open another one, Mac puts the first one back where it came from and puts the new application into RAM. That way the computer doesn't have to keep going into the filing cabinet to do its work and it can operate much more efficiently.

When you create a document, it sits in RAM, too, until you put it in the filing cabinet—your disk. You put the document on your disk by **saving** it. Once it's on your disk, either hard or floppy, it will stay there until you trash it yourself.

Danger!

All that time your document is in RAM, it is in **danger.** At any moment, if there is a power failure, even for a split second, or you accidentally hit the wrong button, or you have a system crash, or the screen freezes, or a virus attacks, or your child pulls out the power cord, or any other catastrophe of considerable dimension happens to befall, then everything in RAM *(memory)* is gone. Just plain gone. No way on earth for a mortal person to get it back.

The prevention? **SOS:** Save Often, Stupid. Well, that's a little harsh—how about Save Often, Sweetie. Save Save Save. Every few minutes, when you're just sitting there thinking about your next marvelous move, Save. In most programs it's as easy as pressing Command S. Then if there *is* a catastrophe, you will have lost only the last few minutes of your work. Of course you won't listen to me until you have experienced your own catastrophe.

Rule #1:
Save Often!

To save a document for the first time, it must be given a name. Under the File menu are the commands **Save As...** and **Save.** At first the subtle difference can be confusing.

Save As...
vs. Save

Save As... is the command you must use *first* to give the document a name, as a document cannot be saved without a name. "Save As..." gives you a dialog box such as the one shown on page 140 (they're slightly different from program to program).

Save As...

Save is the command to use *after* you have named the document and you want to save the new changes onto that same document. *Save* just goes ahead and does it—you will see the Edit menu flash for a quick second. Get in the habit of typing Command S (the keyboard shortcut) regularly.

Save

> There is usually no keyboard shortcut listed in the menu for "Save as...." But if you have not yet given the document a name, then choosing *Save* (Command S) will give you the *Save As...* dialog box because the file must have a name. Most programs will not allow you to name a document "Untitled."

Making Several Versions

Sometimes you might want to create changes in a document, but you still want to keep a **copy of the original without the changes.** For instance, you write a witty letter to Uncle Jeff, then decide you also want to write to Uncle Cliff. You have a few things to tell Cliff that Jeff isn't interested in, but you don't want to retype the entire letter. That's when you'll use *Save As...* a *second* time to give the document a *new* name.

▼ Save the letter to Uncle Jeff. You've probably named it "Witty letter to Uncle Jeff."

▼ Now from the File menu, choose "Save As...."

▼ Change the name from "Witty letter to Uncle Jeff" to "Witty letter to Uncle Cliff."

This puts the original document (to Uncle Jeff) safely away on your disk and opens a new one (the copy to Uncle Cliff) right on the screen. You'll notice the name in the window title bar of your document will change to what you renamed it. Any changes you make to *this* document (Uncle Cliff's) will not affect the original (Uncle Jeff's).

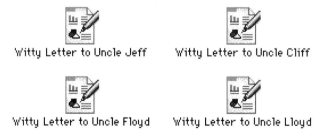

All of these letters are based on the original letter to Uncle Jeff. I just kept choosing "Save As" and giving the new ones new names. The information, layout, type choices, etc., all stayed the same, but now each letter is separate and I can add or delete the details in each.

Sometimes you might make a bunch of changes to a document and then decide you don't like the changes. In this case, check the File menu to see if your application has a command called **Revert.** If so, choose it and the document will revert *to exactly how it was the last time you saved it.*

If there is no Revert command, then *close* the document. When you see the box that asks if you want to save the changes (shown below), click the button that says "No" or "Don't Save." Reopen the document and everything will be exactly the way it was *the last time you saved it.*

Reverting to a Previously Saved Version

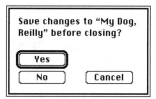

If you click "No," your document will revert back to how it was the last time you saved it.

The "Save As..." Dialog Box

Below and opposite are illustrations of a typical **"Save As..." dialog box.** This is a very important box for you to understand because you will be using it every time you start a new document. **I know all this information looks intimidating, but it's really not that bad and it's very important.** If you spend a few minutes here, *you* will be in control instead of being at the mercy of the computer system.

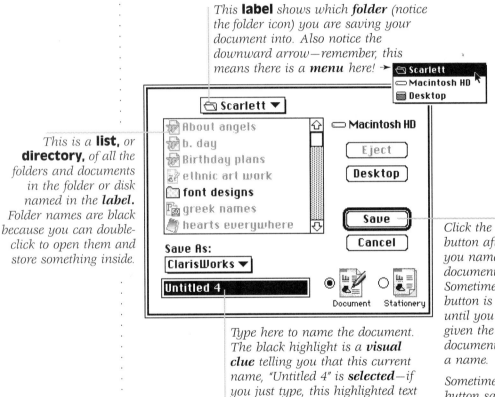

This **label** *shows which* **folder** *(notice the folder icon) you are saving your document into. Also notice the downward arrow—remember, this means there is a* **menu** *here!*

This is a **list,** *or* **directory,** *of all the folders and documents in the folder or disk named in the* **label.** *Folder names are black because you can double-click to open them and store something inside.*

Type here to name the document. The black highlight is a **visual clue** *telling you that this current name, "Untitled 4" is* **selected**—*if you just type, this highlighted text will be replaced.*

Click the **Save** *button after you name the document. Sometimes this button is gray until you have given the document a name.*

Sometimes this button says "OK" instead of "Save."

If you have selected a folder icon, this button says "Open" so you can open the folder to save it inside.

As is typical on the Mac, the dialog box has many **visual clues** that tell you what to do or what to expect. These are just a couple of them. See Chapter 29 for details on "navigating," *which is a critical skill.* It will teach you how to save a document into exactly the folder you need it saved into.

*Look very carefully. What are the two differences between this picture and the one on the opposite page? The differences, the **visual clues,** are important!*

*When a file name is gray, it is a **visual clue** that the file itself is in the folder, but you can't do anything with it.*

*Folder names are black, which is a **visual clue** that you can open them (double-click) to store documents inside.*

A double border around this list is a **visual clue,** indicating that **this list is selected.** If you type a character, you will select the file in this list box that begins with that letter.*

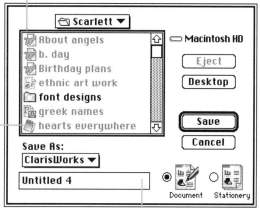

*If this box is white and there is no insertion point flashing, that is a **visual clue** that **this edit box is not selected**—no matter what you type it will not appear in this box.*

To select this edit box so you can type in it, press the **Tab key.**

* Why does this list have a border around it sometimes and not others? If you click in the list, it becomes selected, which *deselects* the name box!

Try this: Open any application, then choose "Save As...." Notice the name box is highlighted (selected). Press the Tab key. Notice the list box is now selected. Press the Tab key several more times to see how that key moves the selection back and forth from the list to the name box.

Use the dialog boxes shown (A or B) to answer the questions.

1. Which dialog box has the list, or directory, selected?

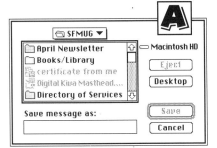

2. Which dialog box is ready for you to name the document?

3. If you were in dialog box A and you typed the letter "B," what would happen?

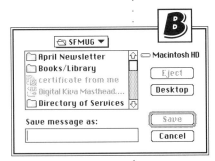

4. What would happen if you were to double-click on the folder named "April Newsletter"?

5. If you were in dialog box A and you wanted to name the document, which key would you press to select the name box (edit box)?

6. What would you press to get the little menu shown here?

7. What would happen if you were to choose "Macintosh HD" from this little menu?

8. Briefly describe two ways to avoid saving your changes.

9. Where does the document hang out before you save it?

10. Which command would you use to save another copy of a document, but with a new name?

Answers on page 371.

PRINTING DOCUMENTS

Printing is usually the point, right? It's all well and good to create all these great things on the computer, but most of the time we need to actually print our creations to make them useful. In this chapter I'll walk you through the printing process, but keep in mind that each of the hundreds of printers for the Macintosh has its own software, so details might look different from what I show here. Please read the documentation that came with your printer!

Also, different applications often create their own Page Setup and Print dialog boxes, so the ones you use might not exactly match the ones I show.

Quick Start

Here are the briefest of directions for **printing your pages.** If it works, then just skip the rest of this chapter. For this very brief quick start, I have to assume you have the printer plugged in to both the wall and the computer with the appropriate cables, and that someone has installed the printer software.

- ▼ Turn on the printer and let it warm up.
- ▼ Open the document that you want to print.
- ▼ From the File menu, choose "Print...."
- ▼ Click the "OK" or "Print" button (or hit the Return key).
- ▼ That's all.

OR:
First Time Ever
Printing to this
Printer

If this is the **very first time** you have ever printed to your printer, you will have to make a brief stop at the Chooser before you print. You only need to do this the very first time, *or* if you are printing to a different printer than usual! After this initial process, you only need to follow the steps above.

- ▼ Turn on the printer and let it warm up.
- ▼ Open the document that you want to print.
- ▼ From the Apple menu, choose "Chooser."

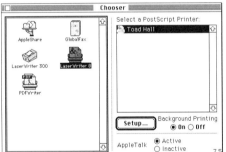

This is the Chooser. Details about it are on the following pages.

- ▼ Click on the icon on the left side of the Chooser that has the name of your printer. If you have a PostScript printer and you see an icon that looks like a printer with a page of ampersands (the "and" symbol), click on it.
- ▼ On the right side of the Chooser, click on the name of the printer (if your printer is not turned on and warmed up, you probably won't see any names listed!), or click on the printer "port" icon (usually the "serial" port).

▼ You might get a message telling you AppleTalk must be on or off. The Mac will turn it on or off for you.

    ▼ If you are printing to a PostScript printer, click the "Setup..." button.

    ▼ Click "Auto setup." Click "OK."

▼ After you have chosen the printer name on the left and the right, close the Chooser (press Command W, Command Q, or click in the close box in the upper left corner of the window).

▼ You will probably get a message telling you that you have changed printers, and to go to "Page Setup." Do that: from the File menu, choose "Page Setup." Don't change anything—just click "OK."

▼ From the File menu, choose "Print...."

▼ Click the "OK" or "Print" button.

Now, if that didn't work, read the rest of this chapter more carefully. It may be that you did not choose the proper printer "driver" in the Chooser, or that you're not sure whether your printer is PostScript or not and so you clicked the wrong button.

Did it Work?

Okay. If you are going to move on through this chapter, make sure your printer is plugged into the socket in the wall. You also need the cable to connect your printer to your Mac. Most printers don't automatically come with a cable to connect it to the Mac (you have to buy it separately), so if you brought your printer home without one you will have to go back to the computer store and get one before you can print. This cable plugs into the printer and into the "port" on the back of the Mac that has a little picture of a printer above it.

Do This Before Moving On!

Also with your printer you got a disk with software on it. Follow the directions in the manual to install the software.

Turn on your printer. It takes most printers several minutes to warm up and get the connection established between it and the Mac, so give it time.

Printers · There are basically two types of printers: **PostScript printers** and **QuickDraw printers** (also called "non-PostScript printers").

QuickDraw printers · **QuickDraw** is a computer programming language that your *Macintosh* uses—it creates what you see on the screen. A printer that can only reproduce what is on the screen is usually called a QuickDraw printer (although there is really nothing "QuickDraw" in the printer itself). The ImageWriter, the HP DeskWriter, and the Apple StyleWriter are all examples of QuickDraw printers, with *resolutions* ranging from about 75 to 400 dots per inch (the higher the resolution, the smoother the printed image).

PostScript printers · **PostScript** is a "page description language," a programming language, that a *PostScript printer* can interpret. A PostScript printer doesn't care what the heck you have on your screen. If the font or the graphic image is created with PostScript, it can look dreadful on the screen but will print beautifully on the page. Personal PostScript printers are the expensive ones, typically around $1,000 to $3,000. They're expensive because they have a powerful computer inside, complete with memory and a specialized CPU (central processing unit, the tiny chip that runs the entire process).

Imagesetters · There are also very expensive (like $100,000), very high-end PostScript printers with resolutions of around 1270 or 2540 dots per inch, such as the Linotronic. These machines, called **imagesetters,** output (print) onto film, not plain paper, and the hard copy looks virtually like traditional typesetting, limited only by the professional expertise of the person who input (typed in) the text. This book was output on a Linotronic.

Service bureaus · Since the high resolution machines are so expensive, you only find them in **service bureaus**—shops where they offer the output (the hard copy, the printed pages) as a service. You take the disk containing your document to them, leave it there, and they print it up for you. It can cost from $4 to $10 a page, but it's beautiful.

The very first time you print from your Mac, *or* if you are hooked up to more than one printer, *or* sometimes if you go somewhere else and print, *or* if you find you are having difficulty printing, you need to go to the **Chooser** to direct the computer to the printer. If none of these situations apply to you, then you can skip this information, go right to "OK, OK, Let's Print" (page 152) and remember these details are here if you ever need them.

Select the Chooser from the Apple menu.

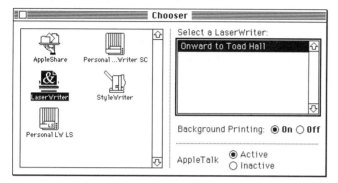

This is the Chooser in System 7 or 7.1. If you are connected to a non-PostScript printer or to a network, your Chooser may look a little different.

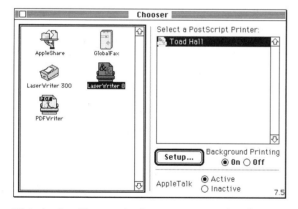

This is the Chooser in System 7.5. Notice the new LaserWriter 8 driver—it is very similar to the LaserWriter icon in the Chooser above. There is now a "Setup..." button for telling the computer specifications about various PostScript printers.

Chooser

Printer drivers

StyleWriter

This is the printer driver for the Apple StyleWriter.

On the left side of the Chooser window you see various icons. These icons represent the **printer drivers** that are installed in your System (a printer driver is the program that tells the printer what to do; it *drives* the printer). For every printer driver in your System Folder (specifically, in the Extensions folder within the System Folder), there will be a matching icon in your Chooser. *Even if you have a printer hooked-up right next to you, you won't be able to print to it unless its driver is in your System Folder.*

▼ In the Chooser, click on the icon representing the printer to which you want to print.

Installing printer drivers

If you don't see an icon for your printer, you must close the Chooser (click in its close box) and **install the driver:**

If you have an Apple printer, find the disk that came with your printer and drag the driver icon onto the top of the closed System Folder; the Mac will put the driver into the Extensions folder. (You could, of course, put the icon directly into the Extensions folder yourself.)

If your printer is not an Apple printer, read the manual that came with your printer for directions on installing the driver. It should be very similar.

If you selected a QuickDraw printer icon, then on the right side of the Chooser you should see a *port* icon, asking which port (sort of like a plug) the cable connected to the printer is plugged into. The picture on the screen should be the same as the one your cable is connected to on the back of the Mac.

Connect to:

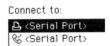

Printer port icons. The cable to your printer is plugged into one of these ports on the back of your Mac, usually the printer port (check the little pictures on the back of your Mac).

[If you have a modem, its cable should be plugged into the port with the little telephone picture on it.]

If you selected a PostScript printer icon or a network server icon, then on the right side of the Chooser you should see the names of all printers that are connected to your Mac and that are turned on.

▼ Click on the port or printer name that your computer is connected to.

▼ *If you are on a network* (which you would be if more than one computer is going to the same printer) or *if you are connected to a PostScript printer,* then make sure the AppleTalk button is clicked **Active.**

If you are the only one connected to a QuickDraw printer, AppleTalk should be **Inactive.**

On older systems, if AppleTalk was previously Inactive, then the Active button may say "Active On Restart." This means that if you click this button, AppleTalk will not really be active until you restart the computer. (Either wait until next time you turn on the Mac, or go to the Special menu and choose "Restart.") In System 7.5, you don't need to restart to switch from Inactive to Active.

In System 7.5, don't worry if you don't know either of the above things—the Mac will tell you if AppleTalk needs to be active or not, and will actually switch the button for you.

▼ Notice in the illustration that two items are *highlighted:* the icon representing your printer, and the name (or the port) of your printer. These two items must both be highlighted! Highlight (select) each one by clicking once on each.

▼ It feels like the Chooser should have an OK button, but it doesn't. I have always wondered why not. So now that you've told the Mac which printer to print to, just close the Chooser window (click its close box or press Command W or Command Q) and proceed with printing your work.

**Background
Printing**

*Also see
"PrintMonitor"*

Background Printing allows the Mac to print to a PostScript printer while you go on with your work. **If you do not** check this button, then you have to wait until the printer has finished all the pages before you have control of your screen again. **If you do** check this button, then the computer sends the information into a "buffer," then lets you use your screen. The buffer sends the information to the printer at the slower rate the printer requires, while you continue with your work. You will notice, during background printing, that occasionally your cursor may freeze or your typing may stop. This is normal behavior because the computer is trying to do two things at once.

You will only see the Background Printing option if you have the PrintMonitor icon and the LaserWriter driver icon in the Extension folder within your System Folder.

PrintMonitor   LaserWriter

*System 7 PrintMonitor
and LaserWriter driver*

PrintMonitor   LaserWriter 8

*System 7.5 PrintMonitor
and LaserWriter driver*

Page Setup

Just about every program that prints documents has a **Page Setup** dialog box where you can set specifications for the document. Before you print, always check this Page Setup feature. Shown on the next page are sample Page Setup boxes, but your particular application may have added other features to its own. They are generally self-explanatory, and if you need information, click the "Help" button—it provides short explanations for each option.

Remember when you went to the Chooser and selected a printer driver and you got this message: This is because you get different options and features in Page Setup depending on the printer driver you chose.

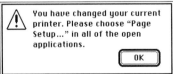

In your document, from the File menu choose "Page Setup..." and click "OK." Then your application knows which specifications are allowed in the document and printing. If you *don't* do this, you might get this message when you try to print:

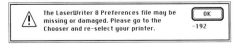

Here are samples of several Page Setups, but remember that you might not see exactly what is here because of a variety of factors. They all say about the same thing, and you really can't click any buttons that will hurt anything—feel free to experiment. Some of the most common features are explained here.

Choose the paper size, how many pages to print on one piece of paper ("Layout"), how much to enlarge or reduce the image, and whether it prints regular or sideways.

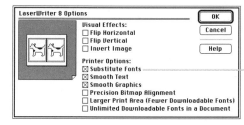

*Notice when you choose certain options, Clarus the Dogcow gives you a **visual clue** as to what to expect.*

Clarus the Dogcow. He says "Moof."

This is the button that turns New York into Times, Geneva into Helvetica, and Monaco into Courier.

*If you are printing to a PostScript printer, **un**check this box.*

Visual clues

*Remember, whenever you see a downward arrow and/or a shadow behind a box, it is a **visual clue** that there is a menu if you press.*

Checkboxes are for clicking in to choose options.

Edit boxes are for typing changes in.

The "Options" and "Help" buttons here really should have ellipses (...) so you know there will be dialog boxes, yes?

Help!

Click the Help button in these boxes! They really are helpful!

These are the dialog boxes that appear when I select the LaserWriter 300 printer driver. Notice the fewer number of options.

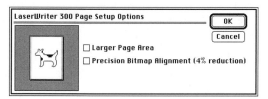

OK, OK, Let's Print! This is the longer, more detailed version of the **printing** process, as opposed to the quick start directions in the beginning of this chapter. You may see different print dialog boxes depending on which printer you are connected to, and the dialog boxes within different applications may look slightly different from what you see here, but basically all you need to do is answer the questions they ask.

1. Save again The first thing you want to do is to **Save** again—as a preventive measure always save just before you print. Also, make sure the printer is turned on (an ImageWriter must have its "Select" button on as well).

2. Go to Chooser if necessary If you haven't printed to this printer before, go the the **Chooser** and select both a printer driver and the name or the port for your printer (see the previous pages).

3. Check the Page Setup Check the **Page Setup** command under the File menu. This sets certain parameters for printing pages. Here is an example of a LaserWriter Page Setup dialog box. Because this box and any Options box that comes with it may vary from printer to printer and from application to application, I suggest you check your manual for specific details on all the buttons, although some options are explained on the following pages.

4. Choose "Print" Now go up to the File menu and choose **Print....** Depending on which application and which printer you are using, you'll get some sort of dialog box (an example below) asking you questions. (If you get a message telling you it's not possible to print, check the previous section on Chooser, and make sure your printer is on.)

A StyleWriter (QuickDraw) print dialog box in System 7.1.

A PostScript printer print dialog box in System 7.5.

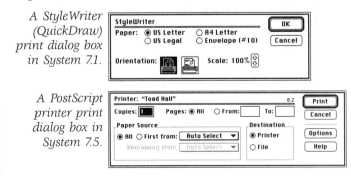

If you click the "Options" button on the previous dialog box, this is what you get. Do you see the five menus (visual clue: shadow and downward arrow)? Check them out.

Even though this looks intimidating, you can usually ignore it. The "defaults" (choices that have been automatically selected for you) will work just fine until you know what you're doing and decide to make some conscious changes.

When you click the last **OK** or **Print** button in the last dialog box (sometimes there are up to three dialog boxes), the messages will be sent to the printer and your brilliant document shall come rolling forth.

5. Click the "OK" or "Print" button

There are so many variations on the Page Setup and Print dialog boxes. Here are explanations of the more common features:

A few details

Copies: Type in the number of copies you want to print. If you're printing more than one copy and you have a **Collate** button to check, the printer will print all the pages in order, then print the next set all in order. If you *don't* click collate, you will get, for instance, 3 pages of page 1, 3 pages of page 2, 3 pages of page 3, etc. But keep in mind that it is faster for the printer *not* to collate than to print all the pages in order and then go back again and print the next set.

Orientation: Your application may use another term for it, but what the Mac wants to know is if it should print upside right or sideways (8.5 x 11 or 11 x 8.5); also known as **Tall** or **Wide, Portrait** or **Landscape.**

Pages: All or **From __ to __:** You can choose to print *all* the pages contained in your document, or just pages 3 through 12 (or whatever your choice is, of course). Choosing **All** will override any numbers in the **From/To** boxes.

Reduce or Enlarge; Scale: Regardless of the precise term your printer driver uses, you can enter a number or press the arrows here to enlarge or reduce the printed page. For instance, enter 50% to print your work at half size. Remember, half of an 8.5 x 11 is 4.25 x 5.5—you must halve *both* directions. On paper, this looks like the image is ¼ the original size; it isn't—it's half of *both* the horizontal *and* the vertical.

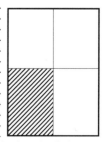

*The shaded portion is 50% of the larger size—half of both the width **and** the length.*

Computer Paper: *This does not refer to pin-fed paper!* Computer paper is 11 x 13 inches. The pin-fed paper that fits through a printer such as the ImageWriter is 8.5 x 11 (letter-size, just all strung together).

Paper Source: If you have more than one paper tray, you can tell the printer which one to choose from. This is one of the details the printer driver tells the computer and printer!

Cover Page: If you ask for a cover page, then before or after your document prints (depending on which button you click) you will get a very useful and handy page with details of this job, like this:

User:	Robin Williams
Application:	ClarisWorks 3.0
Document:	Resignation Letter to the Boss
Date:	Saturday, May 6, 1995
Time:	12:49 A.M.
Printer:	Toad Hall
Pages:	3

If you find this cover page to be a valuable item for you, make sure you also check into the date and time stamping within your application—many word processors can add those important details directly into a header or footer that appears in small type at the top or bottom of each page.

Making a PostScript file

Destination: Ahh, this is an interesting one. It tells the computer whether to send the document to the **printer** as usual, or to create a PostScript **file** on a disk. If you choose to save as a PostScript file, the Mac will save a *copy* of your document in a long and large text file that is nothing but PostScript command codes. If you open this PostScript file in a word processor, it will look like a bunch of gibberish: gsave @2 load stopped not { @1 Ogt { PointsAvailable @1ge / @3 @3 2 mul dup setflat store . . .

But, you can use a "downloader" utility to send this file directly to a PostScript printer to print your pages! Why would you want to do this? Well, do you ever take your documents to a public computer, like at a copy center, to print? Do you ever take or send your documents to another computer that does not have the same fonts? Do you need to print from another computer that doesn't even have the same application you use? Does your service bureau request a PostScript file?

Then make a PostScript file, take that file plus a downloader utility to the other computer and PostScript printer, and download it straight to the printer. It doesn't matter if that other computer has your application or your fonts. Too cool.

PostScript files are huge, though, especially if you choose to include all the fonts. That's your main consideration—whether you can fit it on a disk to take it somewhere else. For instance, a six-paragraph page of text in SimpleText that was 33K turned into a 439K PostScript file (including fonts).

To print a PostScript file, you need a utility like one of those shown to the right. You probably have one on your hard disk, or sometimes when you buy fonts a downloader utility comes on the disk. Just double-click it, go to the File or Utilities menu, and choose "Download PostScript file...." Find your file and click OK to send it to the printer.

Downloader 5.0.4

LaserWriter Utility

Downloader utilities

You can select one or more **documents** from the **Desktop** (Finder) and choose to **print** them. The Mac opens the applications in which the documents were created, prints the files, then quits the applications and returns to the Desktop.

Printing from the Desktop (Finder)

▾ All you need to do is select the file you want to print by clicking once on it. If you want to select and print more than one file, see Chapter 11 on Selecting, page 101. Just make sure that you don't select too many files from so many *different* programs that the Mac cannot open all these applications all at once. You can usually, however, open several documents that all belong to *one* application without experiencing difficulty.

▾ Once the file is selected, you may want to choose "Page Setup..." from the File menu to set some parameters.

▾ To print the file, press Command P (*or* choose "Print" from the File menu, the third command in the list).

You may have heard about "drag-and-drop" printing with Desktop Printers in System 7.5: printing from the Desktop by dragging a document on top of a printer icon without having to go to the Chooser to change printers, without having to open the file, without having to click any buttons. You can only do this if you

QuickDraw GX Printing

have installed the extra part of System 7.5, **QuickDraw GX.** At the time of this writing, QuickDraw GX is not automatically installed for you. I don't discuss QuickDraw GX in this book because its benefits are generally invisible to the user (it "enables" other things to happen), and you have to make a conscious choice to install it which means that most beginners don't even have it anyway. The advantage of drag-and-drop printing is that you don't have to ever go to the Chooser to change printers, and you don't even see your document before it prints. I only have one printer in my office, and I can't even think of the rare occasion where I wanted to print something without taking a look at it first. If you are in a networked office or school lab with a variety of printers, this feature might be great. If you need detailed information about QuickDraw GX, a well as other things like PowerTalk and AppleScript, I suggest you get Bob LeVitus's book, *Macintosh System 7.5 for Dummies.* It's a great book and will answer all your more advanced questions. Tell him I said hello.

Print the Window

When you are at the Finder (Desktop), you can also **print the contents of the active window** (the active window is the one with the horizontal lines in its title bar). Just click once on the window whose contents you want to print. Then from the File menu, choose "Print Window" (it's the very last item in the list). If your window is showing icons, then the Mac will print the icons. Even if not all the icons are visible on the screen, all of them will print. If your window is in a list, the entire list and all the details will print, even if all the details are not visible on the screen. This comes in very handy for keeping track of what's on your floppy disks—just print up a picture of the window and file it away with the disk.

Print the Desktop

You can also **print the contents of the Desktop.** Click once on any icon on the Desktop level, such as the trash can, *or* press Command Shift UpArrow. From the File menu, choose "Print Desktop" (it's the very last item in the list). (If this item still says "Print Window," then you have not selected the Desktop level. Try again.) The Mac will print up as many pages as necessary to display everything that is on your Desktop.

Most **laser printers** spew forth a sample page every time you turn them on, useful for checking the toner level and quality, as well as letting you know how many pages have been printed since you bought the printer. If you don't want to waste paper or toner on this page everyday, simply pull the paper tray partially out before you turn it on. After a minute or two push it back in.

This is, obviously, a temporary measure. If you would like to turn it off permanently (well, permanently until you decide to change it back), you can use the printer utility that came on the disk with your printer. If you have an Apple printer, you can use the LaserWriter Utility that is probably on your hard disk somewhere. If it isn't on your hard disk, it's on one of your original disks for System 7 (if you have "More Tidbits," it's called LaserWriter Font Utility on that disk). In System 7.5, you can use the QuickDraw GX Installer and custom install only the GX utilities. Or the easiest thing to do is borrow someone else's.

If you have an Apple printer and the LaserWriter Utility, follow these simple steps to turn off the startup page. Other printer utilities have a very similar process.

To turn off the startup page, follow these steps:

- ▾ Turn on the printer and let it warm up.
- ▾ Double-click on the LaserWriter Utility.
- ▾ If you get a commercial, click "OK."
- ▾ From the Utilities menu, choose "Set Startup Page..." (for System 7.5); in System 7 or 7.1, choose "Start Page Options...."
- ▾ In this little dialog box, click the button "Off." Then click "OK."
- ▾ From the File menu, choose "Quit," *or* press Command Q.

Saving Laser Printer Toner and Paper

LaserWriter Utility

This file is probably in your computer somewhere. This one only works on Apple printers.

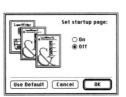

Check this out—you can do lots of things to your printer.

Just click the "Off" button.

PrintMonitor   The **PrintMonitor** is a utility that lets you control background printing, the printing that goes on in the background while you work on something else (see page 150). Through the Print-Monitor you can check on the status of the printing jobs you've requested, cancel documents that are in the process of printing, cancel any that are waiting to print, set a time (the hour and the date) that you want a job to print, or postpone the time indefinitely. You can tell the PrintMonitor to alert you when the printer is out of paper or when to feed in a new sheet of paper during a manual feed.

After you have started printing a document, you will be able to choose "PrintMonitor" from the Application menu (far right of the menu bar). This means if it's a very short print job you won't have much control over it. If you send several files off to print, their names will be listed in the dialog box in order of scheduled printing. You can select a document name, then cancel it or set the print time. From the File menu you can also choose to "Stop Printing," which just *stops* the process (rather than cancels it) until you tell it to resume, also from the File menu. The PrintMonitor will automatically go away when all printing is complete. You can't make it actually go away before printing is finished, but you can just click anywhere else to get its menu out of your way.

If you see the Application menu flashing with the PrintMonitor icon, that's a clue there is something wrong in the process. Press on the Application menu—you will probably see a diamond next to the PrintMonitor name. A diamond next to any name in the menu is a **visual clue** that there is a problem with that application. Choose PrintMonitor and you will get a message telling you what the problem is.

While the PrintMonitor is open, you can get the Preferences dialog box (shown below) from the File menu. I like as much information as possible about a problem, so I choose the last option to display the alert boxes, as well as the diamond in the Application menu and the flashing icon in the menu bar. These are actually the defaults (the automatic choices).

PrintMonitor Preferences

If you are not printing, you can double-click on the PrintMonitor icon in the Extensions folder to open it, then choose "Preferences" from the File menu.

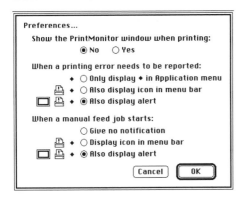

While a job is in the printing process, you can choose "PrintMonitor" from the Application menu to get its dialog box (shown below). You can click in its close box to put it away, but you'll notice it still hangs around, and it is still in the Application menu. Choose another application from the menu, or just click on the screen anywhere and the PrintMonitor will really go away.

Getting and getting rid of the PrintMonitor dialog box

If you find you have trouble printing in the background, try allocating a little more memory to the PrintMonitor application. Details for doing this are on page 302, but here are brief directions: Click on the application icon (it lives in the Extensions folder in the System Folder). Press Command I to get the Get Info box. Change the number in the "Preferred size" box to a higher number, about 50 percent higher to start with.

If you have trouble printing in background

1. Put the tasks below in the proper order for printing to a new printer for the first time:

A. From the File menu, choose "Page Setup...," then click "OK."

B. Choose the name of the printer.

C. Customize any specifications necessary in the Print dialog box, such as the number of copies or the range of pages. Click "OK."

D. Open the document you want to print.

E. Turn on printer

F. Choose the printer driver.

G. From the File menu, choose "Print...."

H. Close the Chooser.

I. From the File menu, choose "Chooser."

J. Click the Setup button, if there is one, choose Auto Setup, click OK.

2. Why does the cursor and typing sometimes get jumpy and fidgety while your pages are printing to a PostScript printer?

3. Is it the QuickDraw or the PostScript printer that is actually a specialized computer?

4. What size is "computer paper"?

5. At the Desktop, when you choose to "Print Window," which window gets printed?

6. How do you get rid of the PrintMonitor after you have closed its window?

7. What are the **visual clues** that tell you the PrintMonitor is having trouble printing?

Answers on page 371–372.

CLOSING AND QUITTING 17

There is a big and important difference between **closing** and **quitting.** You *close* a *document,* but you *quit* an *application.* This is an extremely vital concept to get, so don't skip this short chapter.

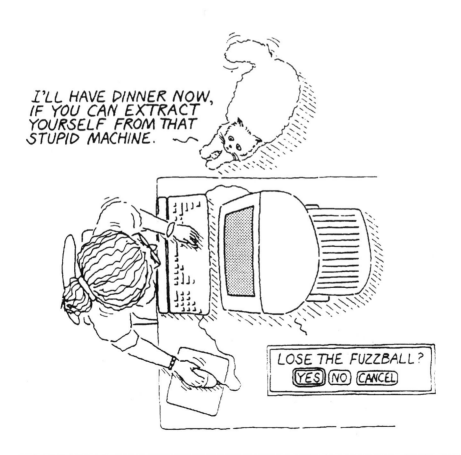

I'LL HAVE DINNER NOW, IF YOU CAN EXTRACT YOURSELF FROM THAT STUPID MACHINE.

LOSE THE FUZZBALL? YES NO CANCEL

Quit vs. Close   At first it seems a bit confusing—what's the big deal, **quitting** or **closing.** Either way, you're finished, right? Wrong.

Essentially, this is what happens: Say you open your word processing application—that is comparable to putting a typewriter on your desk. Then you start a new document—that is comparable to putting a piece of paper in the typewriter.

When you choose "Close" from the File menu, that is comparable to taking the piece of paper out of the typewriter. The typewriter, though, is still on the desk! And on the Mac, both the desk and the "typewriter" are rather invisible. You might *think* the typewriter is gone.

But the typewriter—the word processor—stays on the desk (in the computer's *memory,* called RAM) until you physically put it away. When you choose "Quit" from the File menu, that is comparable to putting the typewriter away.

If your desk gets full, what happens? It crashes. If your computer's memory gets full, what happens? It crashes. It's very important to know whether you want to close or to quit!

Closing a Document   When you are finished working on a document, you can **close that document** window by clicking in its close box or by choosing "Close" from the File menu. Either way, you are just *closing the document* (putting away the paper) and you are still *within the application (the software program).* You still see the menu belonging to the application, even though the rest of your screen may look gray or colored, just like your Desktop, and even if you see windows that belong to other programs or to the Desktop!

If you just *closed* a document window and now you see "Special" in your menu, it does not necessarily mean you *quit* the program—you have just *closed,* but not *quit.* If you click anywhere on your screen, you will pop into the Finder/Desktop, deluding you into thinking you have quit the application!

Choose to close when you are finished with a document and want to start another, or perhaps when you know you are going to come back to this application later.

Usually the keyboard shortcut to close a document is **Command W,** just like closing a Desktop window.

To **quit an application,** you must choose the Quit command. This is always done from the File menu, it is always the very last item. In just about every program you can use the keyboard shortcut: **Command Q.**

If you haven't saved all your changes in any of the open documents, the Mac will politely ask if you want to save them at this point, whether you are closing or quitting. Thank goodness.

Save changes to "Article" before quitting?
Yes
No   Cancel

If you click Yes and you haven't yet even saved the document with a name, you'll get the "Save As..." dialog box (page 140) to name the document before quitting, because nothing can be saved without a name.

Click the No button if you decide at this point you don't want the changes (or the document, if you've never named it).

Click Cancel to return to your document without saving any changes.

Once you have quit, the application is removed from the computer's memory. Quit when you are finished working in the application for the day.

If you hold down the Option key while choosing "Quit," *and keep holding it down,* when you arrive at your Desktop all the windows will be closed!

If you're not sure if you have quit your applications or not:
check the Application menu, the tiny icon on the far right of the menu bar. Any application names that appear besides "Finder" *are still open in memory.* Choose that name, then press Command Q to quit, even if you don't see the application anywhere! Trust me. And read Chapter 19 about Shut Down for more details.

Quitting an Application

The item "Quit" is always the last command in the File menu. If you don't see Quit in the File menu, you are probably at the Desktop/Finder.

This Application menu tells me PageMaker is open.

Circle the correct answer to these questions:

close **quit**   1. To put away a document.

close **quit**   2. To put away an application

close **quit**   3. Press Command W.

close **quit**   4. Press Command Q.

close **quit**   5. Take the "paper" out of the "typewriter."

close **quit**   6. Put the "typewriter" away.

Use this illustration to answer the rest of these questions:

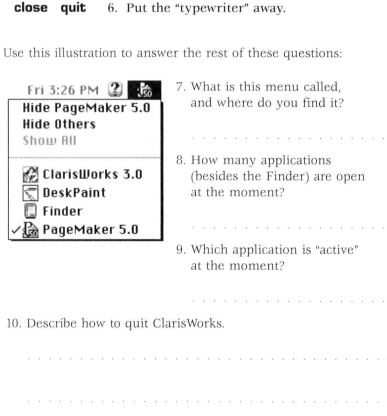

7. What is this menu called, and where do you find it?

8. How many applications (besides the Finder) are open at the moment?

9. Which application is "active" at the moment?

10. Describe how to quit ClarisWorks.

Answers on page 372.

EJECTING DISKS

Disks go in and disks come out. Sometimes they don't come out. Sometimes they get stuck. Sometimes they won't "mount." This short section covers all the tricks to getting floppy disks, cartridge hard disks, and CDs in and out of your Macintosh.

**Ejecting
a Floppy Disk**

There are actually several ways to **eject a floppy disk** (remove it from the floppy disk drive), some of which are preferable to others. Let's start at the Desktop.

Shut Down
Also see page 171.

If you are done for the day and are planning to **shut down** the whole system, then close up all your windows (press Command Option W). From the Special menu choose "Shut Down." This will close any open applications, eject any floppy disks, and turn off the computer. (On older Macs, you will get a reassuring message that it is now safe to turn off the computer.)

**From the menu
or the
keyboard shortcut**

Even if you're not ready to shut down, you may sometimes need to eject a floppy disk to trade it with another, or simply to take your disk and go away. Beginners usually go through the routine of selecting the disk (by clicking once on it) and choosing "Eject" from the Special menu (or using the shortcut **Command E**). This will certainly spit the disk out, but it is not the best method.

*Gray disk icon left
on the screen after
being ejected.*

You may have noticed when you eject a disk by using the menu that a gray version of the icon stays on the screen. That's because the memory of this disk is still in RAM (in *memory,* see page 136). If someone else comes along to use this machine while the gray icon is still showing, when they insert their disk the Mac will very often kick theirs out and ask for the one that just left. That's not a problem if the disk is sitting on the desk, but if Mary took that disk and left for a meeting in Chicago, then you may have a problem.

Try this!

If the computer asks you to insert a disk and you don't have it, try pressing **Command Period.** This will often force that rude question to disappear. You may need to do it a few times, along with clicking OK to a dialog box or two. You can try dragging that gray disk icon to the trash, but sometimes even then you'll get that dialog box asking for it to be inserted.

If the message won't go away with Command Period and you don't have the disk (the disk must be named exactly the same and have exactly the same data on it—you can't fool the System), *then the only thing you can do is to turn off the computer.* Preferably, *restart* instead of turning it off! (See next page!)

▼ If you have a **Restart button** on the front, side, or back of your computer (it's the button on your computer *box*—not your monitor or keyboard) with a tiny triangle on it, push that.

▼ If there is no button, try this: hold down the Command and Control keys, then push the PowerOn button, the big button at the top of the keyboard with a left-pointing arrow. This doesn't work on all Macs, nor does it work all the time.

If you cannot restart, then you have to turn off the computer. There is a button on the back of the Macintosh (not the monitor). Just push it. Wait a minute before you turn it back on. And don't eject a disk with the Eject menu command again!

To avoid the problem of gray disk icons being left on the screen, it is actually preferable to **eject your disk through the trash.**

Aack, you say! Yes, that's a frightening thought, but calm down; it's quite all right. *The trash can doesn't erase anything off your disk.* First make sure you have closed any documents and quit any applications that you used on that disk. Then simply **press on the disk icon, drag it down to the trash, and put it in.** Your disk will safely pop out and leave no gray icon on the screen. The computer now has no recollection of the existence of that disk and you can merrily be on your way and no one will be mad at you for leaving yourself behind. This is especially important if more than one person uses the computer, as in an office or in a classroom. This is the keyboard shortcut:

▼ Select the disk (click once on it).

▼ From the File menu, choose "Put Away," or use the keyboard shortcut **Command Y.**

Some **dialog boxes** give you an option to eject a disk while in an application, such as "Save As..." and "Open." When you want to eject a disk while working, just choose "Save As..." even though you don't really want to rename your current document.

▼ Click the Desktop button.

▼ Click once on the name of the disk you want to eject.

▼ After you take it out, click the Cancel button to get back to your document.

—continued

Restart

Ejecting a disk through the trash

Ejecting a disk through dialog boxes

After ejecting a disk through this dialog box, you can of course insert a new disk if you like. If something from the ejected disk is still open on the screen, though, the Mac will ask for the ejected disk again so it can be put it away; then the disk will pop out again so you can put the new one in.

Mounting and Unmounting

You may hear talk of **mounting** and **unmounting** disks, rather than inserting and ejecting them. The terms *mount* and *unmount* typically refer to hard disks (internal or external), removable cartridge hard disks, and CD-ROMs. It is possible and very common to have more than one hard disk attached to your computer. It is possible to have removable cartridge hard disks that you insert into a cartridge drive sort of like inserting a video tape into a VCR. But even though the hard disk is attached to the computer or you have inserted a cartridge hard disk, that does not guarantee that its icon will show up on the screen. If the icon does not appear (which means the computer cannot "read" the disk), we say that the disk did not *mount*. (You can sometimes hear power users muttering under their bated breath as they wait that suspenseful moment for the computer to find and read the disk, "Mount, baby, mount." Why is it suspenseful? Because sometimes they don't. But that is another book.)

Removing CDs and cartridge hard disks

These hard disks do not eject like floppy disks. A cartridge hard disk and a CD-ROM must be *unmounted* before they can be removed from their drives.

To remove a CD-ROM:

▾ Drag the icon to the trash to dismount it. Now push the button near the CD-ROM slot to eject the disk.

To remove a cartridge hard disk:

▾ Drag the icon to the trash to dismount it.

▾ Push the button on the cartridge drive to stop the disk from spinning. **Wait** until it stops spinning completely.

▾ Push the little lever to the side; hold your hand in front of the drive slot to catch the cartridge as it comes flying out.

If, when you eject the disk, you get a message telling you something is still in use and you don't think it's true, check this: Did you read a Read Me File, or something similar? If reading that file made TeachText or SimpleText or some other word processor open, you probably have to *quit that application* before your disk will let go.

▾ To eject a floppy disk from the internal drive at any time, in any application, press Command Shift 1 (one).

▾ To eject a floppy disk from an external drive at any time, press Command Shift 2.

▾ For a Mac with two internal drives and an external:
Command Shift 1 ejects the bottom internal drive;
Command Shift 2 ejects the top internal drive;
Command Shift 0 (zero) ejects the external drive.

If for some reason, perhaps because of a power outage or a system error, when you turn off the computer your floppy disk is still inside, do this:

Hold down the mouse button. *Keep holding it down* and turn the computer back on; your disk(s) should pop out like toast.

If all else fails, notice that tiny hole next to the floppy drive or the CD-ROM slot? That's paper clip size. Unbend a paper clip and push it in. It's pretty safe, as all you're doing is releasing the mechanism that holds the disk in place—push firmly.

1. If you eject a disk by selecting it, then choosing "Eject Disk" from the Special menu, what happens?

. . . .

2. Why is the process in question #1 not a good idea?

. . . .

3. What is the best way to eject a floppy disk?

. . . .

4. What is the best keyboard shortcut to eject a floppy disk, and to unmount a cartridge or CD?

. . . .

5. Say you inserted a floppy disk and read the ReadMe file on it. You closed the ReadMe file, but now when you eject the disk you get a message telling you the disk cannot be put away because something is still in use. What do you do?

. . . .

6. If you are in an application, how can you eject a disk?

. . . .

7. If someone ejected a disk and then left the room, but they left a gray icon of the disk on the computer, what are the steps to take to get rid of the gray icon?

First, I would:

. . . .

If that didn't work, I would:

. . . .

If that didn't work, I would:

. . . .

If that didn't work, I would:

. . . .

Answers on page 372.

SHUT DOWN

Shutting down is the computer's process of tying up all the loose ends inside itself and parking the hard disk before it's turned off. It is certainly possible to turn the computer off without going through the **Shut Down** process, but you run the risk of losing data and possibly damaging mysterious but important elements. At the very least, turning off your Mac without choosing Shut Down leaves your computer in an unstable state. So follow this simple ritual when you are finished for the day!

Good Housekeeping

When you're done with the Macintosh, it's good housekeeping to close up all your windows on the Desktop. Press Command Option W and every open window will fly away home. This is an especially nice thing to do if more than one person uses the machine, because any windows left open will reopen the next time the computer is turn on.

However, if you don't have to share your computer with anyone, you can take advantage of these windows staying where you left them and perhaps leave your nice, neatly organized hard disk window open so when you return to the Mac you can skip the step of double-clicking the hard disk icon to get to your files. Or leave open the folder that contains the project you will be working on for the next several days.

Quitting All Applications

Before you shut down, check to make sure you have quit from all your *applications:*

*The tiny icon on the upper far right of the menu bar changes, giving you a **visual clue** as to what application you are currently using.*

▼ Press on the Application menu, which is the icon in the far upper right of the menu bar (the *menu bar,* not the Desktop; look *above* the icon of your hard disk).

▼ Look at the bottom portion of that menu. If there is any name at all listed besides "Finder," it means *that application is still open.* There is a checkmark next to the application you are currently in.

▼ To quit any other open application, select it from this Application menu. It may seem that nothing whatsoever happened and you are thinking, "So what?" *But something did happen!* Trust me. Look at your menu bar. I bet it is different than it was twenty seconds ago. And in the far right of the menu bar, the tiny icon has changed. *Even though you may see no other indication of your application*—no window, no document, in fact, you may see windows from *other* applications—*the application you chose from the Application menu is open and ready.* Really.

*Notice there is a checkmark next to PageMaker, plus the PageMaker icon in the upper right, both **visual clues** telling you what is open.*

(If this confuses you, be sure to read Chapter 30, called Very Important Information.)

▾ So now you're in the open application. From the File menu choose "Quit," which should be the very last item. (If the File menu does not have "Quit," then you probably clicked on the Desktop which popped you back to the Finder. Don't scream. Check the Application menu again.)

▾ Repeat this process for every program listed in the Application menu (except Finder).

Now from the Special menu choose **Shut Down.** Actually, to tell the honest truth, if you had left any applications or documents open, the Mac would take care of putting them away, asking if you want to save any open documents. But I do believe that you need to know what is going on so you can be in control.

Shut Down

When you shut down, all your floppy disks will pop out and any extra hard disks will unmount. If you are using a smaller or older Mac, you'll get a reassuring dialog box that says you can now turn off your computer safely. In that case, turn it off with the same button you turned it on. On the larger Macs, "Shut Down" will also automatically turn off the computer.

In **System 7.5,** there is also a Shut Down command at the bottom of the Apple menu. This does the same thing as the command from the Special menu. Its advantage is that you can choose it from within any application—you don't have to be at the Finder.

System 7.5
Shut Down

In **System 7.5.1,** the PowerOn key on the big keyboards (the key you push to turn the computer on) will now also Shut Down your Mac. Fortunately for those with small children and cats, the Mac will ask if you want to save any unsaved documents before it turns everything off.

System 7.5.1

In both **Systems 7.5** and **7.5.1,** if you turn off your computer without shutting down, for whatever reason, you will get a reprimand when you turn it back on. You can disable this announcement through the General Controls control panel (see page 230).

Fri 3:26 PM
Hide PageMaker 5.0
Hide Others
Show All

ClarisWorks 3.0
DeskPaint
Finder
✓ PageMaker 5.0

1. In the illustration above, how many applications are still open (not including the Finder)?

. . . .

2. Describe how to quit each of the open applications you see in the Application menu, above.

. . . .

3. What will happen if you choose "Shut Down" from the Special menu before you have quit each application?

. . . .

4. What is the keyboard shortcut to close all your Desktop windows?

. . . .

5. In System 7.5, what is the advantage of having the Shut Down command in the Apple menu?

. . . .

Answers on page 372.

PART TWO

This section explains features of the Macintosh beyond the basic things you need to know just to get your work done. Many of the items in this section are for customizing your Mac, making your work much easier, and helping you to be more efficient. Everything in this section is important for you to understand, but you may want to take it in small chunks. For instance, read through the Desk Accessories chapter and play with each of the desk accessories. Then in a couple of days read about the Apple Menu and Aliases, and make some aliases to put into your Apple Menu. Next week spend some time with the Find File. Oh, you have many treasures to discover!

EVER SINCE OUR EYES MET IN THE MACINTOSH CLASS, MY FEET HAVEN'T TOUCHED THE GROUND.

OH, FRANKLIN! LET'S INVESTIGATE THE SYSTEM FOLDER LIKE THERE'S NO TOMORROW!

SYSTEM FOLDER

The **System Folder** is a magical thing. It's in charge of running your Mac, and a great number of items work simply because they are inside the System Folder. Many things will *not* work if they are not stored inside your System Folder.

System Folder

The blessed System Folder.

This folder is so special because it contains the System file and the Finder file, as we talked about in Chapter 2. If either the System or the Finder are not in the System Folder, its icon changes, as shown to the right. We affectionately refer to the System Folder *with* the icon as the "blessed" (two syllables) System Folder.

System Folder

*Oh no—this system folder is not blessed! This is a **visual clue** that either the System or the Finder is missing.*

Important: The System Folder is a critical part of the functioning of your Macintosh, and you should never put anything inside of it unless you know for absolutely positively certain that it really truly belongs there. And if you are a student in a school computer lab: **don't touch the System Folder.**

**What's in the
System Folder?**

If you take a look inside the **System Folder,** you'll see other important folders; each folder takes care of some detail of working on the computer.

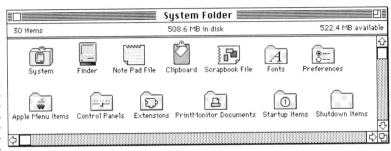

*Notice the information bar tells us there are 30 items in this folder, plus the scroll bars are gray. Both of these **visual clues** indicate that at the moment, there is a lot more stuff in here than you're seeing, like items from applications or other utilities.*

(I like to hide what I don't need or don't understand—I "shove it under the bed" by rolling the window up. This way when I look at this window I feel like I know what I'm doing.)

**You can read this
chapter later!**

You can live a long time without knowing much about these folders and files inside the System Folder. Eventually you will need to know just what these folders are and what they do so you can be in control.

These are some of the icons and folders you will see in your System Folder:

The **System file** (the file that actually runs your Mac, as opposed to the System *Folder*) may be a little different from computer to computer, depending on which version of System 7 you use. You can actually double-click on the System file to see the sounds that are installed in your System. Double-click on any sound icon to hear it.

In **System 7.0,** fonts (typefaces) are also stored in the System file; each font is represented by a document icon. Double-click on the name of a font to see a sample of what it looks like.

In **System 7.1** and above, fonts are not stored in the System file; they are stored in a **Fonts folder** in the System Folder. You can view the fonts in the Fonts folder by double-clicking on their icons. Both the screen fonts and the printer fonts are stored in this folder. When you are ready for greater details about fonts, see Chapter 21.

Don't let these simple icons fool you into thinking this is all the System file does—those fonts and sounds may take up about 150 kilobytes of space, but if you check the Get Info window for the System file, you'll find it consumes more than a megabyte. All the rest of the space is for the inner magic that makes the machine work. *The System file must remain inside the System Folder or you will not be able to start the computer!*

The **Finder** is the program that runs the Desktop and keeps track of all your files. This icon is just as important as the System file, and *it must stay in the System Folder or you won't be able to start the Mac!* If you try to open the Finder icon, you'll just get a message telling you it's none of your business. (Well, not in exactly those words, but that's the effect.)

System File

System

Chicago

Double-click a font icon to see what the typeface looks like.

Finder

Finder

Clipboard
and
Scrapbook File

Clipboard   Scrapbook File

The **Clipboard** and the **Scrapbook File** are stored in your System Folder. The Clipboard stores text and graphics that you "cut" or "copy" temporarily so you can paste it somewhere else. The Scrapbook holds text, graphics, and sounds permanently. You can double-click on either icon to see what is stored within each file, although you don't actually *use* them from here. See pages 212–213 for details on exactly how to use the Scrapbook, and pages 128–129 for how to use the Clipboard.

Note Pad File

Note Pad File

The **Note Pad File** appears after the first time you use the Note Pad "desk accessory" from the Apple menu. The chapter on Desk Accessories, page 203, describes in detail how to use the Note Pad. You don't actually use this file here in the System Folder, although you *can* double-click on this icon and get the Note Pad and type messages into it, but typically you will actually get it from the Apple menu.

Control Panels

Control Panels

The **Control Panels folder** holds all your "control panels," which are tiny programs that let you customize your Mac and the features of many utilities. With the control panels you can alter your Desktop pattern, set the mouse speed, control the repeat rate of the keys on your keyboard, or change the number of colors displayed on your monitor. Because control panels are so important to you and your work and you will eventually be getting into this folder often, you should read Chapter 24 (*after* you're feeling comfortable with your Mac).

Apple Menu Items
Folder

Apple Menu Items

The **Apple Menu Items folder** contains the icons of every item on your Apple menu (the menu on the far left of the menu bar). You can put documents, programs, folders, desk accessories—anything you like—in your Apple menu by dragging their icons to this folder. Of course you should put *aliases,* or substitute icons, of most files into the folder—not the original files! (See Chapter 25 on Aliases for details.)

> You can double-click the icon of any desk accessory to open and use it, whether it is stored in the Apple Menu Items folder or not. See Chapter 22 for details on desk accessories.

(Because the Apple Menu is a key to organizing your work and making your life simpler and happier, you really should read Chapter 23.)

The **Startup Items folder** can be very handy. Any documents or programs that you store in the Startup Items folder will automatically open each time you start your Mac. (Use "aliases," though—substitute icons that go get the real thing! See Chapter 25 on Aliases.) This is great, for instance, if you are busy for weeks on the same project—every time you turn on your computer, you can have that particular project open automatically for you, or at least the folder that contains all the files. Or put an alias of your hard disk icon in here and then every time you turn on your Mac your hard disk window will open.

You can also put sound files in the Startup Items folder, and when the Mac arrives at the Desktop, this sound will play. If your Mac arrived with a microphone, it is extraordinarily easy to make your own sounds (see page 246). You could leave sweet messages for your lover or reminders to your kids, but of course you would never leave a nasty sound to surprise and terrify that boss you don't like. (You can't make an alias of a sound, though.)

Startup Items Folder

Startup Items

The **Shutdown Items folder** in System 7.5 is just like the Startup Items folder, mentioned above: anything in it will activate when you Shutdown. At this point in our Mac life, there aren't a whole lot of things that you want to start when you're shutting down. It's a good place for personalized goodbye sounds. My machine says, "Ooooh, baby baby, goodbyyyye!" My friend, Bob LeVitus's machine says, "Elvis has left the building." You can put in here any sound you create or capture using the Sound control panel.

Shutdown Items Folder

Shutdown Items

The **Extensions folder** holds certain System-related files that help run your Mac or your peripheral equipment. These "system extensions," previously called INITs, must be stored in the Extensions folder or they don't work. This folder also contains utilities that let you share files on a network. See "Installing Items," next page, for details on how to tell if something belongs in the Extensions folder. (If you're running System 7.0, you need to store your *printer font* icons [page 188] here.)

Extensions Folder

Extensions

The **Preferences folder** contains files that have settings about how your programs think you want them to work. You can't open the icons in this folder because they're created by your programs. Don't worry about putting anything in here—your application program and System 7 will take care of that.

Preferences Folder

Preferences

PrintMonitor Documents Folder

PrintMonitor Documents

The **PrintMonitor Documents folder** holds files waiting to be printed. You never put a document in here yourself—under certain conditions, the Mac will try to send a file to the printer but for some reason it can't make it at the moment, or you might tell the Mac to print it at a later, specified time. If so, the computer stores a temporary file in the PrintMonitor Documents folder until it can complete the job. You can ignore this folder completely.

PS Spool File 1

This is what a temporary file looks like in the PrintMonitor Documents folder.

Fonts Folder

Fonts

The **Fonts folder** in Systems 7.1 and 7.5 is where all fonts, including TrueType and both parts of PostScript fonts, are stored. (In System 7, some parts of the fonts are stored in the System file and others in the Extensions folder.) If you're interested, the next chapter tells more than you ever wanted to know about fonts on the Macintosh.

Just a Note

If you find that you are using your Apple Menu Items folder regularly, or the Startup Items folder, or that you often use certain desk accessories, you can create aliases, or substitutes, of these files and put the aliases someplace where they are easier to access, instead of digging into the System Folder. You could put an alias of the Apple Menu Items folder on the Desktop, for instance, and just drop things into it as you need. *The files you put into the alias folder will actually drop into the real folder.* See Chapter 25 on Aliases for details.

When you're ready to add, or **install,** something to your Mac's system, like a font or a desk accessory or a new control panel device or an extension, don't worry about which folder it is supposed to be stored in. Here's what to do:

▼ Select the file or files you want to install. (Click once on the icon; hold the Shift key down and click on separate icons to select more than one.)

▼ Press-and-drag the icon(s) to your *closed* System Folder (as shown to the right).

▼ The Mac will ask if it's OK to put the item in the appropriate folder. Yes, it's OK. Let the Mac figure out which folder it belongs in.

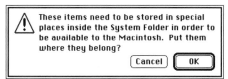

▼ If you have several different sorts of files, the Mac will put each one where it belongs, then tell you where they were placed. How thoughtful. Thank you very much.

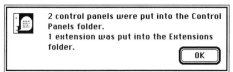

Important Note: When installing items, drag the new item to the *closed* folder icon (even if it's gray) of your System Folder, not to the *open window* of the System Folder. If you drag files to the open window, they will be placed inside the System Folder, yes, *but not in the places they belong.*

Another Important Note: This method of installing files does not work for anything that you want to store in the **Apple Menu Items folder,** the **Startup Items folder,** or in the **Shutdown Items folder.** If you want anything to go into either of these folders, you must drag it there directly.

Installing Files into the System Folder

System Folder

*Drag the files and drop them on top of this **closed** folder icon, not to the open window of the System Folder.*

1. If you are a student in a computer lab at school, what should you put in the System Folder?

2. If you are a student in a computer lab at school, what should you take out of the System Folder?

3. If you are working at home or at your business, should you mess around with the System Folder without knowing what you are doing?

4. Which two files must be in the System Folder so your Mac will work?

5. Do you need to worry about most of the stuff in the System Folder?

6. How do you install fonts, control panels, or extensions?

7. Which are the only three folders in which you might want to put items yourself?

8. If you want a sound to play when you start your computer, where should you put the sound file?

9. Which folder inside the System Folder will you probably use the most, once you are familiar with your Mac?

10. If you are a student in a lab, will you ever touch the System Folder?

Answers on page 372.

FONTS

21

It used to be so easy. Now font technology and font management has become so complex that I have written a separate book on the subject, called *How to Boss Your Fonts Around*. In this chapter I'm going to tell you only the very basic things you need to know. And maybe you don't even need to know these. **If your fonts are working fine and this information bores you or makes you quiver, just skip this chapter.** My sister, Shannon, calls font technology "the F word."

*I'm serious—ignore this chapter unless you **really** want to know the technology of fonts!*

Fonts In the Macintosh user environment, the term **fonts** refers to the typefaces available. Technically and traditionally, that's not exactly what "font" means, but we'll let it pass for now rather than confuse the issue.

At the moment there are two basic font technologies on the Mac: *PostScript* and *TrueType.* First I must explain a little about PostScript printers and non-PostScript printers so the font information makes more sense.

PostScript Printers **PostScript** is a "page description language" from Adobe Systems, Inc., that allows a printer to draw certain fonts and graphics. See, certain fonts and graphics are created in the computer using mathematical formulas and outlines. To the right is an example of the outline for the letter "Q" in a particular font.

This is an example of a PostScript outline character.

Printers print *dots,* though, not outlines or math formula descriptions. They print tiny dots in "resolutions" of, for instance, 300 dots per inch. The more dots per inch, the smoother the edge of the object because the dots are smaller and closer together. Some PostScript printers, called **imagesetters,** print 1270 or 2540 dots per inch (the type you are reading right now was set by an imagesetter).

Anyway, when PostScript fonts or graphics come down the pike from the computer to the printer, the printer freaks out at these outlines. The PostScript interpreter takes over and translates, or *rasterizes,* the outlines into dots so they can be printed. PostScript printers are the expensive ones because they have a computer inside of them (sometimes the computer inside your printer is more powerful than the one on your desk). The Apple LaserWriter IINT and IINTX, the TI OmniLaser, or the QMS-PS are examples of PostScript laser printers.

So a PostScript printer, then, is a printer that has a computer inside of it, and it can interpret the PostScript page description language for complex drawing of fonts and graphics.

Printers that are not PostScript are often called **QuickDraw printers.** This is not because there is anything called QuickDraw inside the printer!

The images you see on the Macintosh screen are displayed using the QuickDraw programming language. A QuickDraw, or non-PostScript printer, has no computer inside of it, and so it can only reproduce what it sees on the Macintosh screen—that's why it's called a QuickDraw printer. The HP DeskJet, HP DeskWriter, and the Apple StyleWriter are all QuickDraw, or non-PostScript printers.

OK. Got that? Now for the F information.

TOGETHER, THIS BOOK AND I ARE A GENIUS!

There are two types of font technologies you will run into on the Mac: **PostScript** and **TrueType.** We'll talk about each one separately, then I'll suggest which one you might prefer to use. Remember, you can skip all this stuff until the day you really think you want and need to know it, which might be never.

PostScript Fonts

Centennial

Screen fonts are usually contained in "suitcases." Screen fonts appear on your screen and their names appear in the font menus.

CenteLig

The outline portion, or printer font, of a PostScript font is what a PostScript printer reads.

Goldw   Jaspe

Printer font icons may look different, depending on which vendor they are from.

A **PostScript font** has two parts to each font. There is a *screen, bitmapped* part which is what appears on your screen: little electronic *bits* of information are *mapped* to the pixels (dots) on the screen, turning the dots on or off so you can see the shape of the letters. The name of the screen font is what shows up in your menu. Screen fonts (bitmapped fonts, same thing) are usually stored in little suitcase icons, although they can actually be kept almost anywhere now. You might also hear bitmapped fonts referred to as "fixed-size fonts."

The second part of a PostScript font is the *outline* part, which is what a PostScript printer reads. This outline portion is actually a mathematically derived outline of the shape of the letter. See, it's like this: On your screen you're viewing the bitmapped font. When the page goes to the printer, the printer says, "Oh, I don't understand bitmaps. I'll go find the outline of that font." It finds the outline, which is sometimes called the *printer font* because that's what the printer needs. The PostScript interpreter *rasterizes* that outline into dots, then fills the outline in with black dots so it looks solid.

If you have a PostScript printer and you use PostScript fonts, then it doesn't matter what your type looks like on the screen.

The type can look like this on the screen:

but it will print like this: Q

That's because the *bitmapped* font displays on the screen, but the printer creates the type from the *outline* font.

(If you have a non-PostScript printer, though [a QuickDraw printer], then if it looks crummy on your screen it will look crummy when it prints. Don't worry—there are a couple of wonderful and easy ways around this. We'll get to it.)

▼ All PostScript fonts are also known as *outline* fonts.

▼ All PostScript fonts are *scalable,* meaning they can be scaled, or resized, to any size you like and they will still print nicely.

▼ Almost all PostScript fonts are *Type 1* (and *all* Type 1 fonts are PostScript).

PostScript fonts
Outline fonts
Scalable fonts
Type 1 fonts

When you buy PostScript fonts, you will get both parts: you will get a suitcase file that contains the screen fonts, plus you will get a printer font for each style of screen font. For instance, if you have Centennial Light, Centennial Light Italic, Centennial Black, and Centennial Black Italic screen fonts in the suitcase, you will have four printer fonts, one for each of those styles. To install them, see page 194.

What Do You Get on a Font Disk?

This disk contains both the screen fonts (inside the suitcase icon) and the printer fonts.

Centennial

Inside the suitcase icon are the four screen fonts, as shown here, below.

Centennial Light 12   Centennial Light Italic 12

Centennial Black 12   Centennial Black Italic 12

Occasionally you may get screen fonts on a disk that are not contained in a suitcase file. That's okay, too.
Screen fonts always have a number (the point size) at the end of the name.

TrueType Fonts

Geneva

This is a TrueType font icon.

Geneva

This is what TrueType Geneva looks like right on the screen. This is 19.3-point type.

TrueType fonts, created by Apple, are also *outline* fonts, although their outline uses a different mathematical system from PostScript's. TrueType fonts are also *scalable,* in that they can be resized to any size you like. TrueType is *not* PostScript, and TrueType is *not* Type 1.

The TrueType screen information and the printer information are built into one file so you don't have two separate icons for each font. *This means that the screen can use the same information that the printer uses and can simulate the look of the printed type on the screen.* TrueType fonts, at any size, will look smoother than you thought your monitor would allow. TrueType fonts, when printed to a PostScript printer *or to a non-PostScript printer,* will print at the resolution of the printer. That is, if you use an Apple StyleWriter with a resolution of 360 dots per inch, your type will print at 360 dots per inch. It's beautiful on the screen and it's beautiful on the page.

This makes it sound like TrueType is better than PostScript, yes? Well, in some cases it is and in some it isn't. Let me explain Adobe Type Manager first and then suggest some optimal combinations of font technology and printers.

Adobe Type Manager is a small program, a "utility" (now included with System 7.5), that makes PostScript fonts appear smooth on the screen, and print smooth even to a non-PostScript printer.

Adobe Type Manager, affectionately called **ATM,** uses the printer font portion (the outline) of the PostScript fonts. It *rasterizes* this outline (turns the outline into dots) and displays it on the screen. Basically, ATM does the same thing the PostScript *printer* does, but instead of outputting it to paper like the printer would, ATM outputs it to the monitor. So your PostScript fonts look as beautiful on the screen as they do on paper.

In fact, ATM will also rasterize the outlines and output them *to a non-PostScript printer* at the resolution of the printer. This means that with ATM, your HP DeskWriter will create smooth type at 300 dots per inch, which looks as good as type from a PostScript Apple LaserWriter!

If you have ATM (and everyone *should*—it's too wonderful to be without), be sure to **read the manual!**

On the screen
without ATM

On the screen
with ATM

ATM makes an incredible difference in the way type looks on your screen, and in the way type looks when you print to a non-PostScript printer.

~ATM 68020/030   ~ATM 68020/030/040

*In Systems 7.0 and 7.1, you need to install two icons to run ATM. You will find an icon that looks like **one** of the above, or similar. The numbers refer to the kind of chip that is running your machine. Unless you have a very old machine, like a Mac Plus or SE, you need the icon with the 020/030 and possibly 040 label.*

~ATM™   ~ATM™

In Systems 7.0 and 7.1, you also need to install one of these (whichever one is on your disk).

In System 7.5, you need to only install the control panel (the one on the right).

Which Font Technology for You? With **TrueType** you get nice smooth type on the screen and nice smooth type on both PostScript and non-PostScript printers. With **PostScript** (Type 1) fonts combined with ATM, you get the same thing. So which font technology should you use?

It's possible to use both TrueType fonts and PostScript fonts on the same machine and in the same document.

> *Just don't keep two fonts with the same name from the two different technologies in your computer!* That is, don't keep both TrueType Times and PostScript Times in your Mac. I'll come back to this later.

Here are suggestions for optimal combinations of font technology and printers.

Non-PostScript printer: one option **If you have a non-PostScript printer** (DeskWriter, DeskJet, StyleWriter, etc.), you will be able to create beautifully typeset pages and see beautiful type on your screen using **TrueType.** If you already have TrueType fonts that came with your machine, then when you begin to invest in more fonts you may want to continue to invest in TrueType fonts.

Non-PostScript printer: another option **If you have a non-PostScript printer,** you will be able to create beautifully typeset pages and see beautiful type on your screen using **ATM and PostScript fonts.** If you already have PostScript fonts, you may want to continue investing in PostScript. There are currently many more typefaces available in PostScript than in TrueType.

> Keep in mind that both TrueType and ATM technologies are centered around type, not graphics. Many graphics use PostScript, and if you have a QuickDraw (non-PostScript) printer, neither TrueType nor ATM can help create those graphics on the printed page. You will not be able to get high-end, smooth graphics on a QuickDraw printer, but then if you are in the market for high-end graphics you would not have bought a non-PostScript printer.

If you have a PostScript printer, the general consensus is to ignore TrueType and use **ATM and PostScript fonts.** One of the reasons for this is that the PostScript interpreter understands perfectly the PostScript fonts; they speak the same language, but the PostScript interpreter has to figure out what to do with TrueType. Also, the larger the point size and the higher the resolution, the more trouble TrueType causes. Which means:

PostScript printer

If you plan to have your **pages printed on an imagesetter** (which is very high resolution), **don't use Truetype.** Imagesetters *really* don't like to deal with TrueType fonts—they create many problems in the output. TrueType slows down the machines incredibly, and sometimes they simply clog it up and won't print at all. Those $100,000 PostScript imagesetters are even fussier than our $1200 laser printers. Check with your service bureau before you show up with a document containing TrueType.

Imagesetters

How to Install Fonts

If the Application menu shows any other applications open besides "Finder," you must close each one first.

System Folder

This is a closed System Folder.

Fonts, PostScript or TrueType, must be loaded into your System before you can use them. I'm going to tell you **how to install fonts,** but then you really must read the Important Note after the directions.

▼ First make sure all applications are closed. Check the Application menu (far right of the menu bar) and make sure there is no other application listed except the "Finder." If there is, select the application, then press Command Q. Do this even if you don't know what I'm talking about and even if, when you choose the application, you don't see any change on your screen. Trust me.

▼ Make sure your System Folder is closed.

▼ Make sure you can see both the closed System Folder *and* the fonts you want to install at the same time.

▼ Whether you have a suitcase or a series of bitmapped fonts (PostScript or TrueType), select them and drag them over to the System Folder. When the System Folder is highlighted, let go of the fonts. You'll get a message asking if you want the Mac to put them where they belong. Of course you do.

▼ If you are installing PostScript fonts, find the printer font icons and drag them, all of them, over to the System Folder and drop them inside also. The Mac will put them where they belong.

You can drop a combination of screen, printer, and TrueType fonts onto the System Folder simultaneously and the Mac will place each one where it belongs. In fact, if you have a folder of fonts, *and you know there is nothing in there except fonts,* you can drop the entire folder on the System Folder and the Mac will take are of everything.

You need to drag all of these items to the System Folder to install the fonts if the fonts are PostScript.

Geneva

When you install TrueType, you only need one icon for each font.

▼ If you have an AFM file (Adobe Font Metrics), ignore it. Do not install it anywhere on your Mac. Leave the AFM file on the floppy disk on the *very* off chance you may ever need it. If you do need it, the application you are using will tell you so.

Carpenter.AFM
Ignore the AFM files.

▼ You might find some sort of "font downloader" utility also on a disk of fonts. If you don't already have a downloader in a folder somewhere, copy this one onto your hard disk, *but not into the System Folder!* If you have a downloader already, you don't need this one unless this one is a more recent version (check the Get Info notes on each file; see page 90).

Downloader 5.0.4   LaserWriter Utility

LaserWriter Font Utility   Download

Even if you don't know what to do with it yet, keep a recent version of a font downloader on your hard disk.

In System 7.0, bitmapped screen fonts and TrueType fonts are stored in the System file; printer fonts for PostScript are stored in the Extensions folder.

In System 7.1 and above, all fonts and all parts of fonts are stored in the Fonts folder within the System Folder. You will need ATM version 3.0 (at least) to use ATM with the Fonts folder.

Important Note: What I just described is the standard, typical way of installing fonts, the way you read about in all the magazines and literature about the Mac. "Oh, just drag those fonts and drop them into the System Folder." The truth is, though, once you start adding fonts to your collection you need to become responsible and knowledgeable about how to manage those critters. Once you acquire a font addiction and start adding massive quantities of fonts, you must buy and use a font management utility because *all those fonts really should not be kept in the System Folder!* If you buy maybe five or ten or even twelve font families, you'll be safe enough with all of them in the System. But any more than that and you're going to need help. You need to manage them. You need to buy either Suitcase or MasterJuggler and you need to learn how to use it. All of this is the topic of another book, *How to Boss Your Fonts Around.*

Resident Fonts

Now, this following bit of information will only pertain to you if you use PostScript fonts and ATM, and it will pertain whether you use a PostScript printer *or* a QuickDraw printer.

PostScript printers have RAM (random-access memory) and ROM (read-only memory) inside, just like your computer. Permanently built into the ROMs is the printer font information for the standard laser printer fonts: Avant Garde, Bookman, Courier, Helvetica, Palatino, New Century Schoolbook, Times, Zapf Chancery, Symbol, and Zapf Dingbats. These fonts are considered **resident** in the printer. When you buy a PostScript printer you are given a disk with the corresponding screen fonts to install in the Mac. Whenever you print using one of these fonts, the printer looks in its own ROM first, finds the printer font information, and prints.

If you use PostScript fonts and ATM, you may notice that ATM does not affect these standard, resident laser fonts—they still appear rough and jaggy on the screen (although they will print smooth on a PostScript printer, they will print jagged on a QuickDraw printer). Well, remember, ATM uses the printer (outline) font to produce the smooth shapes on the screen. *But ATM cannot find the printer fonts for these standard laser faces because the printer fonts live in the ROM of the PostScript printer!* If you want to see these fonts rendered beautifully on your screen, or if you want to print them to a non-PostScript printer, then you need to buy the printer fonts from Adobe. (Personally, I would rather take that money and buy some different fonts.)

When you install ATM using the installer utility, it installs printer fonts for Helvetica, Times, Symbol, and Courier. The others you must buy.

This is what
Palatino looks like
on the screen.

But this is how
Palatino prints to a
PostScript printer.

Palatino will look terrible on the screen even if you use ATM because ATM cannot find the resident printer font.

On a non-PostScript printer, Palatino will look just as bad as it does on the screen.

Now, *this* following bit of information will only pertain to you if you use a **PostScript printer.**

System 7.x (which means any version of System 7) automatically installs **TrueType** Times, Courier, Helvetica, and Symbol. *It is not possible, though, to print TrueType Times, Helvetica, Courier, or Symbol to a PostScript printer.* Most applications call on a font by name. If a document goes down to the PostScript printer and asks for Times, the printer looks in its own ROM first for an outline called Times. It finds one there, of course (see the information on the previous page).

So you may see TrueType Times on your screen, but you will print PostScript Times. *They are not exactly the same face.* You may end up with different spacing, different line endings, different page breaks. If you have a PostScript printer, then you also have the PostScript versions of these four fonts. *Remove the TrueType versions of any fonts with the same names as your printer's resident fonts, and reinstall the PostScript fonts.* The downloader utility usually has a menu item that tells you exactly which fonts are resident in your printer.

Fonts of the Same Name

Is It TrueType or PostScript?

How do you know if you are using **TrueType** or **PostScript**? Well, you can always look at the icons in the System Folder, as explained on the next page. But let's assume you are working in an application and you want to know right then and there.

Type Size

Unless you are using Microsoft Word, you can tell whether the font you are using is TrueType or not through a **visual clue** in the type size menu.

Installed sizes

Have you noticed how some of the sizes listed in the size menu are in outline style (which has nothing to do with *outline fonts*), and some are not (see left)? This can be different for each font. (Unfortunately, Word ignores this important visual clue.)

What the outlined number is indicating is that this particular size for this particular font has been *installed* in the System. Remember the numbers you saw at the ends of the names of the screen font icons on page 189? Generally, type will look its best on the screen in the outlined size, and will print best on a QuickDraw printer in the outlined size. You can ask for any other size, and in some programs type in your own size up to 127 point or beyond, but *if you are not using TrueType or* ATM, it'll look funky on the screen because the computer has to fake that size. The bigger the size, the funkier it looks. And if it looks funky on the screen, it will look funky on a QuickDraw printer because that printer can only reproduce what it sees on the screen.

If all the sizes (except maybe 6 and 8) are shown in the outline style, then the selected text is TrueType.

If just about all (all except for maybe the 6- and 8-point sizes) are displayed in the outline style, **then the currently selected font is TrueType.**

You can also look in your System file or in the Fonts folder within the System Folder to determine whether the fonts are TrueType, and also to determine which sizes of screen fonts are installed. Just double-click on the System file (found inside the System Folder) if you are using System 7.0; double-click on the Fonts folder (found inside the System Folder) if you are using System 7.1 or higher. You can open any font suitcase, no matter where you find it, to check fonts, also.

Times   Zapf Dingbats 12

TrueType font icons have three "A"s; screen fonts have only one A.

If the icon has three "A"s on it, it is TrueType.

If the icon has only one "A," it is a bitmapped font.
The icons with a single A will have a number after the name, such as Zapf Dingbats 12. This means it is the 12-point screen size.

Well, now, I bet you might be wondering why, if you have TrueType New York, you also see **screen fonts** for New York 10 and New York 12 in your System. Yes, I did say earlier that TrueType combines screen and printer font information into the one icon. These screen fonts for TrueType New York (and any others you find that match your other TrueType fonts) are simply there because supposedly it is faster for the Mac to create the font on the screen if it can use the already-created screen font in that size, rather than having to use the TrueType technology to *create* that size. Since most people use sizes 10- and 12-point type most of the time, the screen fonts are merely to speed the process. You can remove these screen versions from your System and I seriously doubt you would ever notice any loss of speed.

New York

New York 10 New York 12

Anywhere you find a TrueType icon or a screen font icon, you can double-click on it to see what that font looks like. If it is TrueType, you'll see it in three sizes. If it is a screen font, you see it just in that size screen font.

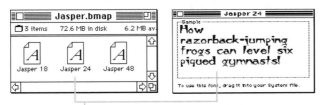

Double-click on the 24-point size screen font icon to display the font in 24-point.

Font Substitution

If you are printing to a PostScript printer and you use the city-named fonts New York, Geneva, or Monaco, your application may automatically **substitute fonts.** This is true even if you are using TrueType city-named fonts.

While in your favorite application, choose "Page Setup" from the File menu. Most applications will display these dialog boxes:

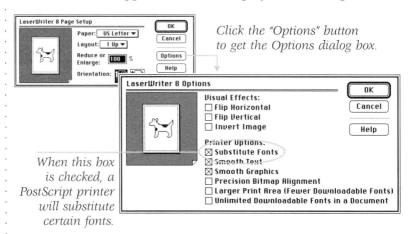

Click the "Options" button to get the Options dialog box.

When this box is checked, a PostScript printer will substitute certain fonts.

Notice the first checkbox button, "Font Substitution"? This box is checked as a "default" (an automatic selection). Unless you consciously uncheck it, this box makes the printer substitute certain fonts. It will substitute Times when it finds New York, Helvetica when it finds Geneva, and Courier when it finds Monaco. Because the city-named fonts are designed for a lower resolution, the words take up more space. The PostScript substitution tries to keep the line as long as it was in the city-named font, but to do that it must add more space to fill out the line. Have you ever noticed printed pages with too much space between the words? Or numbers that looked like they were supposed to align but didn't? Or an underline that was dashed? That's the result of trying to print a font with a city name to a PostScript printer. See the small examples on the next page.

Try this yourself. Type a page with Geneva, New York, and Monaco. Print it to a PostScript printer once with font substitution checked, then print it again without font substitution checked. Put the two pages together and look at them.

TrueType Chicago prints very nicely on a PostScript printer, because there is no corresponding substitute or similarly named printer font living in the printer.

This is a sample of 10-point New York printed with <u>no font substitution.</u>
 G. One potato
 H. Two potato
 I. Three potato

This is a sample of 10-point New York printed with <u>automatic font substitution.</u> The PostScript printer turned it into Times.
 G. One potato
 H. Two potato
 I. Three potato

This is a sample of 10-point Times printed on a PostScript printer. It needs no <u>font substitution.</u>
 G. One potato
 H. Two potato
 I. Three potato

GX Fonts

You may hear now and then about new "smart fonts" called **QuickDraw GX fonts.** The QuickDraw GX from Apple is a new "imaging architecture" for the Mac, meaning it will enable several advanced features for graphics, type, and color. GX fonts will be able to have up to 65,000 characters, rather than the 256 we are now limited to, so they will be able to support languages with many characters, such as Japanese and Chinese. They will have advanced typographic capabilities, so even a Mac beginner writing a letter to grandma will produce a highly sophisticated typographic page. At the moment, even though GX offers these features right now, there are no software packages that can take advantage of it, except a small word processor that you get when you install the QuickDraw GX software, called GXWrite.

If you have not consciously installed QuickDraw GX, then you do not have GX fonts. If you do have GX fonts, you can play around with them for a while, and perhaps eventually there will be more support for them. I'll be writing about them more later, when they are worth taking the time.

Do you care? If you don't, skip this! Go take a nap! Do something useful!

1. Which sort of printer is actually a computer: PostScript or QuickDraw?

. . . .

2. Which technology uses "outlines," PostScript or TrueType?

. . . .

3. PostScript screen fonts are usually stored in little suitcase icons. Do they have to be?

. . . .

4. If you use PostScript fonts, what other software utility should you also use?

. . . .

5. Label the icons below: A) TrueType B) PostSript printer font C) bitmapped screen font

Linos   Linoscript 12   Times (italic)

6. If you will be printing to a high-resolution imagesetter, which font technology is a better choice?

. . . .

7. Describe how to install fonts.

. . . .

8. Why would ATM not work on Avant Garde?

. . . .

9/10. Make two appropriate groups out of the icons below, and state why you grouped them together.

Machine Bold 24   Times (italic)   Machine 24   Times (bold)   Machi

Times   MachiBol   Times (bold, italic)

Answers on page 372.

DESK ACCESSORIES 22

Desk accessories, affectionately known as **DA**s, are handy little tools found in your menu under the Apple. The purpose of a desk accessory is to make life easier. Access them like any other menu item—slide down the list until the name of the DA is highlighted, then let go. Desk accessories all appear in windows, so they can be moved around the screen from their title bars and closed with their little close boxes. You can open any DA while you are in any application.

The Apple menu used to hold nothing *except* desk accessories, but now it can hold anything you want to put in it so not everything you see in the menu is a DA. In fact, it is now difficult to tell which items *are* desk accessories. You can buy an amazing number of desk accessories, many for very low prices. They do all manner of useful and useless things. The following information, however, explains just the DAs that come standard with every Mac.

Alarm Clock
System 7 and 7.1

□ 2:02:10 PM 🔔

Press on the numbers, (which is essentially the title bar) to drag this clock anywhere on your screen.

The **Alarm Clock** won't wake you up in the morning, but it will beep at you while you're sitting at your computer. After it beeps once, the apple in the corner flashes from an apple to an alarm clock. The problem with this alarm is that it doesn't turn itself off—even if you turn off the computer and come back next week, the alarm clock is still flashing; you have to go get it and turn it off yourself.

When the clock is the *active window* on your screen, you can press Command C and **create a copy of the date and time**; set your insertion point down anywhere, even under an icon at your Desktop, and press Command V; the date and time will paste into your document, like so: 1:38:07 AM   11/30/95.

flag

□ 10:39:34 PM ⚑
10:39:34 PM

🕐 📅 🔔

time clock   *alarm clock*
calendar

❏ **To change the settings:** begin by clicking on the tiny flag on the right side of the clock; it will open up to a little control panel. After changing a setting, click anywhere in the clock window to put it into effect.

❏ **To change the time:**
  ▼ Click on the time clock icon on the bottom left.
  ▼ Click on the number in the middle panel that you wish to change (this will cause little up and down arrows to appear on the right).
  ▼ Click on the arrows to move the time forward or backward **or** you can *type* in the numbers once you select them, either from the keyboard or the keypad.
  ▼ Change the AM or PM notation the same way.
  ▼ *Note:* you can press the Tab key to move the selection from hours to minutes to seconds, etc.

❏ **To change the date:**
  ▼ Do the same as for the time, details above, *after* clicking on the little calendar icon.

Arrows with which to change the numbers

□ 7:25:34 PM
🏳 6:15:00 AM ⬍

🕐 📅 🔔

The switch to turn the alarm on or off

❏ **To set the alarm:**
  ▼ Click on the alarm clock icon.
  ▼ Change the time to when you want it to go off, as detailed above (check the AM or PM notation).
  ▼ Click the little switch on the *left* to the up position (you'll notice the zingers around the icon now).
  ▼ When the alarm goes off, you'll get a beep and/or your menu will flash, and the little apple in the menu will flash on and off.

❏ **To close up the clock:**

- ▼ To just get rid of the control panel, click on the flag in the upper right again.
- ▼ To put it away altogether, click in its close box.

❏ **To turn off the alarm:**

- ▼ To turn it off *temporarily,* but leave the alarm set for the next day at the same time, simply get the alarm clock and then click in its close box.
- ▼ To turn it off *permanently,* you must go in and reverse the process of turning it on; that is, click on the alarm clock icon and turn off the switch.

If you are running **System 7.5,** you don't have the little alarm clock as a desk accessory—you have a clock right in your menu that is controlled through a control panel. Full details are in the Control Panels chapter, but if you want to check it out, get the Date & Time control panel from the Apple Menu (slide down to Control Panels, then slide out to Date & Time). It's very self-explanatory.

Menu Clock
System 7.5

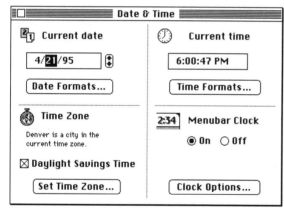

Click on the parts of the date or time you want to change, then click the arrows or type in new numbers.

Remember, when you click a button with an ellipsis (...), you will get another dialog box. Check them out! It's harmless!

This is what my menu clock looks like, now that I've customized it. When I click on the time, it shows me the date for a moment.

Calculator

Calculator

The **Calculator** is a very handy item to have. It operates just like your hand-held calculator, although it has only the four basic functions. Remember, this calculator is a window so it can be dragged around like any other window and put away with its close box. Access it within any application.

- ▼ Operate the calculator with the mouse, keyboard, or numeric keypad.

- ▼ If using the keyboard, make sure you use the real numeral 1 (one) and not a lowercase l (el).

- ▼ The division sign is the slash: /. The multiplication sign is the asterisk: *.

- ▼ The answer can be copied and pasted into your document using Copy and Paste from the Edit menu. You don't need to select the numbers first—if the Calculator is the active window, the Copy command knows what to copy. You can also copy numbers from your document and paste them into the Calculator.

This calculator is extremely limited, though. It won't even add the percent to the sum. If you find you use this little calculator a lot, you might want to check with your local user group or friendly power user for one of the many commercial or shareware (meaning almost free) versions available.

Graphing Calculator

Graphing Calculator

The **Graphing Calculator** is installed in System 7.5 if you have a Power Macintosh. This is a serious tool that, for one thing, can actually graph equations. It does a lot more, but I don't know how to explain it. If you do the sort of work that needs a graphing calculator, then you are probably the sort of person who can figure out how to use this one.

Chooser

Chooser

The **Chooser** is where you choose which printer you wish to use. If you are working at home or at work and are hooked up to only one printer, you need to use the Chooser only the very first time you print. If you have the option of printing to more than one printer, then you need to go to the Chooser each time you want to switch to another printer. For all the gory details on using the Chooser, please see Chapter 16 on Printing.

If you have a CD-ROM drive, you can play audio CDs (yes, music CDs). You can listen to Gregorian chants while balancing your electronic checkbook. Shown below is what the System 7.5 **CD Player** looks like. It's very self-explanatory—it works just like the one in your living room, except you can change its color (check out the "Options" menu after you open the CD Player).

CD Player

CD Player

Click here to repeat the CD.

On a Performa, this item might be called **AppleCD Audio Player.**

To listen to music CDs, though, you might have to also change a couple of settings in the Sound control panel. Try the CD, and if it doesn't work, do this:

▾ Get the Sound control panel:
  From the Apple menu, slide down to Control Panels.
     If there is a little arrow pointing to the right, slide out to the right and choose "Sound."
     If there is no arrow, then just choose "Control Panels" from the menu. When you see the Control Panels window, double-click on the "Sound" icon.

▾ Press on the arrow next to the label, "Alert Sounds"; slide down and choose "Sound In."

▾ Click the "Options" button.

▾ Click "Internal CD" and "Playthrough."

▾ Click "OK," then click in the close box (upper left) to put the control panel away. Now you can play your music.

Key Caps

Key Caps

Key Caps can show you the keyboard layout for every font that is loaded in your System. On a Macintosh keyboard you actually have four separate sets of keys, two of which you know already and two of which only a few people know about. You are about to become In The Know.

▼ After you open up Key Caps, you have a new menu item called "Key Caps."

▼ Pull down the Key Caps menu—this is a list of the fonts that are installed on your System.

▼ Select the font you want; the characters of that font will appear on the keyboard (these are the characters everybody knows about).

▼ To see the Shift characters, press the Shift key (everybody knows these, too).

▼ To see the Option characters, press the Option key (Ha! You are now In The Know).

▼ To see the Shift Option characters, press the Shift and Option keys simultaneously.

Different fonts have different characters in the Option and Shift Option keyboards—some have more, some have less. Most of the Option key characters are consistent in every font, so you can always find, for instance, the accent marks or copyright, trademark, and monetary symbols, etc., in the same place.

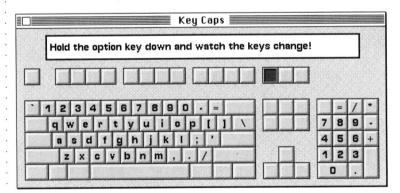

Key Caps is only for finding the *placement* of all the available characters on the keyboard. Hold down the Option key, for instance, and note where the ¢ sign is located.

▼ Once you discover that the ¢ is found under the 4 (the 4 also holds the $ sign), then you can go back to your document and press Option and 4; the ¢ will appear.
It's exactly the same idea as pressing Shift 8 to get an asterisk! Or Shift 4 to get the dollar sign!

It's possible to type the characters on the Key Caps keyboard, copy them (select the characters first, then choose Copy from the Edit menu), and then Paste the characters into your document (they will paste in wherever the insertion point is flashing). This works fine as long as the font you are using in your document is the same font you chose from Key Caps, or at least that they share the same character. Otherwise when you paste the character it will take on the *format* (font, size, style) of the character to the left of the insertion point, which may not be what you want at all.

▼ At the Key Caps keyboard, find the character you want to use.
▼ Remember what font and what keys to press to get that character.
▼ Go back to your document, select the font you want, and press the appropriate keys.
▼ Can you find the apple?

Also see pages 131–133 for more info, including how to type accent marks over letters. There is a very tricky method for discovering the keyboard combination for many of the accent marks that take two steps to create, such as Ê, which takes Option i, and then Shift e. For now, you can use the chart of special characters at the end of the book as a quick reference for typing.

Using Key Caps is a great way for discovering which fonts are installed at the moment in any Macintosh! Just choose Key Caps from the Apple menu, then press on the Key Caps menu item that appears—you will see the fonts that are currently installed and available.

Installed Fonts?

Note Pad

Click here to turn the page forward.

Note to Jimmy

This is a System 7.5 clipping file. Double-click to open it, or open it in another application.

The **Note Pad** is a nice little accessory that allows you to write up to eight pages of notes. This is a great place to leave prearranged messages, notes about particular formatting used in a document, reminders, or more love notes. Any messages in the Note Pad are automatically saved (they will *not* be destroyed on rebuilding the Desktop, as Get Info notes will).

The insertion point is flashing; type into it just as you type anywhere else in the Macintosh.You can backspace/delete, cut, copy, paste, etc. Turn the pages by clicking on the little turned corner on the bottom left; click on the *very* bottom corner to turn the pages backwards.

In **System 7.5,** the Note Pad still has eight pages, but there is a scroll bar running along the right side. This is a **visual clue** that you can type more text than will fit on the page you see, then you can scroll through it. You can select text, then press-and-drag it to the Desktop or into a window to make a "clipping file" that you can open in other applications.

Puzzle
System 7 or 7.1

The completed Apple puzzle. No, I didn't cheat!

The numbers puzzle is much easier.

A custom-made puzzle.

The **Puzzle** is a great relaxer. Be sure to have your sound turned on so you get the prize at the end.

❑ **To switch the Puzzle** from the Apple logo to the numbers, choose "Clear" from the Edit menu while the puzzle is active (click once on it to make it active). Choose "Clear" again to get the Apple logo.

❑ **To view the finished puzzle,** choose "Puzzle" from the Apple menu.
  ▼ From the Edit menu, choose "Copy."
  ▼ Put the Puzzle away by clicking in its close box (*or* press Command W).
  ▼ From the Edit menu, choose "Show Clipboard" to see the completed puzzle. Press Command W to close the Clipboard.

❑ **To paste different new pictures** in the Puzzle to entertain your kids or yourself:
  ▼ Create a graphic in your painting or drawing program, or open some clip art or the Scrapbook.
  ▼ Select the graphic and copy it.
  ▼ Quit the graphics program or close the Scrapbook.
  ▼ Open the Puzzle.
  ▼ From the Edit menu, choose Paste. Zap—a whole new Puzzle!

❑ **To get the original Puzzle back,** choose "Clear" from the Edit menu.

In **System 7.5,** the **Jigsaw Puzzle** is much more sophisticated. It's a regular jigsaw puzzle, but you can still customize it. This jigsaw is more fun for kids than the numbers puzzle, and if they're old enough you can teach them to customize it themselves.

- ▼ Choose "Jigsaw Puzzle" from the apple menu.
  You will get a new menu item called "Options"
  along with the completed puzzle.

- ▼ From the Options menu, choose "Start new puzzle...."
  You can choose to have large, small, or medium pieces.
  Click "OK."

- ▼ So now solve it.

- ▼ Play around with that Options menu—everything is
  self-explanatory.

  Want a challenge? Use the Great Fun Tip to create
  a puzzle out of one of your Desktop Patterns! Ha!

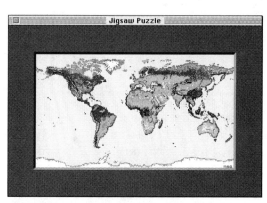

This is the
original
jigsaw puzzle.

This is a custom puzzle.
Copy or create any clip
art and paste it in here.

If you have a Performa,
open any of the clip art
that comes with your
machine. Click on the
clip art to select it, copy
it (from the Edit menu),
then go to the puzzle and
choose "Paste" from the
Edit menu. That's where
this picture came from.

Jigsaw Puzzle
System 7.5

Jigsaw Puzzle

Great Fun Tip!
Open the Scrapbook
or the Desktop
Patterns control
*panel, **and** open*
the Jigsaw Puzzle.
Drag any image
from the Scrapbook
or the Desktop
Patterns over to the
puzzle and let go—
that image is the
new puzzle!

(When you do this,
you are actually
dragging the
"clipping path.")

Another
Great Tip!
View any PICT *file*
by dragging its icon
onto the open Jigsaw
Puzzle! If it displays
as puzzle pieces, just
choose "Solve Puzzle"
from the Options
menu.

Scrapbook

Scrapbook File

The **Scrapbook** is a place where you can permanently store text, graphics, movies (System 7.5), and sounds from virtually any program; then in any other program you can take a copy of it back out from the Scrapbook and paste it into your document. Once you put something in the Scrapbook it is saved to your disk automatically. The Scrapbook holds the entire object or text, even though you can't always see all of it in the window.

You must go through the Clipboard (the Mac's temporary holding place) to put items into the Scrapbook and to take them out.

See pages 128–129 if you want more information on the Clipboard.

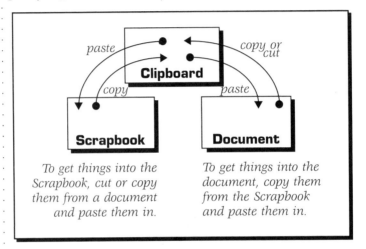

To get things into the Scrapbook, cut or copy them from a document and paste them in.

To get things into the document, copy them from the Scrapbook and paste them in.

❏ **To paste something into the Scrapbook:**
   ▼ From your document, *select* and *copy* the item you want to place (this puts a copy on the Clipboard).
   ▼ Open the Scrapbook from the Apple menu.
   ▼ Paste the item into the Scrapbook (from the Edit menu choose "Paste")—the Scrapbook will make a new page for the new item, and everything else *will move over one; nothing is replaced.*
   ▼ Close the Scrapbook to get back to your document, or just click on any visible part of your document.

❏ **To copy an item out of the Scrapbook:**
   ▼ Open the Scrapbook.
   ▼ Scroll through until the item you want *is visible.*
   ▼ Copy it (from the Edit menu choose "Copy").
   ▼ Close the Scrapbook.
   ▼ Go to your document and paste it in (usually text and sometimes graphics, will insert themselves wherever

the insertion point is flashing; in some applications the item will just be pasted into the middle of the page).

❑ **To delete an item from the Scrapbook:**
- ▼ Scroll through until the item you want is *visible.*
- ▼ From the Edit menu choose "Clear" (Clear *removes* the item *without* putting it on the Clipboard). In **System 7.5,** you can use the keyboard shortcut Command B.

Limitations and troubleshooting

Not every item you see can be pasted into any document of any kind. For instance, you can't usually paste a movie into a spreadsheet cell. If nothing happens when you try to paste from the Scrapbook, one of two things is happening: either it can't be done, or you have inadvertently pasted the item somewhere other than where you expect. For instance, your insertion point might be flashing on page 7, but you are looking at page 15. Remember, when you paste, the item will paste onto the page *where the insertion point is flashing!* In a spreadsheet, it will paste into the selected cell or cells. In a database, it will paste into the selected field. Be conscious!

Scrapbook System 7.5

The Scrapbook in **System 7.5** works exactly the same as the Scrapbook always has, but it is a little fancier, as you can see below. You can see information about each file stored in the Scrapbook, and you can now store QuickTime movies here. There is also a new keyboard shortcut, Command B, to "Clear" (to remove an item from the Scrapbook without placing it on the Clipboard).

text clipping

picture clipping

sound clipping

As in the Note Pad, you can drag a file out of the Scrapbook directly onto the Desktop or into a window, where it becomes a "clipping file." You can open this clipping file in other applications. Eventually, they say, we will be able to drag files out of the Scrapbook directly into our applications without having to copy and paste. Right now, you can drag items from the Scrapbook to the Desktop Patterns or the Jigsaw Puzzle.

These clipping files, made by dragging items from the Scrapbook to the Desktop, can be opened by double-clicking on them, or you can open them in other appropriate applications.

The Scrapbook in System 7.5.

Stickies

System 7.5

Stickies

Stickies are electronic Post-It® notes. Some people like them, some people don't bother with them. Use Stickies for a bit and see what you think. (They don't really turn at angles, as shown to the left.)

From the Apple menu, choose "Stickies." The first time you do this, you'll see these messages:

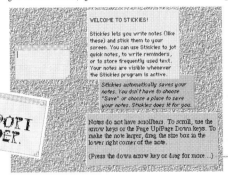

Unfortunately, they left out a step here: first you must click at the end of this sentence before pressing the down arrow key works.

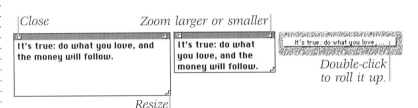

Close   *Zoom larger or smaller*

Double-click to roll it up.

Resize

You'll get this message every time you close a Stickie unless you uncheck "Confirm window closing" in the Preferences.

These little stickies act like windows: you can move them around by dragging their title bars, resize them, zoom them smaller or larger, double-click their title bars to roll them up, and click the close box or press Command W to make them go away. You can change the color, typeface, and typeface size for each note (from the Color and Note menus that appear when a stickie is an active window). You can "import text" (bring in text from a document you created) and "export" text (which saves it as a SimpleText document) from the File menu.

If you choose "Launch at system startup," all your Stickies will automatically open when you turn on the Mac. Then choose "...in the background" so your Desktop windows will be active when you startup, rather than Stickie windows.

From the Edit menu, choose "Preferences..." to customize some of the Stickie features to your own liking (see left).

If you want all your Stickies to be a certain format, make one exactly the way you want it (typeface, size, color) and position it on the screen where you would want a new one to show up. Then from the Edit menu choose "Use as Default."

Remember, *not all of the items in your Apple menu are desk accessories.* You won't often need to know which ones are or aren't except when you are **installing** them and want to know where to put them.

If you need to know whether a file is a desk accessory, click once on the icon, then choose "Get Info" from the File menu and check the "Kind." If the file is *really* a desk accessory, meaning the Mac knows it is a desk accessory and not just something you want to put in your Apple Menu Items folder, then you can just drag the icon and drop it onto the top of the *closed* System Folder. You'll see this polite message:

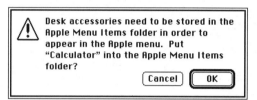

You can also place the desk accessory icon directly into the Apple Menu Items folder, found inside the System Folder. As soon as you drop it in, it appears in the Apple Menu and you can use it.

Keep in mind that desk accessories can also be stored right on the Desktop, if you use one so much that you would like to have it available for instant clicking. You might want to keep an alias (Chapter 25) on the Desktop and the original file in the Apple Menu, or vice versa.

To **close any desk accessory,** click in its little close box in the upper left of its window, *or* press Command W, *or* press Command Q, *or* go up to the File menu and choose "Quit."

Installing Desk Accessories

The Get Info box will tell you if the file is actually a desk accessory.

Closing Desk Accessories

Match the task with the appropriate desk accessory you would need to accomplish the task. One DA might apply to more than one task.

Scrapbook

Calculator

Key Caps

Chooser

Note Pad

Puzzle or Jigsaw Puzzle

CD Player

Alarm Clock (or Date & Time control panel)

Stickies

1. Change the time

2. Play a music CD

3. Find out how to type this character: ©

4. Save a graphic image to put into your letterhead next week

5. Leave little notes all over the Desktop

6. Tell the computer to print to a different printer

7. Add up the itemized list for an invoice total and copy it into the invoice

8. Discover which fonts are installed

9. Keep a to-do list and notes about your garden

10. Hang out and enjoy yourself for a few minutes

Answers on page 372.

APPLE MENU

The **Apple menu** is under the tiny apple *icon* (picture) in the upper left corner of your menu bar. This menu is completely customizable, meaning you can add or delete any item at any time. You have access to anything in the Apple menu from within any other program on the Macintosh.

You can customize your Apple menu by adding files to it that you use frequently. Documents, folders, programs, desk accessories—stick 'em in the Apple menu. This chapter fills you in on all the juicy tidbits of how to customize your menu and how to take advantage of it.

OBVIOUSLY, A REFERENCE TO ADAM AND EVE, OR PERHAPS THE DECLINE OF NEW YORK, OR—I KNOW!—YOUR TRIBUTE TO FRUIT!

I CALL IT "MY FAVORITE MENU."

Apple Menu The **Apple menu** is *meant* for you to customize—it is designed to help make your work easier and more efficient. Take advantage of it! But keep this is mind:

> Except for desk accessories (as you read about in the previous chapter, right?), you should put *aliases* of any item into the Apple menu—don't install the original file!

Aliases An **alias** is a *substitute* for the real thing. When you choose an alias, *it goes and gets the real thing.* You can have lots of aliases for the same item, since all any of them do is find the real object you want—they're "gofers." You know, kind of like your kids: "Jimmy, go fer this and go fer that." Even though I will explain how to create aliases here, you might want to read Chapter 25 for details. Aliases are too cool. And they are a very important part of managing your work.

If you install an alias of a *folder* in the Apple menu in **System 7.5,** it will have an arrow pointing to the side and the contents of the folder will be listed there so you can choose any item (in Systems 7.0 or 7.1, selecting a folder alias from the menu will open the actual folder for you). If you install an alias of an *application* in the Apple menu, selecting it will open the application for you. If you install an alias of a *document* in the Apple menu, selecting it will open the application it was created within, plus put the document on your screen.

This is the Apple menu as it looked when I turned on my new computer. It's such a jumble of stuff that I don't even like to look at it. It's hard to find things. Take a look at the next few pages (particularly pages 222–223) and see what a difference it makes to organize and customize your Apple menu.

Follow these steps to **install any file**, *including desk accessories,* in the Apple menu. If you don't know whether it is an actual "desk accessory" or not, click once on the file, then press Command I to check the Get Info window, (shown on the right). Or you can check the window: when you view the window as some sort of list, the column "Kind" is usually showing (also shown on the right).

Installing Apple Menu Items

▾ Unless the file is a desk accessory, first make an alias of it:

- Click once on the folder, application, document, etc., that you want in the Apple menu.

- **System 7.0 or 7.1:** From the File menu, choose "Make Alias." The Mac will make an alias of the item and place it almost on top of the original.

The Get Info window (above) will tell you what kind of file it is. The window viewed in a list (below) will also tell you.

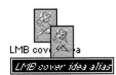

*This is what you will see when you make an alias. Oh, look—the name is highlighted and has a border around it. That must be a **visual clue!** What does it mean?!? ***

How do you know it's an alias? Well, for one thing, the name of the file has the word "alias" at the end of it. But the most important **visual clue** is that the name of the alias file is in *italic*. Alias file names *are always italic.*

- **System 7.5:** There are several shortcuts for making aliases. For one thing, you can select the file (click once on it) and press Command M to make an alias.

  System 7.5: If you are going to put the alias in the Apple Menu Items folder, simply do this: Select the file. From the Apple menu, slide down to "Automated Tasks" and choose "Add Alias to Apple Menu." It's done! You can skip to the next page.

- **System 7.0 or 7.1:** Press-and-drag the alias you made out of the folder and onto the Desktop. (While it's on the Desktop, I like to remove the word "alias" from the file's name.)

---

* The highlight and border mean the file is ready for you to rename— just type.

▼ Now to customize the Apple menu, open the System Folder.

▼ There is a folder in the System Folder called **Apple Menu Items.** You can type **ap** to select it, even if you don't see it.

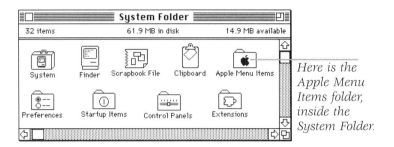

Here is the Apple Menu Items folder, inside the System Folder.

▼ The trick to putting the alias into the Apple folder is that you need to be able to see both the alias of your file *and* the Apple Menu Items folder at the same time; you may need to rearrange windows and the alias file to do so.

▼ Drag the alias and drop it onto the "Apple Menu Items" folder.

▼ The item will appear in the menu instantly; you don't need to restart the computer for it to take effect.

Alphabetizing, or "sorting"

The Apple menu displays items alphabetically, as I'm sure you've noticed. When the Mac alphabetizes, blank spaces and punctuation are "sorted" (alphabetized) in front of any other character. So if you add a blank space or a period as the first character in a name, that file will be first in the Apple menu list. The more blank spaces, the higher on the list the file will be located. (And then some utilities that put themselves into the Apple menu have an option to be alphabetized or to be placed at the top of the list, such as Suitcase, a font management program, which you see in my example.)

Here are some **suggestions for customizing your own Apple menu.**

▾ System 7.x (which means any version of System 7) automatically places an alias of the Control Panels folder in the Apple menu. But if there are control panels that you use regularly, you can make it even easier on yourself by installing aliases of the individual control panels. For instance, if you switch grayscale and/or color levels on your Mac all the time, then install an alias of the Monitors control panel.

▾ Rather than dig into all those folders to get an application that you use regularly, put aliases of your favorite applications directly into the Apple menu.

▾ If you have a folder of important items that is filed within other folders, install an alias of the important folder into the Apple menu. When you choose it, the folder will open and you'll have easy access to all those related files.

▾ If you have documents or templates that you use regularly, such as a fax form or letterhead stationery, put their aliases in your Apple menu.

▾ If you have a floppy disk or cartridge hard disk or CD that you use regularly, or you can even do this to your hard disk, put an alias of it in the Apple menu and you'll get a submenu of all the items on the disk without having to open the windows. Any folders on the disk will have their own submenus. It's really amazing. If you change stuff on the disk, it is reflected in the Apple menu.

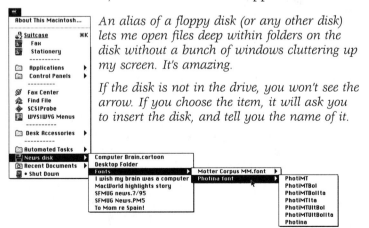

An alias of a floppy disk (or any other disk) lets me open files deep within folders on the disk without a bunch of windows cluttering up my screen. It's amazing.

If the disk is not in the drive, you won't see the arrow. If you choose the item, it will ask you to insert the disk, and tell you the name of it.

Suggestions for Customizing

I keep an alias of the Apple Menu Items folder right on my Desktop so when I want to add something to the menu, I can just drop it into the folder alias.

Hey—Let's Get Really Fancy If you really want to **get fancy** with customizing your menu, you can group the items into clusters and even create separators between the clusters, taking advantage of the fact that blank spaces are alphabetized first, then non-letters, such as hyphens or bullets (• Option 8). I can't stand the cluttered look of the natural Apple menu, especially in System 7.5 (as shown on page 218). It's a mess and it's confusing. Below is an organized menu in System 7.1, and on the following page is an example of an organized 7.5 Apple menu.

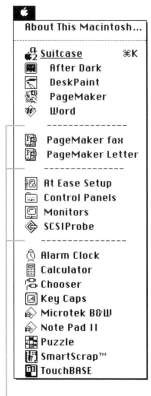

(The font management utility "Suitcase" puts itself first and I let it.)

I typed three blank spaces in front of the name of each of these aliases so my applications are grouped together.

I typed two blank spaces in front of the names of these template aliases.

I typed one blank space in front of the names of these control panels.

I didn't change the name at all of these files (there are no blank spaces). This last section contains all the actual desk accessories—these are not aliases.

I created the separators by making three aliases of a blank page. I typed one, two, three, or no blank spaces in front of the row of hyphens. They each "alphabetized" at the top of the different groups of files because a hyphen precedes an alphanumeric character. **You could, of course, type several hyphens and then a name to indicate the cluster. For instance, instead of ------------, the divider might be ------Desk Accessories -----.**

You don't see an icon to the left of the row of hyphens because I turned the icon into a white box, which essentially makes it invisible. See page 86 for details on changing icons.

System 7.5 adds several items to the Apple menu, which are discussed on the next page. These items are wonderful, but it does clutter the list, as you can see by the picture of it on page 218. As I customized my list, it got longer and longer, and even though it is organized, it still got so long it ran off the bottom of my 20-inch monitor. Fortunately, a simple new feature made my life easier: when you put an alias of a folder into the Apple menu in System 7.5, you get a "hierarchical" menu, one of those little menus that comes off the side. So I made folders inside my Apple Menu Items folders for all my applications, and one for all the desk accessories, and look how much shorter my menu is! And still just as convenient.

Customizing the Apple Menu in System 7.5

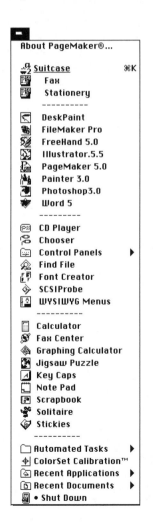

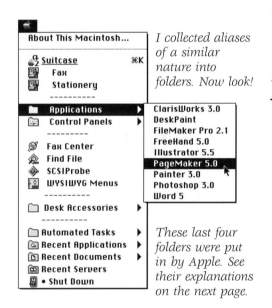

I collected aliases of a similar nature into folders. Now look!

These last four folders were put in by Apple. See their explanations on the next page.

Why would you put aliases of your applications in the Apple menu when you could put aliases on your Desktop and double-click them to open without having to go to a menu? For the simple reason that you can get to aliases in the Apple menu at those times when you can't see your Desktop.

System 7.5 Apple Menu Options

System 7.5 puts several folders into the Apple menu for you. You have control over whether these folders show up or not, and you have control over how many files each one will keep track of. The control panel named **Apple Menu Options** lets you decide if you want the little side menus (hierarchical menus) or not.

These folders are automatically placed in the Apple menu.

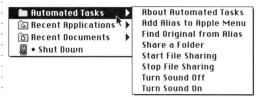

This is great. I use the task, "Add Alias to Apple Menu" and "Find Original from Alias" often. These are all pretty self-explanatory. Once you start file sharing, you will appreciate the automated task of turning file sharing on and off. If you have kids playing games on your computer, you will appreciate this quick and easy way of turning sound on and off.

I don't use this menu item as much, since I have aliases of all my applications in my Apple menu anyway. If you don't find it very useful either, go to the Apple Menu Options control panel and set the number of recently used items to 0 (zero)—that will remove it from your menu.

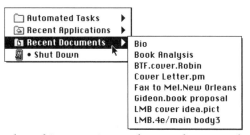

I love this menu item. The Mac keeps track of the documents I have opened and lists them here. Rather than having to dig back through folders to re-open something, I can just select it from this menu. You can control how many recent documents you want the Mac to keep track of.

Use the **Apple Menu Options** control panel to customize those "Recent" folders, and to turn on or off the hierarchical menus. To get this control panel, slide down the Apple menu to "Control Panels," then out to the side to choose "Apple Menu Options."

System 7.5 Apple Menu Options Control Panel

If you don't want the hierarchical menus at all, check the "Off" button.

```
═▢═══ Apple Menu Options ═══
┌─ Submenus ──────────────────────┐
│                                 │
│   ● On  [▣]     ○ Off  [▣]       │
│                                 │
└─────────────────────────────────┘
┌─ Recent Items ──────────────────┐
│ ☒ Remember recently used items  │
│                                 │
│   Documents:      [ 15 ]        │
│                                 │
│   Applications:   [ 5 ]         │
│                                 │
│   Servers:        [ 0 ]         │
│                                 │
└─────────────────────────────────┘
```

If you uncheck the box "Remember recently used items," then those three extra folders for Recent Documents, Applications, and Servers will not appear at all.

You can change the number of items you want the Mac to remember. If you type in "0" (zero), then the folder will disappear from your menu altogether. Anytime you want it back, just type in another number.

If you are file sharing, you can choose to see the servers you last used. If you are not file sharing, set this to zero to remove the folder from the menu.

The Mac actually stores these "Recent" folders in the Apple Menu Items folder in the System Folder, and when you open an application or document, it makes an alias of it and puts it in the appropriate folder so the item shows up in your Apple menu. The first item in is the first item out (FIFO, first in, first out). That is, if you have your "Recent Documents" set at 10, then when you open the 11th document the Mac eliminates the first one (which is the oldest, most long-ago item) to make room for the new one. But you don't need to worry about it at all—it's all taken care of for you.

Who cares?

1. When you start to customize your Apple menu, are you going to install original files or aliases?

. . . .

2. What is an alias anyway?

. . . .

3. Where do you put desk accessories or aliases when you want them to show up in the Apple menu?

. . . .

4. Which of the following items can be stored in the Apple menu as aliases: folders, applications, documents, floppy disks, CDs, hard disks

. . . .

5. How can you force a set of items to be grouped together in the Apple menu?

. . . .

6. In System 7.5, what is the fastest and easiest way to get an item into the Apple menu?

. . . .

7. In System 7.5, how can you get rid of the folder in the Apple menu called "Recent Servers"?

. . . .

8. If you know that a file is technically a "desk accessory," do you need to make an alias of it before you put it in the menu?

. . . .

9. What is the visual clue that tells you a file is an alias?

. . . .

10. Can you name three items that you, personally, would find useful having in the Apple menu?

. . . .

Answers on page 373.

CONTROL PANELS

The **Control Panels** concept is a very important feature of the Macintosh that lets you customize the look and feel of your computer, plus give you added features. Each control panel controls a certain aspect of the Mac, such as what you see in your windows and how the items are displayed, what sound you hear and how loud it is, whether or not you want to share folders and files with other people on other computers, and many other features. A certain number of control panels are provided by Apple, and you will run into others provided by other vendors.

Control panels are stored in the Control Panels folder found in the System Folder. *Most control panels will not work unless they are stored in this folder!* You can open the Control Panels folder and double-click on any file to open the panel itself. Most of the features are self-explanatory, and different sorts of computers have different sorts of control panels. In this chapter I'll go through the most common ones so you can quickly get an idea of what they do and how you can control your Mac.

AFTER SPACING OUT ABOUT HIS ANNIVERSARY,
JAKE ADJUSTS HIS MEMORY.

Control Panels

Control Panels

Control Panels are stored in this folder, found in the System Folder.

Control panels are accessible through your Apple menu (an alias of the Control Panels folder was automatically installed in the Apple Menu Items folder for you).

In Systems 7 and 7.1: When you choose "Control Panels" from the Apple menu, the Control Panels folder opens and you can double-click on any file within it.

In System 7.5: There is a little arrow pointing to the side next to the Control Panels item, indicating another menu (an *h-menu,* remember?). You can slide on out to the side and select the control panel you want without having to open the entire folder. If by chance you *do* want to open the whole folder, just let go when "Control Panels" is highlighted in the menu, without sliding over to the side.

If you find you are using certain control panels regularly, you may want to put an alias of the panel itself directly into the Apple menu (see the previous chapter).

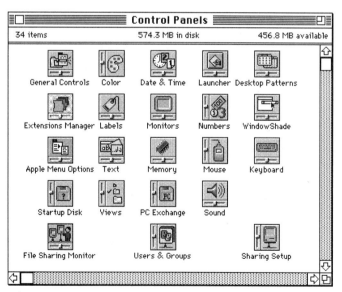

These are some of the Control Panels that are standard with most Macs.

The control panel called **General Controls** lets you control several details. You can change the pattern and the colors of your monitor, the time and date, the menu blinking, etc.

On the **Performa** models, the General Controls panel does not give you the option to edit the Desktop pattern. You do have a number of beautiful patterns, though, much more complex than these, to choose from.

The General Controls panel in System 7.5 is quite different from this one—details of it are on next page.

General Controls

This is an enlargement of the selected pattern you see on your Desktop. You can edit the existing pattern, or change it altogether, by drawing in this box with the mouse. The tiny bar above the colored box below indicates which color you will edit with.

Click the tiny right or left arrows to view the existing patterns. Click on the pattern itself to change your screen. Double-click the pattern to save it; otherwise it will disappear when you view another.

If you have a color monitor, double-click on one of these colored boxes to get the Apple Color Wheel, where you can choose another color for that box.

Choose how fast the insertion point blinks whenever you are in a typing mode.

Choose whether, when you let go of a menu selection, the highlighted selection flashes or not. I like at least one flash to let me know I really did choose the menu item.

Click on any of these numbers or dates, then type in the numbers you want to change them to, or use the tiny arrows that appear. Click the calendar or clock icons to set the changes. The time you set here will change the Alarm Clock, and vice versa.

The Mac uses the time and date you set here to label all the documents you create with a time and date.

General Controls
System 7.5

The **General Controls** panel in **System 7.5** has added some interesting features. Below is a screen shot of the entire control panel, and I'll go through each item separately. This panel is a good example of the difference between radio buttons (the little round ones) and checkboxes (the square ones). Their different shapes are not arbitrary—they are **visual clues.**

Radio buttons indicate you can choose *one and only one* of the options, like on a car radio. As you choose one, any other button turns off.

Checkbox buttons indicate you can choose *any number* of the options, including *none of them or all of them.* If you click in a box, you see a check (X); if you click on the check, it is removed. (This is a toggle switch—it toggles back and forth between on and off as you click on it.)

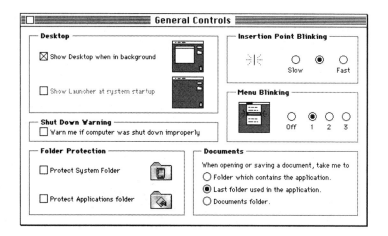

Desktop

If you choose **Show Desktop when in background,** then no matter which application you are in you will be able to see the Desktop and all the icons on it while you are working on your documents. This is confusing to beginners because if you accidentally click on that Desktop, you will pop out of your application and over to the Desktop without knowing what happened. More advanced users like to have that option.

If you **un**check that option (click in the checkbox), then the only way to get back to the Desktop (Finder) is to choose "Finder" from the Application menu (the icon on the far right end of the menu bar).

If you choose **Show Launcher at startup,** then guess what—the Launcher will show up when you start your computer. The Launcher is this interesting little panel upon which you can place your favorite applications and documents. Then when you want to use one of them, you just click once on its icon on the Launcher panel. Supposedly this is easier for beginners—you don't have to know how to navigate around the computer. But unless you have version 2.5 (at least) of the Launcher, putting new items onto the Launcher and taking other items off is a rather complicated procedure.

All the details about the Launcher are on pages 238–241. If you like it and use it, you can choose in this control panel whether or not you want it to automatically appear when you turn on (startup) your Mac.

Shut Down Warning

Sometimes the computer crashes, freezes, bombs, or otherwise stops functioning properly. Usually when this happens you have to either turn off the computer or push the restart button (if you have one). Remember, the Mac doesn't like to be turned off unexpectedly. It likes to go inside itself and tidy up important things before shutting down. So if you had to follow undesirable procedures because of some problem, when you next turn on the computer you get a message telling you the Macintosh was shut down improperly. Well, if you **un**check the box to **Warn me if computer was shut down improperly,** then you won't see that message anymore.

Insertion Point Blinking

The **insertion point** is that little flashing bar that appears whenever you can type. You can choose how fast it blinks. If you choose "Slow" it can get lost on the page because it is gone for so long. Fast is rather annoying to many people.

Menu Blinking

When you choose a menu item, the menu blinks either one, two, or three times. You can choose the number, or choose to have no blink at all. I like to have at least one blink as my **visual clue** that I really did get the right menu item.

Folder Protection

If you check either of these boxes, **Protect System Folder** or **Protect Applications folder,** no one can throw away anything from those two folders, nor can they move items out of them, nor can they rearrange files. You can still save documents into either folder, though.

The Performas have folder protection on as a default (it's automatically on when you get your computer). This can be incredibly annoying to beginners who have no clue how to change it.

If you try to change anything in those folders, you get a message like one of these (and I do wish they would learn proper punctuation so I don't have to keep fixing the screen shots of these dialog boxes):

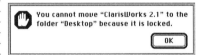

*What a confusing message. What's locked—
the folder "Desktop" or ClarisWorks? I have
no folder named Desktop anyway. And
they're lucky I fixed the bad punctuation
in this message.*

In **System 7.5.1** (a minor update to 7.5), you get a more thoughtful message (still with bad punctuation) that tells you how to fix the problem:

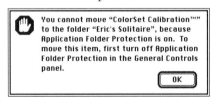

In the **Documents** setting you can choose where your "Open" and "Save As" dialog boxes automatically open to. The choice **Folder which contains the application** is really a silly option— you don't want to store the documents you create in the application folder. For instance, if you are writing budget reports for work, you don't want to store all the database reports in the folder with the database, and the spreadsheet reports in the folder with the spreadsheet application, and the word processing document in the folder with the word processor. No, you want a folder for the Budget in which you store all the related files.

The choice **Documents** folder forces you to save anything you create in a folder called Documents that will be automatically created for you on the Desktop. This might be okay for a while, but as soon as you figure out how to organize your files with folders and how to save them into their own folders, you will never want this Document folder again.

The choice **Last folder used in the application** is the lesser of three bad choices. When you Save or Open you always see the last folder you used in this particular application.

I wish there was a choice called **None of the above. Leave me alone. I can do it myself.**

Documents

Documents

When opening or saving a document, take me to
○ Folder which contains the application.
◉ Last folder used in the application.
○ Documents folder.

Color

Color

If you click on "Sample Text," you'll see the names of the programmers.

The **Color** control panel only works if you have a color monitor or a grayscale monitor (a grayscale monitor is one that can show varying shades of gray instead of just black and white). Press on the arrow to get a menu of color choices. The color you choose for "Highlight color" will appear whenever you select text, whether you are in an application or in a dialog box. The color you choose for "Window color" will be the color of the border and sometimes a few details of the windows. Keep in mind that a colored border around your windows takes more time to create than a black-and-white window. If you choose "Other...," you will get the Apple Color Wheel where you can create and select any color possible. Just play with this wheel—move the scroll bars up and down, press on the arrows, drag around in the wheel itself. (To change the color of *icons*, use the Labels control panel. To change the number of colors you see on your *screen,* use the Monitors control panel.)

Date & Time
System 7 or 7.1

Date & Time

Use the **Date & Time** control panel to change the date and time, if necessary (this will change the date and time in the Alarm Clock and in the General Control panels, and vice versa). Just click on the day or time and press the arrows or type the numbers. To accept the new information, click anywhere, close the control panel, *or* press the Return key.

This control panel also lets you change the *formats* for the date and time. Click the button "Date Formats..." or "Time Formats..." to get a list of options. As you change options here, a sample of the new format will appear in the bottom portion of the box. If you have any other language versions installed in your System, you can choose to display date and time in that language's standard format: choose the language from the "Date Formats" menu by pressing on the arrowhead (it probably says "U.S." at the moment). As soon as you make any changes to these boxes, the Format menu will display "Custom."

When you use a program in which you can automatically insert the date or time, the numbers will appear in the format you have determined here.

Date & Time
System 7.5

Date & Time

The **Date & Time** control panel in **System 7.5** has been expanded, as you can see in the dialog box below.

▼ Click on any of the numbers and you will get little arrows. Click the up or down arrows to move the selected number higher or lower. Or you can just type some numbers in to replace the selected ones.

▼ Any button you see with an ellipsis (three dots ...) gets to another dialog box where you can set the specifications for all those things.

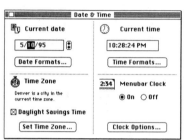

Just go poke around in all the dialog boxes—they are very self-explanatory. You can change the typeface for the clock that shows up in the menu bar, you can change the time zone you're in (which is especially handy if you take your computer traveling), you can click the Daylight Savings Time box to move your clock ahead one hour, or uncheck it to change the time back one hour. Have fun!

Desktop Patterns
System 7.5

Desktop Patterns

The **Desktop Patterns** control panel lets you choose a pattern for your Desktop from among an amazing variety of choices, ranging from very beautiful to very distracting to very disgusting. Just click on the scroll arrows to view them, then click the button at the bottom to turn your Desktop into that pattern. You will

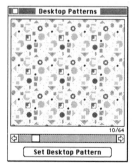

see it change right before your eyes. When you find one you like, just close the control panel.

You can change the background pattern on some of your **desk accessories,** like the Scrapbook, Calculator, or Find File. When you find a pattern you like, hold down the Option key and the button turns into "Set Utilities Pattern."

Just press on the image and drag it to the Desktop Patterns!

Add your own patterns! If it's in the Scrapbook, just press-and-drag the image and drop it onto the Desktop Patterns control panel. Or copy an image and paste it into the Desktop Patterns. It will make the pattern automatically, even if the original image is large. Too cool!

Keyboard

Keyboard

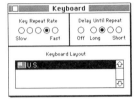

If you notice you seem to type double spaces between words often, or perhaps double letters as in "tthe" or "yyou," you might want to lengthen the delay.

The **Keyboard** control panel gives you control over several features on your keyboard.

▾ Every key on the Macintosh keyboard will repeat, meaning if you hold the key down it will continue typing that character across the page. "Key Repeat Rate" lets you control just how fast that key repeats across the page.

▾ If you click the "Off" button under "Delay Until Repeat," then the keys will not repeat at all, no matter how long you hold them down.

▾ From "Long" to "Short" gives you control over how long you can hold your finger on a key before it starts to repeat. This is wonderful for people who are heavy on the keys—set it for a long delay so even if your fingers plod along on the keys you won't end up with extra characters all over the place.

▾ If you have a file in your System Folder that provides you with another keyboard layout, perhaps for another language or for a Dvorak keyboard, the names of the different layouts will show up here and you will be able to switch between them.

Labels

Labels

The labels you create in the control panel, above, will appear in the Label menu on the Desktop, shown at the top of the next page.

The **Labels** control panel allows you to set up a labeling system for the files on your Mac, which you can apply from the Labels menu at the Desktop. It allows you to connect groups of icons that are related to each other, but that may be stored in different places. For instance, you may have a series of lectures you present in different fields. You can store the lectures each in the folders for the respective fields, but apply a "Lecture" label to them so you can search for and group them together. Applying a label applies its corresponding color, also.

The label (and color) is *in addition* to the icon's name. It's just attached to the file; it does not appear in the name. In your Desktop windows, you can choose to display the "Label" as another column in the list of information (use the Views control panel; see page 250). If you choose to display label information in the *windows,* then your View *menu* will also have the option to view "By Label." Perhaps you have a folder with lots of files in it from a variety of topics. You can label some or all of them, then when you view "By Label" all the files from each topic will be grouped together.

To change the name of any of the existing labels:
- ▼ First open the Labels control panel (double-click on the panel "Labels" in the Control Panels folder).
- ▼ Select an existing label (you can press the Tab key to select each one).
- ▼ Type the name of the new label.
- ▼ Close the control panel window (click in its close box *or* press Command W). The revised label will instantly appear in the Labels menu.

To change the color of any of the existing labels:
- ▼ Open the Labels control panel (double-click on the panel "Labels" in the Control Panels folder).
- ▼ Click once on the colored box. The Apple Color Wheel will appear on your screen. Don't worry about how complicated it looks—just play with it. Click on the little arrows, drag the slider bar (just below the wheel) back and forth, and press-and-drag right in the wheel itself. You'll see the new color you are creating in the box in the upper right called "New." If you want the original color back, just Cancel.

To apply a label and color to an icon:
- ▼ At the Desktop, select the icon or group of icons.
- ▼ From the Label *menu* (not the control panel), choose the label or color of your choice.

Note: If you apply a label one day and then later change the name of that particular label in the control panel, all icons with the original label attached will change to the new label! For instance, say I labeled 12 documents with the label "Love Letters." If I go to the control panel and change "Love Letters" to "Dog Food," every document that had the label "Love Letters" will now have the label "Dog Food."

You can use Find File (Chapter 26) to search for items of a certain label or color. You might be surprised to discover that many applications apply colors (which also applies a label) to certain files. I wish they wouldn't do that because it makes my own label-organizing less effective.

Finding by label or color

Launcher

*System 7 or 7.1;
early Launcher
versions*

Launcher

*Launcher 2.5 and
above is very different
from the original
Launcher! Details are
on the following
pages.* **Look at the
pictures of the
Launcher**—*read
the directions for the
one that matches the
one on your screen.*

The **Launcher** control panel opens a special "window" that has buttons on it. You click the buttons *once* to open, or "launch" applications and documents. It's meant to be useful for beginners, and as long as everything you need is already on the Launcher, perhaps it is useful. But if you have to change items, then you get into some serious Mac-using which is contrary to the beginner concept of the Launcher. The newer version of the Launcher, version 2.5 or above, is much easier to use!

You can remove buttons from the Launcher that you don't use, and add others. If you are a brand-new beginner, you may want to get help for this—at least find someone who knows how to open folders and move things around and make aliases. Or you can just follow the directions.

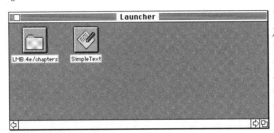

This is a window, just like the windows you know and love. Move it, scroll it, close it just like any other window.

You can add buttons representing documents or applications or even folders to the Launcher.

To add items to the Launcher window:

▾ Find the document, application, utility, etc., that you want to appear in the Launcher window. You'll probably find it on the hard disk somewhere. Click once on the file to select it.

▾ From the File menu, choose "Make Alias." This makes a copy of the icon with the same name (a copy of the *icon,* not of the file itself—read Chapter 25 on Aliases), but the new name is in italic and has the word "alias" at the end.

▾ Press-and-drag the alias icon over to the Desktop somewhere.

▾ Open the System Folder by double-clicking on it.

▾ Inside the System Folder, locate the Launcher Items folder (you can type "la" to find it quickly). Don't do anything to the folder—just make a note of where it is.

Launcher Items

*This is the folder
you need.*

▼ Remember that alias you put on the Desktop? Drag it over to the Launcher Items folder and drop it in (just position the pointer over the folder so the folder turns dark, then let go).

▼ Close the window to the System Folder. This new item instantly appears in the Launcher window and you can just single-click on it to launch the file.

To remove items from the Launcher window:

▼ Open the System Folder by double-clicking on it.

▼ Find the folder called "Launcher Items." (You can type the characters "la" to find and select the folder.) Double-click to open it.

▼ Press-and-drag any icon out of the folder. You can throw the item in the trash because it is just an "alias" of the real thing—it is not the original document or application. (Well, as long as the name is in *italic* it is not the real thing. Read about aliases in Chapter 25.)

▼ Close the Launcher Items folder and the System Folder. You'll notice that the items you removed no longer appear in the Launcher window.

You can make an alias of a folder and put it into the Launcher. When you click on the button of a folder from the Launcher window, it opens the actual folder that is on the hard disk. You cannot put items *into* this folder button on the Launcher—you can only put items into the real folder on the hard disk.

To put the Launcher away and not let it come back, click in its close box (upper left of the window). Then:

▼ From the Apple menu, choose "General Controls."

▼ Make sure there is no checkmark in the checkbox, "Show Launcher at system startup."

▼ Close the General Controls panel (press Command W).

If you ever want to use the Launcher again, choose it from the Control Panels item in the Apple menu. If you want it to show up automatically when you turn on your Mac, go back to the General Controls and check that box again.

Click this box here, part of the General Controls control panel.

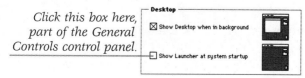

**Launcher
version 2.5
or above;
System 7.5.1**

Launcher

The newer **Launcher,** version 2.5 or above, is much more useful and much easier to customize. If your Launcher looks like the one below, you have the newer version of it. You might want to put an alias of the Launcher right on your Desktop so you don't have to keep going to the Apple menu to get it.

*Category
buttons*

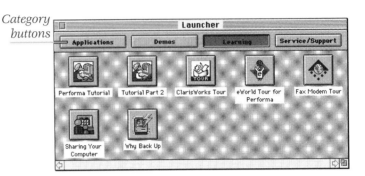

To add and delete buttons from this Launcher, you don't have to make aliases yourself or dig around in the System Folder at all!

To add an item to the Launcher:
- ▾ Open the Launcher if it isn't open already (from the Control Panels item in the Apple menu).
- ▾ Find the file you want to add. It can be a document, an application, a folder, etc. You can't put sounds on it.
- ▾ Drag the icon of the file onto the category button where you want the file to be placed. (If that category is open, you can just drag it right onto the Launcher window.)

To remove an item from the Launcher:
- ▾ Hold down the Option key.
- ▾ With the Option key held down, drag the icon from the Launcher to the Desktop, or if you are going to throw it away, drag it straight to the trash.

  Remember, all these things in the Launcher are aliases, so it is completely safe to throw them out! Your original files stay right where you left them.

To move an item to a new category:
- ▾ Hold down the Option key and drag the item to one of the other category buttons. Let go.

Drag a document icon over these buttons.
Any button that highlights will open the file. For
instance, drag a SimpleText document over these
icons and see how many of them will open it.

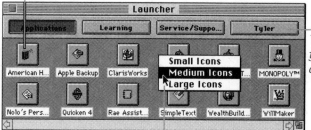

You can make
your own
categories!

Command-press to get this little
menu to change the size of the icons.

To put a file into a folder on the Launcher:

▾ Do you have a folder on the Launcher? You can put
one in any category. Make a folder on your hard disk,
then drag it to the Launcher.

▾ Drag the icon from your hard disk and drop it on top
of the folder button on the Launcher. (Anything you
put in the Launcher folder will really go into the real
folder on the hard disk.)

To resize the Launcher buttons:

▾ Hold down the Command key and press the mouse
pointer inside the Launcher window. This will make
a little menu pop-up. Keep holding the mouse button
down and choose another size.

To open category button folders:

▾ Hold down the Option key and click on
a category button. Its original folder will
appear.

To make new category buttons, and remove others:

▾ In the System Folder, open the Launcher
Items folder.

▾ Make a new folder. Start the name with
a bullet (press Option 8 to type a bullet).
It will now appear in the Launcher.

▾ To remove a category from the Launcher, take the
bullet off of the name in the Launcher Items folder.

Any folder name
starting with a • will
appear as a category.

Memory

Memory

*This control panel assumes you know what **memory** is in the first place. Read the chapter called "Very Important Information" for a better understanding of the difference between hard disk space, memory, and virtual memory.*

Use the **Memory** control panel to set a *disk cache* (pronounced "cash") for your Mac, turn *virtual memory* on or off, turn *32-bit addressing* on or off, and (on some Macs) create a *RAM disk.*

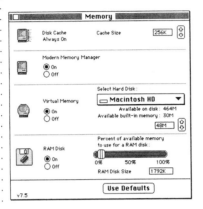

The **disk cache** is a part of the memory your Mac uses to hold information about the most recent things it's done on your disk, like getting files and saving them. Getting this data from the disk cache is much quicker than going back to the disk to retrieve it. The Mac will set a default (an automatic choice) for the cache size, depending on how much memory is available. You can override this default by changing the Cache Size yourself. It might seem like setting a larger cache size would be better, but generally it actually isn't because then that much memory is unavailable to any applications you open. The nerds I most respect recommend setting it at the lowest level possible and forgetting about it.

Virtual memory

You should really read Chapter 30, called "Very Important Information," so you understand memory and **virtual memory.** The basic idea behind virtual memory is that you can use some of your hard disk space as memory. If after reading that chapter you want to turn on virtual memory, this control panel is where you do it.

32-bit addressing

If your Mac can hold more than 8 megabytes of memory, then you will see the section for **32-bit addressing.** If you don't know whether or not you have more than 8 megs of memory (RAM, random access memory) installed, choose "About This Macintosh..." from under the Apple menu while you are at the Finder. Next to the item "Total Memory," the Mac will tell you how much RAM is installed. If this number is more than 8,192K, then you should turn **on** 32-bit addressing. If the Total Memory is something like 12, and your System Software is taking up something like 6 or 9 megs, the System is reporting that high amount for itself because 32-bit addressing is not on. (Look up 32-bit addressing in the Jargon section if you're not quite sure what it is.)

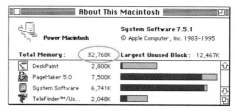

If you ever run old software that is not "32-bit clean" (it's a long story, trust me), you may run into problems if 32-bit addressing is turned on. "Problems" like crashing your computer. Software that is not 32-bit clean will usually run okay if you turn off 32-bit addressing, although if the software is really old it just may not work with the System itself.

The total memory is given in kilobytes—just take the number before the comma, which is approximate megabytes. For instance, this Mac has 32 megs of RAM installed.

Some machines (the SE30, Mac II, IIx, IIcx) cannot use more than 8 megs of memory anyway, even if you install it and turn on 32-bit addressing. You can get the software called Mode32 from Connectix, now available from Apple, user groups, and bulletin boards, to help one of these Macs access more memory. System 7 itself is supposed to help those machines access more memory.

The **Modern Memory Manager** is on Power Macs only, and is instead of the 32-bit addressing option. It should be on.

Modern Memory Manager

A **RAM disk** is a pretend hard disk made out of memory. (Virtual memory is a hard disk pretending it is memory; a RAM disk is memory pretending it is a hard disk.) Not all Macintoshes can do this, but if you see it in your Memory control panel, your Mac can.

RAM disk

When you create a RAM disk, you are telling the computer to take some of your real memory and set it aside. The Mac will create an icon of a floppy disk on your Desktop, and then you can copy things to this disk, or save things onto it. Why? For speed. RAM disks are blazingly fast. If you copy your favorite application to a RAM disk, you will notice a decided difference.

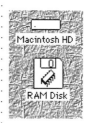

But RAM is temporary, remember? Anything stored in RAM or on a RAM disk will disappear when you shut down or when you crash or when the lights flicker. (It will stay during a restart, though.) So you don't ever want to save an important document to a RAM disk.

After you restart, you will see the RAM disk on your Desktop. It will appear in your Save As dialog boxes, also.

To create a RAM disk, click it On. Move the slider to the amount of RAM you are willing to give away, and restart. The floppy icon will appear on your hard disk.

Monitors

Monitors

The **Monitors** control panel lets you choose how many of the available shades of gray or colors your screen will display, assuming you even have a choice. The number of grays and colors to choose from depends on your monitor, how much RAM and video RAM you have, and what kind of video card is in your computer. If you're short on RAM, choose to display fewer colors.

Just press on the menu in the tiny picture and drag it to the other monitor, if you have one.

If you have **more than one monitor** attached to your computer, this control panel also lets you determine which monitor should function as your main one. Press on the tiny menu bar in the control panel and drag it to another monitor. Whichever one has the menu bar is the one that will function as your main monitor. This change won't take effect until you restart the Mac.

You can also drag the picture of the second monitor around and put it on the same side of your main screen as your second monitor is positioned on your desk. The mouse will move off the main screen in that direction. (Now, don't ever go into your boss's or your sweetheart's Monitors control panel and switch the second monitor picture to the opposite side of the main monitor—that would be naughty.)

If you have a "multi-sync" monitor, you can change the "resolution" of your screen. Click the "Options..." button and you will see your resolution choices. It doesn't really change the resolution—it makes things appears smaller and farther away (which might make you think it is in higher resolution) or it makes things bigger and closer (which might make you think it is in lower resolution).

Mouse

Mouse

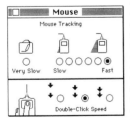

Use the **Mouse** control panel to switch to a tablet speed, if you use a tablet (a tablet is a pad on which you use a pen-shaped stylus; you would know if you had one). The terms "Slow" and "Fast" are a little misleading. The "slower" the "Mouse Tracking," the farther you have to move the mouse across the desk to get the cursor to move across the screen. Slower speeds are good for drawing. If you set it to "Fast," you have to move the mouse a much smaller distance to get it to move all the way across the screen. It may drive you nuts to work on someone's computer who has the mouse tracking set to one of the slower speeds. Now you know what to do about it.

The "Double-Click Speed" lets you set the speed at which the mouse will interpret two clicks as a double-click (as opposed to two single clicks). If you're kind of slow with your finger, set it to the slow speed. If you set it to the fastest speed (the far right button), you may find that the mouse sometimes thinks a single click is a double-click.

Use the **Numbers** control panel to determine how numbers and currency will display. This can be important in international work, where numbers in the thousands may be separated with a period instead of a comma. The format you choose here will affect cells and fields and headers that use a currency or number format automatically.

Numbers

Numbers

The Mac has several built-in **networking** features, and there are three control panels that let you change those settings. These are explained in Chapter 27 on Sharing Files, page 271.

Networking Control Panels

> **Sharing Setup** lets you set your user name, choose a password for yourself, and turn on your Mac's ability to share files over the network.

Sharing Setup

> **Users & Groups** lets you restrict access to your computer to specific people or lets everybody see what you've been working on.

Users & Groups

> **File Sharing Monitor** shows you what's being shared and lets you know just who's looking in your folders.

File Sharing Monitor

The Macintosh **Easy Open** control panel enables you to open a document in applications other than the one in which it was created. Don't worry about this one yet—come back in several months. Its default (automatic) settings are all you need for now. If you are having trouble importing graphics or text into other applications, try turning this off.

Macintosh Easy Open

Macintosh Easy Open

PC Exchange controls which applications on your Mac will open PC documents (PC meaning any computer except a Macintosh). For instance, the default is that .TXT documents will open in SimpleText. Click the "Add..." button to assign other applications to document types.

PC Exchange

PC Exchange

Sound
System 7 or 7.1

Sound

Use the **Sound** control panel to determine the volume of all the sounds that come out of your Mac. Just move the slider bar on the Speaker Volume up or down. If you set the bar at zero, the menu bar will flash instead of beep. You can also choose what noise you want to hear instead of the beep. Click on the name of a sound to hear it. The last one you choose before you close the control panel is the sound the Mac will use when you need to be beeped.

If you *don't* have one of the Macs that came with a microphone, then your control panel won't have the bottom portion you see in the example. If you *do* have a microphone, then you can have lots of fun. Plug the mike into the little port on the back of the machine (there's only one spot the plug will fit into). (If you have a phono jack adapter, you can directly record sounds from other sources, such as music CDs and tapes.) Click the "Add..." button, then record sounds using the buttons as you would on a tape recorder. When you save the sound, it will automatically appear in the list and you can select it.

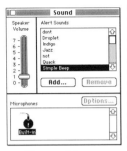

If your Mac came with a microphone, you'll have the "Add" button and the bottom portion shown here.

These sound files are actually kept in the System file (the Mac puts them there for you). My uncle recorded himself hollering, "Woman—get back in the kitchen!" and moved the sound from the System file to the Startup Items folder so when my aunt turned on the machine she got yelled at. (Don't worry—she didn't get mad, she got even.)

When you click the "Add" button, you get these controls for recording the sounds.

In **System 7.5,** this control panel has several more options.

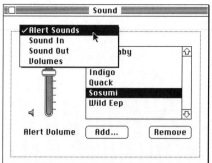

This is the Sound control panel in System 7.5. Press on the "Alert Sounds" to get a menu of other sound controls.

You can make your own sounds just as in the previous version of this control panel; click "Add."

When you choose **Sound In,** you will the option to choose other methods of inputting sound, such as through your microphone or AV connector.

When you choose **Sound Out,** you have the option to choose the built-in speakers or other playback devices to hear the music and other sounds.

When you choose **Volumes,** you have control over the master volume for your Macintosh and for built-in headphones, if you have them.

If you have more than one hard disk attached to your Mac that has a System Folder on it, or perhaps more than one *partition* to your hard disk, you can use the **Startup Disk** control panel to determine which hard disk to use to start your computer. Each attached hard disk that contains a System will appear as an icon in the control panel; click on one to choose it. You need to restart the computer for the new disk to become the startup disk. You can always tell which hard disk is booting the computer—its icon is always first in the upper right corner.

Startup Disk

The **Text** control panel is only useful if you have more than one language installed in your Macintosh. If you do, they will be listed in the menu here in the control panel and you can choose the one you need to work with.

Text

Text

WindowShade

WindowShade

The **WindowShade** control panel gives you control over how you want the windows on the Mac to roll up. What? Well, in **System 7.5** you can double-click on the title bar of any window—at your Desktop, in your applications, anywhere—and the window will roll up to display just the title bar, kind of like rolling up a windowshade. Like this:

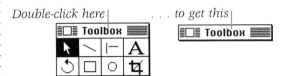

Double-click here ... *to get this*

In the control panel, you can choose whether you want the window to roll up with two or three clicks, or not to do it at all. If you click any of the "modifier" keys, then you will have to hold down that key or keys *in addition* to the two or three clicks that you choose. If you put a checkmark in the box, "Make sounds when using Windowshade," you'll hear a little wooshing sound as the windows roll up and down.

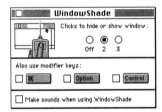

Apple Menu Options

Apple Menu Options

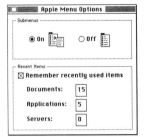

The **Apple Menu Options** control panel determines whether your Apple menu has *hierarchical menus* or not. Hierarchical menus are the little submenus that come off to the side, indicated by a little arrow. In this control panel you can turn them off altogether if they annoy you.

If you check the box to "Remember recently used items," then you will have three new folders in your Apple menu. One will create a submenu that holds aliases of the last number of documents you opened, one holds applications, and one holds servers (which is only useful if you work in a heavily networked environment where you have access to several other computers through your own). The number you type in is how many items the Mac will remember. If you type in "0" (zero), the folder will disappear from the menu.

I find it useful to have the Mac remember the last 8 or 10 documents I used. I am not connected to any servers so I typed zero in that one, and I have aliases of all my applications in my own Applications folder in the Apple menu, so I don't need the Mac to keep track of those.

If you have any number of files typed in the "Documents" box, the Mac will monitor *all* the files that are opened, including all the filters of some programs that use them. If it seems that your desktop publishing applications are taking an unusually long time to launch, come to this control panel and type in a zero in the Documents edit box.

Extensions Manager

The **Extensions Manager** control panel is an extremely valuable one, but it's not something you should fool around with if you don't know what you're doing.

Extensions Manager

Extensions are tiny little programs that work behind the scenes (usually) to do all kinds of little tasks for you. Because there is such a wide variety of extensions and because they go directly into the system, they have a long history of causing minor to major trouble when they conflict. This Extensions Manager helps you control conflicts by allowing you to turn groups of them on or off, depending on what you are doing. It also manages control panels.

You can create sets of extensions and control panels so when you restart the Mac, customized groups of extensions will load, depending on what you are doing and what you have determined is conflicting with what you are doing. How do you determine what is conflicting? By turning certain ones off through this Extensions Manager and restarting to see if the problem persists. If you think you have an extension conflict, find your local power user or ask at your local user group for someone to help guide you through to the solution. Heed this warning.

System 7.5: If you have a clue about what you're doing and you want to control extensions, hold down the Spacebar as you boot or restart. Hold it down until you get the Extensions Manager. Choose the set, "System 7.5 Only," then close the window to resume startup.

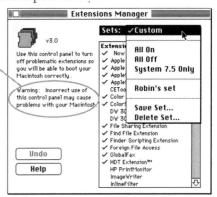

Views

Views

The **Views** control panel allows you to customize the windows on your Desktop. This is a very useful control panel, and one that is good practice for beginners to work with.

Keep in mind when you choose a font for your windows that fonts with city names are easier to read on the screen (fonts like Geneva, New York, Boston, etc.). Also, when you choose a size, the size number that is in outline style (like 12 as opposed to **12**) will be easier to read on the screen also.

If "Always snap to grid" is checked, as you move icons they will pop into the nearest little invisible cubby. If you *don't* want an icon to snap, hold down the Command key and move the icon. If this item is *not* checked, then when you hold down the Command key and move an icon, it *will* snap to the grid! The point is, whether "snap to" is checked or not, using the Command key will override it.

Press on this box to get a menu of all the fonts you have installed. The one you choose is the one that will be used in your Desktop windows.

Press this arrow to get a list of font sizes. Choose one, or type in a number.

Views

Font for views: **Geneva** ▼ **9** ▼

Icon Views

▢ ▢ ▢ ▢ ⊙ Straight grid

▢ ▢ ▢ ▢ ○ Staggered grid

☐ Always snap to grid

List Views

◇ ◇ ◇

⊙ ○ ○

☐ Calculate folder sizes
☒ Show disk info in header

☒ Show size
☒ Show kind
☒ Show label
☒ Show date
☒ Show version
☒ Show comments

Choose whether the invisible grid that icons will snap to is straight across or staggered (see next page). They will only snap to if that checkbox is checked.

You can choose to see the size of folders in a list view, but then it takes much longer to open windows.

If you check this, your icons will always snap to the nearest empty spot in the underlying invisible grid.

Choose this to have two lines of information in the window header— disk information and view information. See the next page.

Click any number of these to determine what information you want displayed in your window when you view as a list. The ones you choose here will also appear in the View menu at the Desktop.

Just under the title bar there is very useful **information.** *If your window is showing icons,* you'll see how many items are in that window, how much space is being used and how much space is left on the disk. *If your window is not showing icons,* then the information bar indicates how your files are currently being organized, but not how much space is on your hard disk. You can customize the bar so you can see *both* lines of information, as shown in the example below. Click "Show disk info in header."

When you choose a **list view** for your Desktop windows, you no longer have the advantage of seeing the **icons** which give you so many visual clues about the file's function—all you see are generic little icons that give you a hint that the file is a folder or a generic document or application. But if you click one of the larger icon sizes in the control panel, as shown to the left and below, you can have the best of both worlds—you can view the contents as a list, but still see the specific icon for the file.

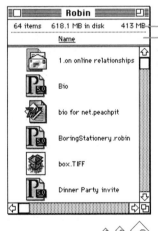

Notice in this information bar I can see both lines of information while the window is in a list view.

Click the largest icon to view your window as shown above.

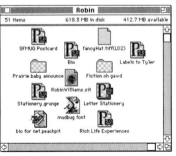

A staggered grid leaves more room for long file names, which is especially handy if you have enlarged the font size.

Which control panel would you use to accomplish the following, and which settings would you set?

1. Make the mouse move quickly across the screen without your hand having to move much at all.

2. Change the pattern of your Desktop.

3. Start file sharing between several computers.

4. Change the size of the type in the windows on the Desktop so you can read it.

5. Change the colors of the labels so you can color your icons to match your office.

6. Change the time that shows up in your menu in System 7.5.

7. Fix it so you *don't* see the icons on the Desktop when you are working in an application and so when you accidentally click on the pattern in the background, you *don't* pop to the Desktop.

8. Use fewer colors on your monitor to save memory.

9. Record your own sounds to surprise and startle your coworkers.

10. Get rid of the "Recent Servers" option in the Apple menu.

Answers on page 373.

ALIASES

Aliases are one of the greatest features of the Mac. An alias is a fake *icon* that *represents* the real thing. When you double-click on an alias, it goes and gets the real thing for you. Aliases only take up about 2 or 3K of disk space, so you can store multiples of them all over the place, wherever they come in handy.

Say you have an application you use frequently—your word processing program, for instance. You can make an alias of ClarisWorks or WordPerfect or whatever you use and put it just about anywhere. You might want to put it right on your Desktop. Or in your Apple menu. Since you can have many aliases of the same file, you can put the same alias in several places! Learn to use and take advantage of the seriously cool feature.

PUZZLED BY PERSISTENT BACK PAIN,
PAUL SELECTS THE "CHIROPRACTORS ALIAS."

Aliases You can make **aliases** of programs, documents, desk accessories, disks, folders, control panels, the trash can, etc. Aliases provide a wonderful tool for organizing your work; anything you want to use can be only one click away from wherever you are. Remember, an alias is just a picture that goes and gets the real file. It's a go-fer.

Using Aliases Here are ideas for **using aliases** (exactly *how* to make an alias is on the next page).

- ▾ Put an alias of a Control Panel that you use over and over again out on your Desktop or in your Apple menu.

- ▾ Use aliases to store documents in two or three places at once, including right on your Desktop. For instance, you may want to keep budget reports in folders organized by months, as well as in folders organized by projects.

- ▾ If you have a document you use frequently, put an alias of it in the Apple menu: just open your System Folder and drag the alias into the "Apple Menu Items" folder.

  On **System 7.5,** use the "Automated Task" to do this for you: select the file you want an alias of, then from the Apple menu slide down to "Automated Tasks," then slide out to "Add Alias to Apple Menu." The Mac will make an alias, take the word "alias" off the end of the name, and put it in the Apple Menu Items folder.

- ▾ In fact, if you find you use your Apple Menu Items folder regularly, make an alias of the folder and leave it on your Desktop. Dropping a file in the alias folder automatically puts it into the real folder.

- ▾ If you have an application, a document, or a folder that you want to open automatically whenever you turn on your Mac, put an alias of it in your "Startup Items" folder, found in the System Folder.

- ▾ Leave aliases of applications neatly organized directly on your Desktop or in your hard disk window. This way you don't have to dig into folders to open the applications. This also makes all your applications available to you for the **drag-and-drop trick of opening files,** including files from other programs. Remember: you can drag any document onto the icon of the application to open the document. Many applications can open files created in other programs

This America Online alias sits on my Desktop so I can quickly pop in to check my mail.

this way, so if you come across a file from a program you don't have, or perhaps you don't know where it came from, you can drag it over the top of all these aliases that are sitting on your Desktop. Any icon that changes color when you drag the document on top of it will open that document.

▼ Use the drag-and-drop trick mentioned above to open those ubiquitous "ReadMe" files that are on every disk of software. These files open automatically in Teach-Text or SimpleText if you have it, but I like to *print* the ReadMe files. I hate to print them in the font they show up in within TeachText because the type is too big and it takes too many pieces of paper, but Teach-Text doesn't let me change the font. So I drop ReadMe files onto an alias of my word processor and I am happy. Now that Simple Text can change the typeface and size I am also happy.

▼ Some of the more advanced uses for aliases aren't apparent unless you're on a network. For example, you can make an alias of your file server so you can connect to it quickly. And you can make an alias of your hard disk, copy it onto a floppy (since the alias is only about 2K), and take it to somebody else's computer on the network. Then you can quickly connect back to your own computer just by clicking on the alias on the other computer (provided you have set up the sharing privileges first; see Chapter 27 on simple networking and sharing). This concept is sometimes called the "office-on-a-disk."

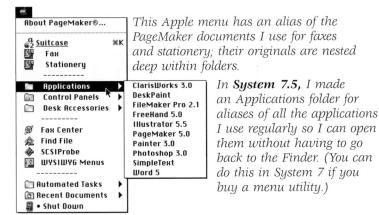

This Apple menu has an alias of the PageMaker documents I use for faxes and stationery; their originals are nested deep within folders.

*In **System 7.5,** I made an Applications folder for aliases of all the applications I use regularly so I can open them without having to go back to the Finder. (You can do this in System 7 if you buy a menu utility.)*

Finding files with aliases

▾ **Use aliases to find files that you keep stored on floppy disks or cartridge hard disks.**

■ Make an alias of an original file; *the original file must be on the floppy or the cartridge already.* Be sure this floppy disk or cartridge disk has an identifiable name, and be sure you put a label on the disk with this name so you can find it again.

■ Drag the alias from the floppy to your hard disk. Now you can eject the disk and store it safely.

■ When you double-click on the alias you have on your hard disk, you will get a dialog box asking for the floppy disk that contains the original file (that's why you named the disk memorably and actually labeled it, right?).

▾ In **System 7.5,** you can put an alias of an entire floppy disk, cartridge, or CD in your Apple menu and you will get hierarchical menus (those little submenus with the arrows) of all the files on the disk. You don't have to open all the windows to get to things. There is an illustration of this on page 223.

▾ Since aliases only take up about 2K, you can keep a folder of many of the files you use only occasionally but that you do want to keep track of. This folder of aliases is your "secretary" who knows just where everything is filed. (Also see "Finding the Original File," page 259.)

Making an alias is so easy.

▼ Select the item you want to make an alias of (click once on it).

▼ From the File menu, choose "Make Alias." In **System 7.5,** press Command M instead of going to the File menu. You now have an alias.

▼ The new alias icon will look the same and will be named the same, with the word *alias* added. An alias name is in italic so you can always recognize the file as an alias.

(I like to remove the word "alias" from my files because otherwise the name is too long. Move the alias out of the folder the original is in before you change the name because you can't have two files with the same name in one folder.)

▼ Drag the icon to wherever you want to keep it. Rename it if you like. The new file does not have to have the word "alias" in its name. *And it doesn't matter if you move the original file*—the alias can always find it.

▼ To put the alias in your Apple menu, drag the alias icon to the "Apple Menu Items" folder in your System Folder and drop it in.

Making Aliases

MerryWives   *MerryWives alias*

The alias looks just like the original, but the name is italic.

MerryWives

I like to remove the word "alias" so the name is shorter.

MerryWives

Even when you view your windows by name, an alias looks like an alias.

Details Making aliases is easy, but there are a couple of **details** you should understand.

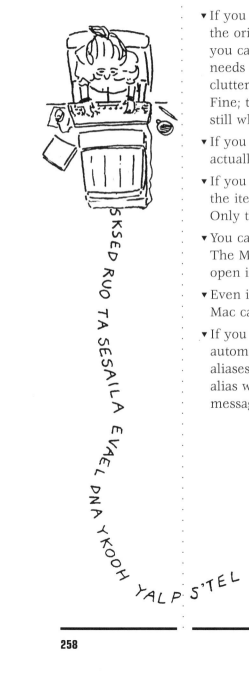

- An alias isn't really a *duplicate* of anything but the icon; it's just a *representation* of the real thing. If you double-click on an *alias* of Word, you'll start your *original* Word program running, even if the original Word is stored in a completely different folder.

- If you delete an alias of something, you don't delete the original—it's still stored on your hard disk. So you can keep on revising your filing system as your needs change. Don't want that alias of Budget Charts cluttering up your Project Plans folder any more? Fine; throw it away. The original Budget Charts is still where you left it.

- If you put an item into an *alias* of a folder, the item actually gets put into the *original* folder.

- If you put an item into an *alias* of the trash can, the item actually gets put into the *original* trash can. Only the original trash can will bulge.

- You can move an alias and even rename an alias. The Mac will still be able to find the original and open it whenever you double-click on the alias.

- Even if you move or rename the *original* file, the Mac can still find it.

- If you eliminate the *original* file, the Mac does not automatically eliminate any of the representational aliases you created. When you double-click on an alias whose original has been trashed, you will get a message telling you the original could not be located.

To find the original file belonging to an alias, follow these steps:

▼ Click once on the alias.

▼ From the File menu, choose "Get Info," *or* press Command I.

▼ The Get Info dialog box tells you where the original is located (see below).

▼ If you want to have the Mac go get it and bring it to you, click the button "Find Original." The window the original is stored in will be displayed and the real icon will be highlighted.

▼ If you click "Find Original" *or* if you double-click on an alias that has its original stored on a floppy disk or a cartridge hard disk (see previous page), you will get a message telling you which disk to insert.

Click here and the Mac will find and display the original file.

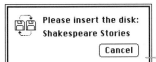

If the original file is on another disk and the disk is not in the computer, you will get a message telling you which disk to insert.

In **System 7.5,** use the Automated Task in the Apple menu **to find an original of an alias:**

▼ Select the alias (click once on it).

▼ From the Apple menu, slide down to "Automated Tasks."

▼ Slide out and choose "Find Original from Alias."

▼ The original will appear in front of you.

1. What is an alias, anyway?

. . . .

2. How large, in file size, is a typical alias?

. . . .

3. What are the two steps involved in creating an alias?

. . . .

4. In System 7.5, what is the quickest way to put an alias into the Apple menu?

. . . .

5. If you throw away an alias, what happens to the real item?

. . . .

6. If you throw away the real item, what happens to all its aliases?

. . . .

6. In System 7.5, what is the easiest way to find the original of an alias?

. . . .

7. If you're working on a Mac that doesn't have System 7.5, how would you find the original of an alias?

. . . .

8. If you want the document for a particular project to automatically open on your screen every day this week, where would you put its alias?

. . . .

9. If you put a file into an alias of a folder, what happens to that file?

. . . .

10. What happens if you make an alias, then rename the original?

. . . .

Answers on page 373.

FIND FILE

Find File is a wonderful timesaving and frustration-reducing feature that allows you to search for any file on your disk. Have you ever saved a document and then wondered where it went? Or have you needed to find all the letters you wrote last Tuesday? Or do you want a file that is buried five folders deep and you're just too lazy to dig down? You can also do a search-within-a-search, like find all the letters you wrote last Tuesday whose titles start with "Memo to." It's just too great.

The Find File feature in System 7 or 7.1 is very different from the Find feature in System 7.5. So read the introductory material that applies to both, then skip to the section for the version you have on your Mac.

You Can Find:

You can find any file if you know any of this information:

▼ A few characters in the file's name, or what characters start or end its name.

▼ Any of the words that may be in the file's Get Info comment box (Get Info details on page 90).

▼ The date you last changed the file, or when you created it.

▼ What label/color you assigned to it.

▼ What kind of file it is (an application, a folder, an alias, etc.).

▼ The version number.

▼ Whether it's locked or not.

▼ Whether its size is greater than or less than so many kilobytes.

Simple Finding
System 7 or 7.1

When you want to find a file and you know its name, or at least several characters (a "string" of characters) in its name, you can just do a **quick-and-easy simple find.**

See pages 266–267 for details on how to use Find File in System 7.5

▼ From the File menu, choose "Find..." (*or* press Command F). You'll see this dialog box:

▼ If you know the name or even part of the name of the file you're looking for, just type the characters in the Find box (it doesn't matter whether you use capital letters or lowercase letters).

▼ Click the Find button, *or* hit the Return key. When Find File finds a matching file, it will display it for you. If the file was deep in folders, Find File will put it right in front of your face. If a matching file can't be found, you'll hear a beep.

▼ If the file isn't exactly the one you want, just leave it there and press **Command G** (which is the shortcut for "Find Again"). **This will put the wrong file away, back where it came from,** and another file with the name you want will be displayed. Keep pressing Command G to put the wrong one away and find another one. When the Mac has found every file with that string of characters, you'll hear a beep.

Instead of searching for som ething one file at a time, you can click the button **More Choices** to bring up a fairly sophisticated Find utility.

More Complex Finding

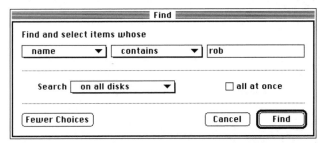

More Choices

Click "More Choices" to really have some fun.

Now there are a great many more options. Notice the downward-pointing arrowheads next to "name" and "contains," plus the tiny shadow behind the words. These are **visual clues** that if you press on these words you will see menus. These pop-up menus hold more choices. As you select different options in the first pop-up menu (currently displaying "name"), the options available in the other menus change. Try it and see.

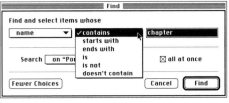

When "name" is my search criteria, the second menu has options for text, and I can type into the third box.

Notice how the options change in all three spaces, depending on what you select in the first menu. Spend a few minutes checking this out so you have a better idea of what your options are for searching.

When "date created" is my search criteria, the second menu has options for dates, and I can click the arrows (or type) to change the date.

When "label" is my search criteria, the last box becomes a menu which will show all the customized labels.

All At Once

⊠ **all at once**

Click this box to display all the found files simultaneously.

Even if your window was in an icon view, Find File creates a list, then expands the folders that have a file you want.

If you check the **all at once** checkbox, Find File will find and display, simultaneously, every occurrence of whatever you've specified so you can see all the matching files at the same time, without searching individually for each one. It does this by making a list of the items in your hard disk window (if that's where you searched), and then expanding the appropriate folders. When you scroll down the list, you will see that every matching file is highlighted.

Maybe you want to apply a label or a color to all of these files at once; since they are all selected, just choose the label or color from the Label menu. Maybe you want to throw them all away; drag *one* of the icons to the trash and they will all follow, whether you can see them or not (remember, *the tip of the pointer* must reach the trash can; it doesn't matter whether the icon reaches it or not). Maybe you want to store them all into a new folder; just drag one of the files into the new folder and they will all go. *As soon as you click anywhere except a highlighted icon, all the selected files will be deselected!*

If all the files cannot be displayed at the same time, the Mac will tell you so. When you press Command G to see the rest of the selected items, the first group of files is deselected.

> If Find File has expanded a lot of your folders (as in the illustration above left) and you want them all compressed again, press Command A to select all the files in the window, then press Command LeftArrow.

Restricting Searches

You can also choose **where you want Find File to search.** Narrowing your search can save a lot of time. See the downward-pointing arrow in the label next to "Search"? You can press on the arrow to get the menu of places to search—just the Desktop, just your hard disk, just a floppy disk, just the active window, or perhaps just the files you've selected (select the files and folders *before you choose Find File*). What you see in this menu is affected by what is selected on your disk and whether the "all at once" button is checked or not.

Back to Simple Finding

You can **get back to the simple Find box** by clicking the button "Fewer Choices."

In a **search within a search** you can look for items that meet one set of criteria. Then search just those selected files for the next set of criteria. For example, suppose you have a lot of files that have "Chapter" in their names, but you only want to locate the chapters you wrote after March 17, 1995. Here's how:

- ▼ First, search "all at once" for all files whose "name" "contains" the word "chapter." Find File will find and highlight all the matching files.

  Don't deselect the files! (which means don't click anywhere!)

- ▼ From the "Search" pop-up menu, choose "the selected items."

- ▼ Change the search criteria to "date created" and "is after."

- ▼ When you choose "date created," today's date will be shown. To change the date to March 17, click once on the part of the date you wish to change, then click on the little arrows (or you can type new numbers in).

- ▼ Click the "Find" button, or hit the Return key. Find File will display only those files that have the word "Chapter" in their names that were created after March 17, 1995. It's too cool.

Don't limit yourself to using "Find…" only when you are looking for a particular file. This feature can also be a lot of help if you're reorganizing your filing system. For instance, you can search by "date created" to see which of your files are outdated. Or if you're making backups, you can first search by "date modified" to see which files you haven't backed up since the last time. Or you can search for a file you want to use simply because you don't want to go digging through folders to get to it: Hit Command F, type a few letters of the name, hit Return, when the file appears, hit Command O to open it. Oh, there are all kinds of ways to be lazy—I mean efficient.

Search within a Search

Widen or narrow your search as you choose.

Other Search Ideas

Finding Files
in System 7.5

Find File

System 7.5's **Find** feature is incredibly more sophisticated and useful than the one in System 7.

If you really have an attachment to the Find File feature in version 7 and 7.1, you can still get it in System 7.5: hold down the Shift key as you choose "Find File" from the File menu. Or press Shift Command F. To find the next item, press Shift Command G.

To get Find File in System 7.5, do any of these things:

▾ At the Desktop, from the File menu choose "Find...."

▾ Or at the Desktop, press Command F.

▾ Or from the Apple menu, choose "Find File." This is handy when you want to find something but you are not at the Desktop.

This is what you will get:

The default is to choose to look on the hard disk. Press on this to get the menu of your options of where else to look.

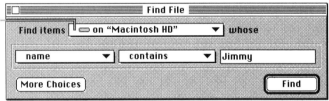

Type in a name, click "Find" (or hit the Return key), and you will get the dialog box below. It shows you all the files at once that are on the disk you chose (from the very top menu, see note to the left of the above dialog box).

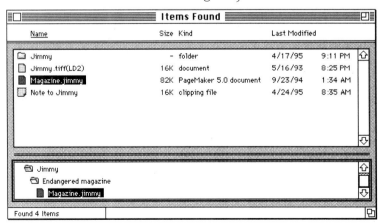

Before we move on to the details of using the "Items Found" dialog box, take a look at your other options for finding files.

▼ Press on the very top menu to choose where the Mac should look for your files. Don't ignore this menu! If Find File found nothing and you know something is on the disk with your specifications, check this menu—maybe it is just looking in the wrong place.

▼ Start from the far left menu to choose options for narrowing your search. As you choose an item in the first menu, the second and third menus change. Check them out! Hold down the Option key when you press on that first menu, and you'll even get more options (see right), including "contents," which lets you search through you files for certain words.

▼ Press "More Choices" to do a search within a search. This can narrow down your search to just the one file you need. Keep pressing "More Choices" until the button is no longer black (that's a **visual clue** that you are seeing all your options).

This choice lets you search for a phrase within the file! It can be slow, but it's handy.

Notice that as you choose different options, your other parameters also change.

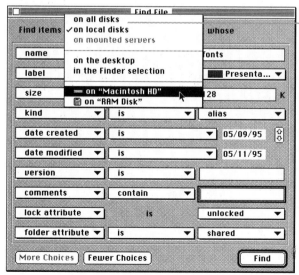

Don't forget you can choose to find items in particular places. Limiting your search will speed it up.

When "More Choices" is gray, you have no more choices. Press "Fewer Choices" to close up the dialog box one option at a time.

Found Files

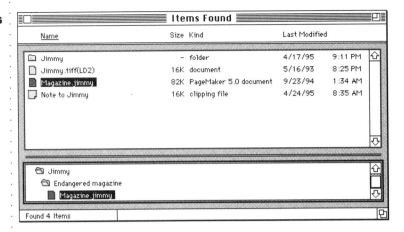

Once you have found files, you can do lots of things with them right from here.

- ▼ **To find out where a file is stored,** click once on it. The disk and folders it is stored within will appear in the bottom portion of the window. I wish that little part was bigger.

- ▼ **Throw a file in the trash** by dragging it from the top half of the window to the trash can. Notice the trash can bulges, indicating it's in the trash. But its name still appears in the window until you empty the trash because the Mac is telling you where the file is now.

- ▼ **Move a file** by dragging it out of the top half of the window to wherever you want to put it.

- ▼ **Open the file** right from the window by double-clicking on it. *Or* press Command O to open it, *or* choose "Open Item" from the File menu.

- ▼ **Open the folder that contains the file** by pressing Command E, *or* choose "Open Enclosing Folder" from the File menu.

- ▼ **Print the file** by pressing Command P, *or* choose "Print" from the File menu. If the Print command in the File menu is gray, that file is not printable.

- ▼ **Get Info on a file** by pressing Command I, *or* choose "Get Info" from the File menu.

- ▼ **Make an alias of a file** by holding down the Command and dragging the file anywhere, including the Desktop.

Find File is a window, acting very much like any other window on your Desktop.

> Notice you have **scroll bars** along the right side. That's a **visual clue,** right? You know you can press on the scroll arrows and see more information in the little parts of the windows.
>
> There is a **resize box** in the bottom right corner so you can resize the window.
>
> There is a **close box** in the upper left to close it.
>
> There is a **zoom box** in the upper right so you can zoom it larger or smaller.

These are all the familiar features you know and love on any window on the Mac, yes? You know what you're doing.

To change the view of the found files:

▼ From the View menu, choose a view.

Or—do you see the names of the views across the top of the Find File window? Just click on the name of the view you want.

To change the font and size of the text in the Find File window:

▼ While Find File is open, go to the Edit menu. Choose "Preferences...."

▼ Choose and font and a size. Click OK. You won't see the changes until you click OK.

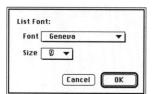

*Notice the shadow behind these boxes? Remember, that is a **visual clue** that there are menus behind those items.*

1. Do you have to type in the exact and entire name of the file you're looking for?

. . . .

2. Do you have to type caps and lowercase as exactly in the file name?

. . . .

3. Do you have to type spaces in exactly the right place?

. . . .

4. How do you tell Find File where to search?

. . . .

5. How would you find a file you wrote in March '95 that you know had the word "budget" in the file name? You have hundreds of reports with the word "budget" in the names.

. . . .

The following questions pertain to System 7.5 only:

6. If you are not at the Desktop, how can you get Find File?

. . . .

7. Once Find File has found several items for you, what is the easiest way to open one?

. . . .

8. What keyboard shortcut can you press to open the folder that contains a found file?

. . . .

9. How can you trash an item that Find File displays?

. . . .

10. Find File founds lots of files. How can you organize them in the Find File window so they are grouped according to what sort of file they are?

. . . .

Answers on page 373.

SHARING FILES

This chapter is only for you if you have more than one Mac in the same house or small office. If you do have more than one Mac, it is incredibly easy—in fact, it's so easy it's spooky—to **share files** between Macs. You can just drop a file into a shared folder and it instantly appears on the other computer. This works even if the other Macs are not using System 7.

You must be networked together (your Macs must have some sort of cable connecting them to each other or both to the same printer), but networking a couple of Macs is a simple procedure. There are entire books written on networking, and the procedure *can* get very complex, so complex that people make a living being network specialists and in a large office there is usually a *network administrator*. I am only going to explain the simplest method to get a couple of Macs talking to each other. I do this in my office with one other person and it is the coolest, most efficient way for us to get work done.

HI, MY NAME'S DAD, I'LL BE YOUR CHEF TONIGHT. WHAT'S SOUNDS GOOD?

CARRYOUT!

File Sharing Software

You need to have installed the **file sharing software** that came with System 7. If you didn't install it, you can run the Installer again from your original disk (have that power user friend of yours help you), click Customize, and install it. It's probably already there—if you see the control panels Network, Users & Groups, File Sharing Monitor, and Sharing Setup in your Control Panels folder, and if you see Network Extension, File Sharing Extension, and AppleShare in your Extensions folder, then you probably have everything you need.

AppleTalk and LocalTalk

The Mac has the **AppleTalk** networking software built into it that allows you to connect with other kinds of networks, and it's free. **LocalTalk**® is the hardware and the connectors built into the computer (you will need to buy a cable, explained in Step 2). If you use EtherTalk® or TokenTalk®, you need other help.

Step 1: Turn AppleTalk On

Before you begin to connect, make sure **AppleTalk is turned on** or nothing will work anyway.

- ▾ From the Apple menu, choose "Chooser."
- ▾ If it isn't already on, click on the button "Active."
- ▾ Close the Chooser (press Command W *or* click in its close box in the upper left corner of the Chooser window).

Step 2: Connect the Computers

The first thing you must do before you can actually share files is connect the two computers together with a cable. All you need are LocalTalk-compatible cables that you can get at your computer store or through mail order. I use the PhoneNET kit from Farallon because it's much cheaper and then I can use plain ol' telephone cables from the hardware store when I need to rearrange things. (You can get extra long telephone cables and connect computers in different rooms to each other and to the same printer.) Just follow the directions in the kit you buy. Both the computers in my office have PhoneNET connectors plugged into the printer ports on the backs of the machines. Then

This is one possible arrangement. Even if the printer is off, the two computers can talk to each other.

You could also hook Mac A into Mac B, then Mac B into the printer.

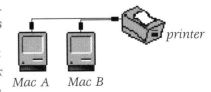

Mac A   Mac B   *printer*

telephone cables are plugged into the connectors. Both of these cables (one from each machine) plug into another connector that plugs into the printer (see the illustration on the previous page). It's really not much different from connecting your VCR and your CD player and your television together.

Now you must **name the Macintosh** and the owner. Generally the biggest computer will be your *file server*, or the one to which the other computers will connect. In large offices or school labs, there are one or more computers that do nothing except act as file servers. In your home or office, one of the Macs will be considered the file server, but to you it will still be your working Mac.

Step 3: Name the Mac

Name the Macintosh (I'm going to refer to this serving Mac as Mac A) through the Sharing Setup control panel, found in the Control Panels folder (get it from the Apple menu). Double-click the Sharing Setup icon to open it.

Sharing Setup control panel

Sharing Setup

▼ Type your name in the edit box "Owner Name."

▼ Make up a password, up to eight characters, which will give you control over whether other people have access to your files. I use my name because I can never remember a password.

If you can't open the Sharing Setup control panel, check that you have the File Sharing Extension and the Network Extension in your Extensions folder inside the System Folder. If not, have someone help you install them and restart.

▼ After you type the password, the letters turn into bullets (●●●●). You had better remember this password, including which letters you typed capital or lowercase.

▼ Type a name for your Mac. This is the name that the person on the other computer (Mac B) needs to know to connect to you. This name will appear in their Chooser when they try to share your files. If you are connecting several Macs together, create memorable and distinct names. Notice I named this one "Jewels," after my sister-in-law, Julie.

▼ Click the "Start" button to turn File Sharing on. (If the button says "Stop," then file sharing is already on—don't click it!)

Turn on file sharing

*After you click the "Start" button, the button turns into "Stop." Notice in the message box to the right of the button it now says "File sharing is on." Notice also that the folder has a dark tab and has wires coming out the bottom, a **visual clue** that information is flowing in and out.*

Program linking

You probably don't need to worry about "Program Linking" right now. Program linking doesn't mean that *you* link to the program (that's just called "sharing"); this button allows *programs* to link to each other, to talk to each other, to instruct each other, to share information. Different applications implement this in different ways; most can't do it at all. Check your manual for details. I've never used it in my entire life.

Step 4: Make a Folder to Share

Make a folder (or several folders) *or* select an existing folder and give it sharing privileges (instructions below). Anything you put in this folder will appear on the hard disk of Mac B. The person on Mac B can put items into this folder on their own computer, and the files will show up on your Mac A.

▾ Click on a folder to select it. You can select more than one folder at a time.

▾ From the File menu, choose "Sharing...."

▾ Click to put an x in the box "Share this item and its contents." Click the close box *or* press Command W to put this dialog box away.

If you want the other person to be able to read these files and/or perhaps to make changes to the file, you can grant permission right here. Just check the boxes of your choice.

To make a shared folder in System 7.5:

▾ From the Apple menu, slide down to "Automated Tasks" and choose "Share a Folder." If you didn't have one selected, the Mac will make one for you.

▾ Now the folder will look like this:
The dark bar in the tab and the wires
coming out the bottom are good **visual**
clues that this folder is willing to share. Anything you
drop into this folder will also share, even without
specifically telling it to.

Now the *other* Macintosh, Mac B, needs to **connect** to *your* **Step 5: Connect**
Macintosh, Mac A. Once you do this, you won't need to do it **the Other Mac**
again unless the file-serving Mac turned off the sharing. I highly **to Yours**
recommend you make an alias of your server icon so if the
sharing does get turned off, you won't need to repeat this process
(steps for making the alias are on page 257).

The file-serving Mac (Mac A) must be turned on.

▾ On Mac B, get the Chooser from the Apple menu.
You should see this:

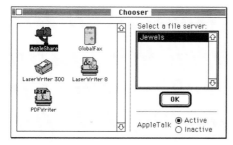

*The AppleShare icon is
critical. You must have
the Appleshare file in
the Extensions folder
in your System Folder.*

▾ Click on the AppleShare icon. (If you were on a big
network with "zones," you would see all the zones
listed here also. But right now we're just talking two
computers.)

▾ You should see the name of the file-serving Mac
(Mac A, that we named "Jewels" a few minutes ago)
in the box on the right. Click on that name.

▾ If the AppleTalk button is not already Active, click
to turn it on. You cannot share files without it.

▾ Click the OK button. This will give you the dialog
box shown on the next page:

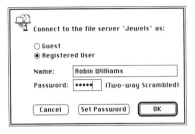

▼ If you know the password that you typed in Step 3, type it in here.

You can also just "log on" (connect) as "Guest" (that means click the Guest button). If you want, you can use the control panel Users & Groups to set up registered users and passwords so you can limit the access to your shared folders. If you are concerned about security, then you may want to do that. But you can always be a Guest. Click OK.

▼ If you click "Guest," you'll see a little dialog box; just click OK and you'll see this next one:

▼ Now you have the option of selecting which of the shared folders on the other computer you want access to.

Users & Groups

Use this control panel if you want to set up users and groups of users to have password-protected access to the shared folders.

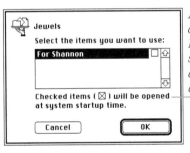

*After the first time you connect to the file-serving Mac (Mac A, Jewels), this shared item will only open at startup **if** Mac A has already been turned on.*

▼ After you choose the files you want, click OK. On your Desktop you should see an icon like this for each folder you have chosen to share:

For Shannon

On Mac B, you can now double-click on this "file serving icon," which is a representation of the folder on the file-sharing Mac A. It opens to a window just like any other folder.

▼ On Mac A, the shared folder icon changes when Mac B has successfully connected (a **visual clue**):

For Shannon

Can you believe how cute this is— little happy people sharing files?

All you need to do now to **share files** between computers is to put the files in any of the shared folders on either Mac. As long as a file is in one of the folders, both Macs can use it.

Important note: Let's say I'm working on Mac A and I put a file into the shared folder so You on Mac B can use it. When I put the file into the folder, I am actually just *moving the original file* into it because I am on the file-server Mac. You, on Mac B, want to use that file. You double-click on your shared folder and see the file. *Don't double-click on the file!!!* You are actually looking at the original file that is on *my* disk, and if you open it, you will be using *my* computer! **Copy the file to the hard disk of Mac B and then open it!**

You, on Mac B, when you put files from your hard disk into the shared folder, you'll see that the computer instantly copies the files from your hard disk onto the hard disk of Mac A.

While the computers are file-sharing, you'll notice they go through little spasms and your typing will stop for a second or two, menu commands take longer to happen, and other little annoying tricks will irritate you because the computers are trying to do two things at once—the work you want, plus send a file.

Step 6: Share Files

For Shannon   For Shannon

On Mac A   On Mac B

Once Mac B connects to Mac A, Mac A's folder icon has happy faces because it is so happy to be the Boss of Sharing Files.

Disconnecting

For Shannon

This is the file server icon on Mac B.

File Sharing Monitor

This control panel keeps track of who is sharing what.

You can **disconnect** yourself from the "network" in several ways:

▼ When either computer shuts down, file sharing is automatically disconnected.

▼ Or: drag the icon of the *file server* on Mac B to the trash. This is similar to ejecting a disk through the trash. You will not see any icon of the file server in the trash can window, so you cannot go get it to reconnect.

▼ Or: click once on the file server icon on Mac B to select it, then press Command Y (the keyboard shortcut for "Put Away" from the File menu).

▼ Or: on the file-serving Mac A, go back to the Sharing Setup control panel and click the "Stop" button.

▼ You can selectively disconnect users on Mac A through the File Sharing Monitor: From the Apple menu, choose "Control Panels," and get the File Sharing Monitor control panel. Click once on the name of the connected user you want to disconnect, then click the "Disconnect" button. You will get an option to determine how many minutes before the person is actually disconnected.

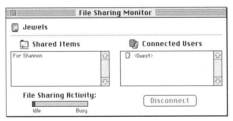

To turn off file sharing in System 7.5:

▼ From the Apple menu, slide down to "Automated Tasks."

▼ Choose "Stop File Sharing."

To turn on file sharing in System 7.5:

▼ From the Apple menu, slide down to "Automated Tasks."

▼ Choose "Start File Sharing."

To reconnect Mac B to the file-sharing Mac A, you *can* go through the process of getting the Chooser and logging on again. Or you can do this great trick:

> When you *are* connected, make an alias of the file server icon on Mac B that represents the shared folder. To make the alias, click once on the icon, then from the File menu, choose "Make Alias."
>
> Keep this alias wherever you like. When you need to connect to Mac A, just double-click the alias. This trick will also work if you make an alias of some file in the shared folder.
>
> In **System 7.5,** of course, you can skip all this and just use the technique at the bottom of the previous page!

You can choose to share your hard disk, then make an alias of it. You can put this hard disk alias on a floppy disk, since it is only about 2K. Then you can put this disk into any other computer that is on the network (that is, any of the computers that you have strung together with cables), double-click the hard disk alias, and be connected to your own hard disk through this other computer. Too cool. This concept is what you have probably heard of as the **office-on-a-disk.**

The only trick to this is that you can only share your hard disk if the hard disk contains no other folders that are shared.

- ▼ If you know which folders are being shared, select each one and turn its file sharing off, using the "Sharing..." command from the File menu.

- ▼ If you're not sure which folders are shared, check the File Sharing Monitor control panel. Choose "Control Panels" from the Apple menu and open the "File Sharing Monitor." This dialog box will tell you, on the left-hand side, which folders are being shared. You can't turn them off here—you can just make a list of the shared items, then go to each one individually and turn sharing off, using the "Sharing..." command from the File menu.

  If you are on **System 7.5,** you can use Find File from the Apple menu or File menu. Search for "Folder Attribute" is "Shared." Select all the folders that show up in the list, then select "Sharing..." from the File menu and turn off sharing for each one.

Reconnecting

For Shannon   *For Shannon alias*

Double-click the alias to automatically start file sharing without having to go through the Chooser.

Office-on-a-Disk

File Sharing Monitor

Use this control panel to monitor what is being shared and by whom.

You luck out!
No quiz today!

Choose the badge
you deserve.
Cut it out
and wear it
with pride.

Mac Merit Badges

OTHER FEATURES
28

This section explains some of the other features of the Macintosh that don't fit neatly into any other category and that don't rate a chapter of their own.

Balloon Help is a feature available on the Desktop. More and more applications are also incorporating Balloon Help into their programs. The idea of Balloon Help is that you can simply point to items you don't understand, like tools or menu commands or parts of a window, and a little balloon shows up explaining what that item is and sometimes what to do with it. It's nice in theory and sometimes they actually do provide answers that help. You'll find that you can't leave this feature on for very long, though, because those balloons popping up in your face all the time become quite annoying.

Turn on Balloon Help through the Help menu, which is that little question mark on the far right of the menu bar. You don't have to be at the Desktop—you can be in almost any application.

- ▼ Press on the question mark to pull down the menu. (If you pull down this menu in an application, it won't say "Finder Shortcuts" or "Macintosh Guide.")
- ▼ Choose "Show Balloons."
- ▼ Move your cursor over the screen and see what pops up. You can slide down menu lists, also, and get balloons for commands. Not all applications use balloons.
- ▼ **To turn off Balloon Help,** choose "Hide Balloons" from the Help menu.

Balloon Help

This is an example of a helpful balloon.

Turn on Balloon Help

This is the Help menu.

*In **System 7.5,** it's called the Guide menu.*

Publish and Subscribe

Edit

Undo	⌘Z
Cut	⌘H
Copy	⌘C
Paste	⌘U
Find...	⌘F
Replace...	⌘H
Go To...	⌘G
Create Publisher...	
Subscribe To...	

The first step is to select the text and make an edition through the "Create Publisher..." command.

The feature called **Publish and Subscribe** is an interesting concept. It works like this: In your application, say your word processing application, you create a document. This document needs to be shared with several other people on the network because they need to approve it. So you select the text and **publish** it (similar to *saving* a document). When you publish the text, the text is then called an **edition.** You save the edition in a folder, just as you would any other file.

John, Shannon, and Scarlett need to read and approve this file. So in their applications (it does not need to be the same application or even the same type of program), they choose to **subscribe** to this edition (which is similar to importing or pasting). Now John, Shannon, and Scarlett each have the same information on their screens.

The magic part is that even though neither John, Shannon, nor Scarlett can edit the edition, they can call you and tell *you* how things need to be changed. You make the changes on the *original* edition. When John, Shannon, and Scarlett next see their editions on their own [networked] computers, *the changes will have already been made, automatically.* The subscribed editions remain *linked* to the original file and will continue to automatically update any changes.

Each application may have its own method and dialog boxes for publishing and subscribing, so you will have to check with your manual for the specific steps to accomplish this in your software. Not all applications take advantage of this feature yet, either.

This is an example of creating an edition in Word.

Other people can choose to subscribe to this edition, which remains linked to the original.

The **Power Macintosh** is Apple's line of faster and more powerful computers. They don't look or feel any different from any other Macintosh. If you buy extra parts, a Power Mac can use both Macintosh software and DOS software. Eventually Apple won't even be making the regular Macintoshes.

Power Macintosh
PowerPC

Power Macs are sometimes called **PowerPC**s. Originally, their official name *was* PowerPC, but Apple soon realized that was a dumb mistake. So they changed the name to Power Macintosh. Still, the chip that runs the computer is called a PowerPC chip, which is why you see the word "PowerPC" on the front of them, as well as "Power Macintosh."

The first number in a Power Macintosh model is the model name, and the second number is the speed of the machine in *megahertz* (megahertz, MHz, refers to the speed at which a computer operates). So a Power Mac 8100/100 runs at a speed of 100 megahertz, which is significantly faster than the Mac IIcx I had until a month ago, which ran at 16 MHz.

Power Macs are much faster than regular Macs because they use a different kind of a chip and a different kind of information processing. Software must be written specifically for a Power Mac or it cannot utilize the enhanced speed. Software written especially for a Power Mac is called "native." The Power Macs can *run* all other Macintosh software, but they won't be significantly faster. Software written specifically for Power Macs, though, won't run on a regular Mac. You'll hear of software called "fat," which means it will run on either chip.

Native software

SimpleText with Voices

SimpleText   Voices

SimpleText is a little word processor that comes with your Mac system. It replaces TeachText, an even simpler word processor. If you've used TeachText before, you'll be pleased to know that in SimpleText you can now change the font, the style, and the size of the type. It will open certain kinds of graphics. But the greatest thing about it is that it reads to you. This is too cool. In the Sound menu, slide down to "Voices." You probably only have one voice at the moment, and it's probably Fred. Look at my menu, pictured to the left—I've got lots of voices. I found them on my Power Mac 8100/100 in a folder called "Voices" in the Apple Extras folder. I took them out of the Voices folder and dropped them all into the Extensions folder in the System Folder. Then they appeared in my SimpleText menu.

Even if you've only got Fred, you can do this: Type some text. Go to the Sound menu and choose "Speak All," or press Command H. The voice you have chosen will read the text to you. It's really amazing. If you have these other voices, type a long paragraph with no punctuation and then have Good News or Bad News or Pipe Organ read it to you. It's really too hilarious to type something very naughty and have one of these robots read it out loud. Jimmy, one of my sons, types in inappropriate messages, calls his friends, and has Whisper or Zardoz read it into the phone. Darn kids. You can type Command Period to interrupt the speaking.

Talking to Your Power Mac

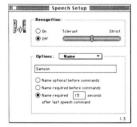

PlainTalk™ for Power Macintosh

What I also discovered in that same Apple Extras folder was a folder called "PlainTalk for Power Macintosh." This is **voice recognition software** for your Mac! Free! Voice recognition software allows you to *tell* your computer what to do, without picking up a mouse or touching the keyboard. You can name the computer, and then say, "Samson, open Word, new document, font Garamond, 10 point, new paragraph." Well, I don't know if will actually know *those* commands, but you can teach it an incredible number of things. A lot of commands are already built in. Just install it and go play with it. Amazing.

It seems to need the special microphone that sits on top of the monitor or it won't work (this mike came with my Power Mac). The folder installs the software you need, and you'll find the Speech Setup control panel in the Control Panels folder. I understand you can get the five PlainTalk 1.3 installation disks from the Apple Assistance Center at 800-767-2775.

NAVIGATING  29

Whenever you save a document, the Mac creates an icon to represent your file. This file has to go somewhere on the disk. Have you ever saved a document and wondered where it went? Have you ever lost things? Have you opened up a document only to discover that it does not contain the last several hours of your work on it, and you know you saved the document beyond that point?

The problem is that you aren't quite clear yet on how to **navigate** through the dialog boxes with all the different levels and folders on the Mac to get where you want to be, either to open the correct document or to save it where you will find it again. Navigating is one of the most important skills you can master. It seems so befuddling at first, and then one day it will just click and make perfect sense. Once you learn how to navigate you will never misplace documents when you save them, you will always be able to find the clip art you're looking for, you will always be able to find the extra report you wanted to open along with the one currently on the screen, and you will amaze your friends and co-workers as you whip through those lists knowing exactly where you are going.

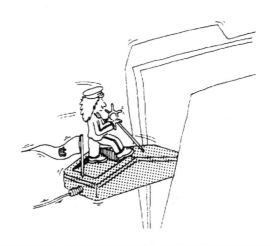

Visual Reference

It helps to have a **visual reference** to show how things are organized on the Mac. Let's follow the document "Scarlett's Art" through the navigation channels.

Take a look at these folders inside of folders where the file **Scarlett's Art** is stored. Imagine the Desktop to be your office. In your office is a filing cabinet, called the Hard Disk. In the filing cabinet are lots of folders. Each of these folders can have folders inside. Think of each of these things—the Desktop, the Hard Disk, each folder—as a separate *level* where you can choose to place a document. For instance, you sometimes want to file a document in a very specific and narrow compartment, nested into a number of folders with each folder getting more specific than the last, as in the case here for Scarlett's Art.

> The **Hard Disk** *is on the* **Desktop.**
>
> **Personal** *is a folder in the* **Hard Disk** *window.*
>
> **My Kids** *is inside the folder* **Personal.**
>
> *The* **Scarlett** *folder is inside the folder* **My Kids.**
>
> **Scarlett's Art** *is inside the Scarlett folder.*

The patterned background is the Desktop level. If you save at the Desktop level, your icon will show up on this patterned background.

*This is the **Hard Disk** level. If you save onto the Hard Disk level, your icon shows up in the window.*

*The **Personal** folder is open (that's why it's gray).*

My Kids *folder is open.*

*The **Scarlett** folder is open.*

*The artwork file, **Scarlett's Art,** is inside the Scarlett folder.*

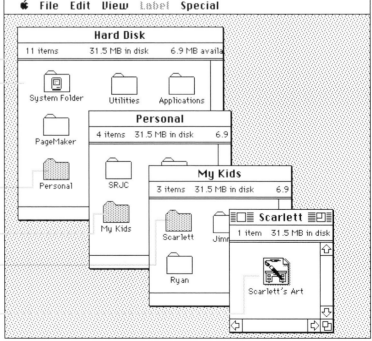

Since you have been working on your Mac for a while, you have created your own folders for organizing your own information. (Well, you *should* be creating them—just press Command N to make a new folder in the *active* window; read Chapter 10 on Folders, page 93). Making a folder on the computer called "Personal" is the equivalent of marking "Personal" on a manila folder and sticking it in a drawer in the filing cabinet (Hard Disk) in your office (the Desktop/Finder). When you open that folder in your real office, what do you see? You see all the documents you've stored in there, right? When you double-click on a folder on your Hard Disk, that's what you see—all the documents stored in that folder.

▾ The trick to navigating through dialog boxes is to understand that **the dialog box is just a different way of looking at the contents of the folder.** When you choose to see that folder in a dialog box, the list (sometimes called the directory) displays all those files.

Different Ways of Looking at the Same Thing

Scarlett's Art is inside the Scarlett folder.

*The **Scarlett** folder is inside the folder **My Kids.***

My Kids** is inside the folder **Personal.

***Personal** is a folder in the **Hard Disk** window.*

*The **Hard Disk** is on the **Desktop.***

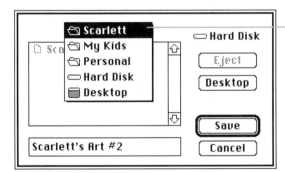

Take a minute to look carefully at this menu and notice the order is exactly like the order you see in the picture on the opposite page—this is a list of the folders that Scarlett's Art is "nested" into. This list just looks upside down compared to the one opposite. But they both lead back to the "root level," which is the Desktop.

You could view the same thing another way: At the Desktop, hold down the Command key and press on the name of the open folder. You see the same hierarchical list telling you where this particular folder is nested.

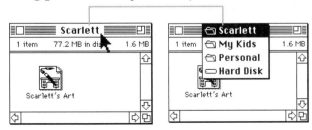

Where Does the Document Go?

This is how you save a document into exactly the spot you want so when you quit you know where the document went. Okay?

So here you are in your word processor. You choose "Save As..." from the File menu.

If you name this document and press the Save button right now, the document icon would appear on the disk whose name is shown on the right of the dialog box, and in the folder or disk whose name is in the label above the list.

The name on the right side of the dialog box is the name of the disk you are viewing. At the moment it's probably the name of your hard disk. If the icon, however, looks like a floppy disk, then you are viewing the contents of a floppy disk that is inserted into your computer.

You can save on any one of several different "levels" on a disk: on the Desktop (on a hard disk), on the disk itself (hard or floppy), or into any folder (each folder is a separate level).

The document will be saved onto this disk and into this folder.

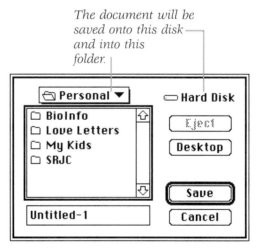

*If the "Eject" button is black, that's a **visual clue** that the disk you are viewing is a floppy disk, CD, or a removable cartridge.*

If you want to save onto the Desktop of the Hard Disk, click the button "Desktop." Whether you were viewing a floppy disk or the Hard Disk, clicking this button will take you to *the Desktop level of the Hard Disk.*

If you save onto the Desktop level, the document icon will be displayed on the far right of the screen.

Click here.

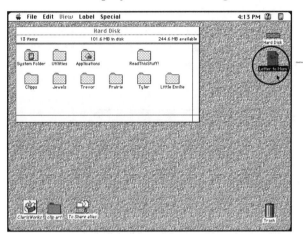

If you want to save into the Hard Disk window (meaning you want your file to be visible in the window of the Hard Disk, not in any folder), click the button "Desktop" to make sure you are viewing your Hard Disk. Then in the list, or directory, double-click on the name of your Hard Disk.

If you save onto the Hard Disk, the icon for your document will be displayed in the window for the Hard Disk.

Before you click the Save button, you should see the name of your hard disk here.

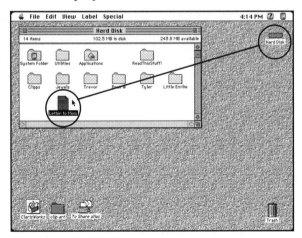

If you want to save onto a floppy disk or a cartridge disk,
then make sure that floppy disk is inserted or the cartridge is
mounted. If you don't see the name of the floppy disk on the
right of the dialog box, you must first navigate over to the disk:

▼ Click the button "Desktop." The name of any other
disk should be visible in the list box, or directory.
Double-click on its name.

If you save onto the other disk, the icon for
your document will be displayed in the disk window,
which is the window you see when you double-click
on that disk's icon.

*Before you
click Save, you
should see the
name of the
floppy disk here.*

*If you want to save
into a folder on
this floppy, double-
click its name.*

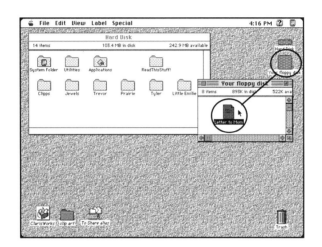

*You can't save
anything onto
CD-ROMs from your
Mac yet—the ROM
stands for "Read
Only Memory,"
which means you
can only "read" from
it, you cannot "write"
to it, which means to
save things onto it.*

If you want to save into a particular folder, you must first navigate to the folder.

- ▾ If the folder is on the Hard Disk, then first make sure you are viewing the Hard Disk: click the button "Desktop." Then double-click on the name of your Hard Disk.

- ▾ If the folder is on another disk, then first make sure you are viewing the other disk: follow the steps on the previous page.

Now you must find the folder. Do you see the folder listed on the disk? Yes? Then just double-click the name of that folder. Its name will appear in the label with a tiny icon of an open folder. **That open folder is your visual clue that if you were to save right now, the document would end up in that folder.**

Is the folder you want inside another folder that you see in the list? Then double-click the other folder first. Then the one you want will be available for opening.

If you save into a folder, the icon for your document will be displayed when you open the folder's window.

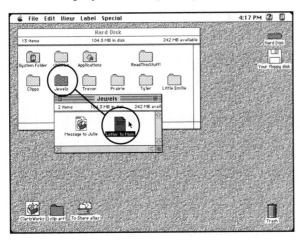

An example of this process is on the following page!

*Remember, you can only find folders **that you previously created.** If necessary, go back to the Finder by choosing "Finder" from the Application menu (far right of the menu bar) and create a new folder where you need it. See page 94. A few applications have a button called "New Folder" in the Save As dialog box!*

After you double-click the folder's name, you should it here.

For Instance

Okay. You want to save a new document into a particular folder. For instance, let's say you are working on a new database of the Boy Scout Roster for Jimmy. You created this new database by double-clicking on the database program, FileMaker Pro.

a So when you choose to save the Boy Scout Roster, the Save As dialog box automatically opens to the folder in which FileMaker Pro is located.* Well, you don't want to store this database file in that folder—you want to store it into Jimmy's folder. Remember where Jimmy's folder is? Right—it's in My Kids, which is in the Personal folder on the Hard Disk. So you need to navigate over to that folder.

b You know the Personal folder is on the Hard Disk so you press on the menu bar in the label and slide down to Hard Disk.

c Now in the list you see all the files on the Hard Disk. Find the folder called Personal and double-click the folder name to open it.

d Now Personal is in the label and all the files in *that* folder are listed. You want the folder called My Kids, so double-click My Kids to open it.

e Now in the list for My Kids you see Jimmy's folder. Double-click Jimmy to open it.

f Now the label has Jimmy's name in it, and you know if you click the Save button this file will be stored into Jimmy's folder.

g This is just the same as digging through folders on the Desktop! It just looks a little bit different.

This menu list shows the same folders inside of folders that you have on the Desktop.

* *In System 7.5, you have a little bit of control over where the Save As and Open dialog boxes go to, by using the General Controls Panel. If you haven't already, you might want to read that section, page 228.*

On a Performa, the default (the automatic choice) is to open the dialog box to the "Documents" folder. If you find this annoying (yes), see page 343.

Why is it that sometimes file names appear in a list box and sometimes they don't? It depends on which dialog box you are viewing and what program you are in.

When you view a **Save As... dialog box** in any program, the directory shows you every file that is in that folder or on that level. This lets you know what else is there and gives you a chance to make sure there is not another file by the same name. Other file names are in gray, just to let you know they are there. Folder names are in black (a **visual clue**) because you can double-click to open the folder and save the document inside.

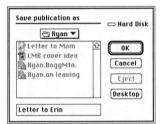

In this typical "Save As..." dialog box, you can see a list of all the other files stored in this folder. If there were another folder inside the Ryan folder, it would appear as black, indicating I can double-click to open it to store this file inside.

When you use a dialog box to **open** a file (or perhaps to **import** another file, such as a graphic), the directory only displays the names of files *that the current application is capable of opening or importing.*

This dialog box is displaying the same folder as in the picture above. The other two files you can see above are not showing up here because this is a PageMaker ***Open*** *dialog box, and these are the only two files in the folder that PageMaker can open.*

Keyboard Shortcuts for Navigating

You can use **keyboard shortcuts to navigate** through the folders at the Desktop and in the dialog boxes.

▾ **In any window on the Desktop:** If you press Command UpArrow, the window in which this folder is stored will pop forward in front of your face. For instance, if you are looking at Scarlett's folder, you can press Command UpArrow to bring the folder My Kids forward. You can keep pressing Command UpArrow all the way to the Desktop level. (Press Command Shift UpArrow to get straight to the Desktop.)

▾ **In any dialog box:** If you press Command UpArrow, the dialog box will display the folder in which *this* folder or document is stored (meaning you will go up one level in the hierarchy). It will display the next folder and list the files in it. You can keep pressing Command UpArrow all the way to the Desktop level.

- If a folder in the list is selected, you can press Command DownArrow to open it (which moves you one level lower in the hierarchy).

- Press the DownArrow to select files in the list.

- Type the first letter or several letters to select specific files in the list.

- Press Command D to select the Desktop level where you can find any attached hard disks or inserted floppy disks.

- Press Command RightArrow or LeftArrow to cycle through the disks or volumes you have connected or inserted.

- Press Command Period to Cancel.

- Press Command E to eject a disk.

- Press Return to Open or Save.

▾ **In a "Save As..." dialog box:** When you choose "Save As...," the dialog box opens and the edit box where you type the name of the file is automatically selected (it's *highlighted*). *If you type while the current name (which may be "Untitled") is highlighted, or while there is an insertion point flashing in the edit box,* then what you type will appear in the edit box.

The edit box for giving the file a name is highlighted. Whatever you type will replace the name that is here.

But if you click in the directory (the list box), the *directory* becomes highlighted—notice the double border around it. *If you type while the directory is highlighted,* the letters you press will select any file with those letters, or the next file in the alphabet.

The directory, or list, is selected, indicated by the double border around it.

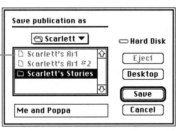

To bounce back and forth between selecting the directory for choosing other files or folders, and selecting the edit box for typing a name, press the **Tab key.** For instance, if the edit box is highlighted or has an insertion point in it, but you want to select a folder in the directory by typing its first letter, then press the Tab key. When you have selected the folder and want to name your new file, press the Tab key. *This will drive you nuts for a while. Eventually, in about a year, you'll get used to it and you'll start remembering to hit the Tab key to switch to the mode you need— selecting files or typing a name.*

1. What does "navigating" mean, anyway?

. . . .

2. If the Desktop is analogous to your office, what is the Hard Disk analogous to?

. . . .

3. Finish this sentence: The "Open" and "Save As" dialog boxes are just another way of looking at . . .

. . . .

4. How do you know which disk you are saving onto or trying to open a file from?

. . . .

5. How do you know which folder you are saving into or trying to open a file from?

. . . .

6. If you choose to save onto the Desktop, where would you find your icon?

. . . .

7. If you save into a folder, how do you find the file?

. . . .

This is the name edit box.

8. In the dialog box to the left, why are some of the files names in gray and some in black?

. . . .

9. In the dialog box to the left, if I start to type the name "Family Vacation," what will happen?

. . . .

10. In the same dialog box, if I want to change the file name, which key can I press to select the name edit box?

. . . .

Answers on page 374.

VERY IMPORTANT INFORMATION

It used to be so easy. And you used to not have to worry about what wasn't easy. But now you have no choice. Now you have to be conscious. Now you have to take responsibility for certain things on your Mac. Sigh.

This chapter covers several aspects of the Macintosh "operating system" that are all inextricably inter-related: hard disk space, memory, multi-tasking, and virtual memory. I know, you don't wanna know this stuff. But believe me, if you don't understand this particular information you will constantly find yourself frustrated and confused. Spend a few minutes here to empower yourself and gain control over your Mac.

Hard Disk vs. Memory

I have worked with thousands of new and not-so-new Mac users and have heard so many people wail in confusion, "My Mac keeps telling me I'm out of memory, but I have 32 megabytes left on my hard disk!" Well, I myself have a hard time figuring out all this technical stuff so I create analogies. What follows is my personal analogy for answering the heart-breaking cry, "What the heck is the difference between **hard disk** and **memory** anyway?"

Think of the hard disk in your computer as a filing cabinet in your office. Picture each megabyte of space as one drawer, so if you have an 80MB **hard disk,** your filing cabinet has 80 large drawers. Well, if you are working in your office and you need something out of the filing cabinet, you don't climb into your filing cabinet to work on it—you take the information out of the file drawer and put it on your desk, right? Well, the computer does the same thing. The computer cannot climb into the hard disk to work any more than you can climb into your filing cabinet. It does the same thing you do—it takes things out of the hard disk and puts them on its desk, but its desk is called **memory** (**random access memory,** or **RAM,** to be precise). When you turn the computer on, it goes to the hard disk, just like you go to your filing cabinet, and gets the System out of the hard disk and puts a copy of it into the memory (onto its desk) to run the machine. When you open an application, such as your word processor, the computer gets a copy of that word processing application and puts the copy into memory (kind of like taking a typewriter out of the filing cabinet and plopping it on the desk).

Well, you can see that the bigger the desk, the more things you can work on at once, or the bigger the project. The System that runs the machine, plus the typefaces and extensions you are using, and a few other items are all automatically placed (loaded) into RAM (onto the "desk") when you turn on the computer. All these things take up a certain amount of space. When you open an application, that application goes into RAM. When you work on a document, everything you haven't yet saved onto a disk floats around in RAM. When you work on large graphic files, like scans of color photos, there is an extraordinary amount of information that has to be held in RAM for the computer to be able to work on the image.

If RAM gets full, **you will crash** (well, that's *one* reason for crashing). Sometimes you will get a warning, but often the System just goes belly up, "unexpectedly quits," or gives you some sort of "system error" message. It's like you put one thing too many on your desk and the desk just collapsed. Type 1 errors are usually out-of-memory problems.

Why do you crash?

You can tell very easily how much memory you have in your Mac. At the Desktop/Finder, go to the Apple menu and choose "About this Macintosh." You will get the dialog box shown below (although yours will look a little different). Do you see where it says "Total Memory"? That's how much RAM you have installed in your Mac. On the right, you see how much is still free at the moment. The number is in *kilobytes,* showing thousands. Just take the first part of the number. Here, it shows I have around 32 megs of RAM. (You read the first chapter on Ks and megs, right?)

How much RAM do you have?

This is how much RAM is in your Macintosh.

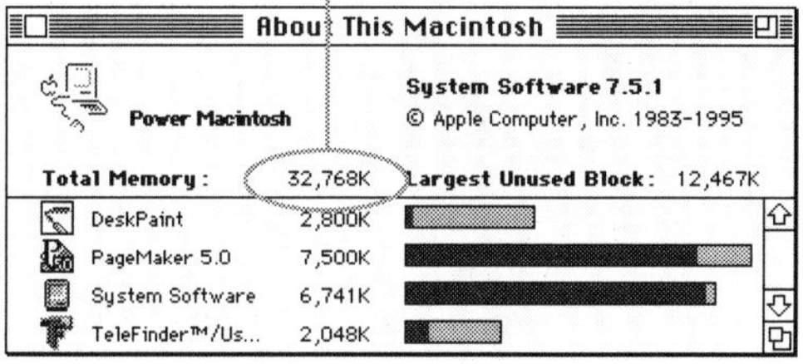

About This Macintosh	
Power Macintosh	**System Software 7.5.1** © Apple Computer, Inc. 1983–1995
Total Memory: 32,768K	**Largest Unused Block:** 12,467K
DeskPaint	2,800K
PageMaker 5.0	7,500K
System Software	6,741K
TeleFinder™/Us...	2,048K

Eight megabytes is about minimum if you are running any version of System 7. You can function with less than that, but you will bump into "running out of memory" problems often. Increasing the amount of RAM in your computer is the single most effective way to increase the potential of your Mac. On most Macs it's just a matter of ordering SIMMs (RAM chips) from your favorite catalog, opening the case, and popping them in. Well, you should read the directions, though, before you actually do it, of course.

Suggestions

If you don't have a lot of memory in your computer, here are a couple of suggestions to avoid running out of it:

Quit, don't just Close

1. Quit the application when you are finished using it (press Command Q). Don't just *close* the document you were working on by clicking in the little close box or by choosing "Close" from the File menu. Closing makes you *think* the application is put away because you don't see it anymore. But you must actually *quit* the application (you can also Quit from the File menu) so the computer can remove it from RAM.

It's like this: When you open a word processing application, it's as if you pulled a typewriter out of the filing cabinet and put it on the desk. When you *close* the document you were typing, you have essentially *put the piece of paper back into the filing cabinet (the hard disk), but the typewriter itself is still sitting on your desk (in RAM).* If you then open a spreadsheet application, you have essentially pulled a large calculator out of the filing cabinet and put it on the desk. When you close the worksheet for the day, you have *put the paper documents back into the filing cabinet, but you have left the calculator itself still sitting on the desk.* Well, eventually this desk is going to get so full of applications (appliances) that it will collapse. For instance, if you still have the typewriter *and* the calculator *and* the System sitting on the desk, and then you put an easel on the desk to paint a picture (like a paint program), the desk will collapse, and you will get a message that "the application has unexpectedly quit," or the entire System may crash. SO—the point is, *quit* the application itself (which puts the appliance back into the filing cabinet); *don't just close* the current document (which just puts the piece of paper back into the filing cabinet).

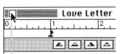

Clicking in the close box (as shown here) or choosing "Close" from the File menu does not put an application away!

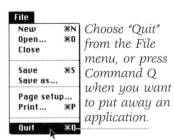

Choose "Quit" from the File menu, or press Command Q when you want to put away an application.

So let's say you haven't been quitting—you've just been closing documents—and now you're getting messages or clues that you are running out of memory. You need to know how to check to see which applications are still open. In the upper right corner of the menu bar is the **Application menu.** Press on it to see a list of all the applications *that are still open on your Macintosh.* If you see any application name besides "Finder" on the bottom half of that menu, *that program is still open.* Do any of the open applications in this list surprise you?

Choose one of the open applications (besides Finder) **and notice the menu bar change.** Even if you see no other change, you will see the menu bar change. You might still see the Desktop and the trash can, but *you are now in that program.* Really. You no longer see "View Label Special" in the menu, right? Check the Apple menu and you'll notice that it says "About [the name of your program]." To put this application away, either choose "Quit" from the File menu, or press Command Q. Even if you still don't see the program, trust me. Press Command Q and watch your menu bar change.

Do you ever find you are working in a program and suddenly it disappears? Or the menu bar changes? Or you closed a document and now you're back at the Desktop when you didn't want to be? That's because the Macintosh has a form of simple **multi-tasking** (not true multi-tasking) where you can have several things going on at once, such as having those several applications open at the same time. The important thing to know is that all it takes is a click of the mouse to pop you back and forth into the various applications. *It happens inadvertently all the time!* You may be happily working away on a letter when you accidentally click on the patterned background of your Desktop (you didn't even know it). The Mac thinks that since you clicked there, you want to go there. So suddenly all your Desktop windows flash in front of your face.

You can go back to your open application just as easily as you left if you can see a window from the program. Just click on the window you were working on. Now the Mac thinks you want to go back to your document and suddenly there you are. If you can't see a window, use the Application menu.

Which applications are still open?

This is the Application menu. This icon will change to indicate which program is currently active (open in front of you).

There will be a checkmark next to the name of the application that is active right now, the one that is open in front of your face. Even if you don't see it any-where, trust it. Look at your menu bar.

Save Regularly

Check the Application Heap

DeskDraw®

To change the application heap, the program must be closed.

Enlarge this number by selecting it and typing.

2. Save regularly. The entire time you work on a document, anything you do not *save* sits in RAM (and you know that anything in RAM will disappear when the computer crashes, right?). When you *save* the document, the current information is stored onto the hard disk and just the parts the computer needs still sit in RAM. It's possible to work on a document for several hours without saving and fill up RAM so it crashes. Oooh. SOS—Save Often Sweetie. Just hit Command S every couple of minutes.

3. Check the application heap. If you find that you crash regularly in a particular application, you may need to change the application heap for that program (details below). The application heap is the amount of memory that the computer sets aside just for that program. If the heap is set too low or just at the bare minimum, the program information gets poured into that amount and takes its chances on finding any more when it needs it, like when it needs to perform a complex maneuver such as checking spelling or flipping a graphic. You don't want to set the amount too high or you may not have enough memory for the other things the computer needs to do or for other applications that are open at the same time. Experiment to discover the amount that keeps you from crashing or "unexpectedly quitting."

▼ Make sure the application is not open. (If its icon is gray, it is open. Check the Application menu, choose the application, and Quit.)

▼ Click once on the application icon to select it.

▼ Press Command I to see the Get Info box.

▼ In the bottom right corner, select the "Current size" number and change it. Add about 10 to 15 percent more than the "Suggested size."

▼ Close the Get Info window and continue with your important work.

This leads to the topic of **virtual memory.** If you don't have any interest in knowing what virtual memory is, you can ignore the rest of this chapter and still lead a very happy and productive life. If you haven't yet read the first part of this chapter, you might want to do that now because the analogy continues.

You read all the time about the miracle of virtual memory enabling you to use extra hard disk space as memory space, which many people think is the answer to the problem of not having enough memory installed in the computer. It's not. Virtual memory should only be used as a temporary stop-gap measure. This is what happens:

When you turn on virtual memory (in the Memory control panel, if your Mac allows it), you are giving the computer permission to pretend that a certain amount of hard disk space is memory. Of course, you must have that amount of hard disk space free. That is, if you have an 80 MB hard disk and you want to use 5 megs for virtual memory, you must have at least 5 megs of your hard disk available. You've probably read articles that say you shouldn't use more virtual memory than you have real memory. That is, if you have a machine with 4 megs of RAM, you shouldn't ask for more than 4 megs of virtual memory.

So let's say you have four megs of RAM. When you ask for four megs of virtual memory, it's as if you are pretending that four of the drawers in your filing cabinet are part of your desk. Now, the computer cannot really use those four megabytes of hard disk space as memory any more than you can use those four drawers as part of your desk. What would you do if your desk was so full that you had to pull four drawers out and set them next to your chair so you could use them for the overflow? Wouldn't you probably put things in the drawers temporarily while you didn't need them and then switch them with something else from the actual desk when you did need it? That's exactly what the computer does.

Let's say you open your word processor and you start to work on your 563-page manuscript. That is comparable to you pulling the typewriter out of a file drawer and putting it on your desk,

If your Mac allows virtual memory, you can turn it on in the Memory control panel. Notice in this example I can't use virtual memory because there is not enough hard disk space available.

plus putting the entire manuscript in a pile also on the desk. Then you decide you also want to do some page layout for this manuscript so you get out your drafting table and put it on the desk (the *computer* gets the page layout program and puts it into memory). Now you want to paint a picture, so you get the easel out of the filing cabinet. Well, whoops, there's no more room on the desk. You don't want to pack up the typewriter and put it back into the filing cabinet, so you just plop the typewriter into one of those extra drawers you pulled out earlier and that are sitting next to your desk. The computer does the same thing— *those four drawers on the floor next to the desk are virtual memory* ("pretend" memory). If the *real* memory (the real desk) is limited, the computer has to swap things back and forth from the virtual memory to the real memory, just like you would have to swap things back and forth to make room on your desk. When you decide you need to use the typewriter again, you must swap either the drafting table or the easel to make room (this is why you don't want to use more virtual memory than you have real memory—you can't fit more in the extra boxes than you can fit on your desk).

Now, this swapping is a little faster than having to go all the way back to the filing cabinet for you, and a little faster than having to go all the way back to the hard disk for the computer, and having to set everything all up again. But it is still inefficient! What if you found you were working like this every day? Wouldn't you think that maybe you should just buy a bigger desk? You should. If you need that extra desk space, that extra memory every day, then you need to get a grip on reality, grow up, and buy the extra memory. Don't depend on virtual memory as a way of life.

HARD DISK.

MEMORY.

RAM

← MEMORIES
OF DINNER.

The **Power Macintoshes,** however, use virtual memory in a different way. Because of the way it uses memory and the way applications written for Power Macs comply with strict specifications, the computer can take advantage of a feature called "file mapping" when virtual memory is turned on. Even if you set virtual memory to the minimum amount, you will (they say) get better performance from applications that are written especially for the Power Mac.

Power Macs and Virtual Memory

If you want to set more than the minimum amount, Apple recommends that you set no more than half of your real, physical RAM. That is, if you have 24 megs of RAM, don't set aside more than 12 for virtual memory.

You control virtual memory on your Mac through the **Memory control panel,** which is explained on page 242.

Controlling virtual memory

So the **upshot of the analogy** is this:

The Upshot

- ▾ Your **hard disk** is like a filing cabinet where you store your work and your "appliances" (your applications).

- ▾ **Memory** is like your desk where you actually do your work.

- ▾ **Virtual memory** is like a makeshift addition to your desk, a temporary solution until you get it together to buy a bigger desk (more memory).

  (*Except* if you are on a Power Macintosh, then you are supposed to get better performance if you turn on virtual memory and set it to at least the minimum amount.)

Circle the choice that most pertains to the phrase.

1. Filing cabinet   RAM   hard disk   neither   both

2. Temporary storage   RAM   hard disk   neither   both

3. System running   RAM   hard disk   neither   both

4. System stored   RAM   hard disk   neither   both

5. "unexpectedly quit"   RAM   hard disk   neither   both

6. "disk is full"   RAM   hard disk   neither   both

7. Permanent storage   RAM   hard disk   neither   both

8. Document you   RAM   hard disk   neither   both
   have saved

9. Document you   RAM   hard disk   neither   both
   are working on

10. Desk   RAM   hard disk   neither   both

11. Application menu   RAM   hard disk   neither   both

12. Application heap   RAM   hard disk   neither   both

13. Application size   RAM   hard disk   neither   both

14. Virtual memory   RAM   hard disk   neither   both

Answers on page 374.

VISUAL CLUES

The Mac, with its famed graphical user interface, provides many **visual clues** to tell us what's going on. Most of these clues, though, aren't documented anywhere and we have to just kinda figure them out as we go along. Some of the clues are loud and clear, like the picture of the bomb; you might not know exactly why you bombed, but you know something is bad. The trash can is another easy visual clue, as are the icons of a hard disk or floppy disk.

But many of the visual clues are much more subtle. And to beginners especially, there is so much information going in through the eyes that it takes a while to absorb everything. I want to point out some of the clues the Mac is constantly providing, which should help you work more efficiently.

ROBIN, I'M GETTING THAT SCREEN AGAIN.

Ellipsis in the Menu

The ellipses indicate that the command will show you a dialog box.

Whenever you see a menu item followed by an **ellipsis** (three dots **…**), it indicates that if you choose that menu item you will get some sort of dialog box. Dialog boxes always have a Cancel button in them, so it's a great way to explore a new program—choose any menu item with an ellipsis, check out its dialog box, then click Cancel and you'll never wreck anything. Any menu item that is *not* followed by an ellipsis will just execute when you choose it, which has the potential to create unexpected results if you don't know what you're doing.

Occasionally you will find applications where the programmers did not follow the rules, and it's frustrating to try to predict what will happen when you choose the item. If you find menu items that are unpredictable because they don't have an ellipsis when they should, write to that company and ask them to please be more considerate.

Default Button

Any button with a thick double border around it is the **default button** ("default" means it is the automatic choice). This means if you hit the Return or the Enter key, the button with the dark border around it is the one that will take effect.

Typically (not always) the default button is the safest option, as in the Cancel button, above.

Highlighted Text

Simply type to replace any highlighted text.

When **text is highlighted** (text on a black or colored background), it's a visual clue to you that you are in typing mode and whatever you type is going to replace the highlighted text. *You don't need to hit the Delete key first—just type.* This is true in every dialog box, in every program that uses type, in every Save As box, etc.

Save As Dialog Boxes

In the **Save As dialog boxes,** have you noticed that sometimes the name of the file is highlighted, and sometimes it isn't? Have you tried to type a new name before and nothing happened? That's because you're missing a valuable visual clue.

When the text is selected (highlighted), it is ready for you to type a new name. If the text is not highlighted, then the list box, or directory, above the name is selected. The visual clue is the border around the list box. Look carefully at the illustrations below. When the list box is selected, you can type a letter or two to select files within the list box. In a Save As dialog box, the only files that will be black (which indicates you can select and open them are folders or other disks. All the other files you see are in gray just to show you what is there.

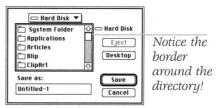

Notice the border around the directory!

Press the Tab key to toggle the selection between the name and the directory!! Try it!

The very buttons themselves are visual clues. **Radio buttons** (the little round ones) are called radio buttons because they act like your car radio in that you can only choose one option at a time. Clicking on any radio button deselects any previously selected button in the same list. And you have to select at least one—it's not possible to have no radio button selected.

Radio Buttons vs. Checkboxes

When a button is a **checkbox,** it's a clue that you can choose more than one. In fact, you can choose from none to all of them.

You can actually click anywhere in the word, not just within the tiny checkbox or circular button, to turn the buttons on or off.

You can select only one radio button.

Style:
- ⦿ Transparent
- ◯ Opaque
- ◯ Rectangle
- ◯ Shadow
- ◯ Scrolling

You can choose any number of checkbox buttons.

- ☒ Lock Text
- ☐ Show Lines
- ☒ Wide Margins
- ☐ Auto Tab
- ☒ Fixed Line Height
- ☐ Don't Wrap
- ☐ Don't Search
- ☐ Shared Text

In dialog boxes, whenever you see a shadow behind a little box it means if you press on the name in the box you'll get a **mini-menu,** or **submenu** (sometimes called a **pop-up menu** because it pops up into your face). These are kind of subtle, so you have to know to look for them. Some pop-up menus are indicated by little arrows (a stronger visual clue), in which case you can press on the arrow itself.

Mini-Menus

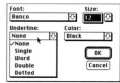

Press on any box with a slight shadow behind it to see the mini-menu.

Mini-Menus above a List

The label above a list box tells you where the items visible in the list are located.

Along the same lines as the previous clue, the **label above the list** in any dialog box (such as when you Save As, Open, Export, etc.) has that little shadow behind it, indicating a menu lurks beneath. Now the visual clue is strengthened with a little downward arrow.

In the label there is always a tiny icon, either a Desktop icon, a disk icon (either hard or floppy), or an open folder icon. This tells you where the items visible in the list are located. For instance, if the icon is an open folder, the items in the list are found within that folder. And if you press on that label with the open folder icon, you will see the menu showing the hierarchy—that is, where that folder is located, perhaps within another folder which is within another folder which is located on the hard disk. You can, of course, select any other folder or disk in the menu to open it and display its contents.

Command-press to see the hierarchy of any window on the Desktop.

By the way, you can also see the **hierarchy of any window on your Desktop** (also known as the Finder). This feature is completely clueless: hold down the Command key and press on the name in the title bar of any active window.

Matching Icons

DeskPaint™   PalmTree

Document icons usually match the application icon.

Robin'sData

A blank document is also a clue.

Icons, of course, are major clues. You've probably noticed that Desktop icons can generally be grouped into several categories: disk icons, folder icons, document icons, application icons, and system icons. Document icons (usually shaped like pieces of paper with the top right corner turned down) often match the application they were created in, which is a very thoughtful and helpful visual clue. See Chapter 9 on Icons.

If a document icon is **blank,** it is often a clue that the application in which the document was created cannot be found on the disk (see page 82 for elaboration).

You can customize any of your icons, thus potentially weakening this system of recognition. Is the icon to the right a folder, a document, an application, an init, a graphic file? Be careful. (See page 87 for details on changing your icons.)

Robin

Customizing icons is fun, but you lose the visual clue to its function.

The Mac lets you know when you are about to **change the name** of a file on the Desktop/Finder. When you single click on the *name* of the icon (*not* on the picture) *or* select an icon and press the Return key, a border appears around the name, which is the visual clue that what you now type will replace the current name. If you wait long enough before you type, you'll notice that the pointer turns into an I-beam when you position it over the name.

Changing File Names

The border around the name indicates you can now change its name. If you make a mistake, press Command Z.

A **gray icon** is a visual clue that the disk, folder, or application is already open. If you don't see its window anywhere, double-click on the gray icon to bring the window or application to the front. (You don't see any sign of your application? The visual clue that your application is active is in the menu bar; see page 84.)

Gray Icons

DeskPaint™   VisualClues

Gray icons indicate the file is already open.

Sometimes a **disk icon is gray** because you ejected the disk using the menu command or you pressed Command E. Ejecting a disk this way leaves it in the computer's memory, and it may ask for the disk again later. See page 166 for details. To prevent leaving the shadow of that disk on your screen, drag the disk out through the trash rather than use the menu command (it's perfectly safe!), *or* select the disk icon and press Command Y (the shortcut for "Put Away") to eject the disk.

LMB fonts

A gray disk icon may indicate a disk has been removed from the drive, but not from memory.

View Clue

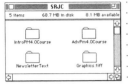

The name of the view in which the window is organized is underlined.

When you view the items in a window in some sort of list, such as By Name, By Size, By Kind, etc., notice that the particular **view** you have chosen is **underlined** in the information bar. You can simply click on one of the other categories in the information bar to switch to that view. See Chapter 8 on Desktop Windows for details.

Number of Items

You instantly know one item is missing from view.

When you view a window By Icon or By Small Icon, the information bar tells you the **number of items in the window,** indicated in the upper left of the window, under the close box. We usually take that for granted, but I have seen countless people complain that their document is missing while the info bar says "5 items" and the window only displays 4 icons.

Scroll Bars

You know there are more items within this list that are not visible at the moment.

Scroll bars, whether in a window or in a dialog box, may be white or gray. When the scroll bar is white, it's a visual clue that you are seeing all the items in that list, or viewing all the icons in that window—nothing is hidden from sight. If a scroll bar is **gray,** it indicates there are other items that are not currently visible, and you need to press the scroll arrow to display them.

On a color or grayscale monitor, the difference between white and gray scroll bars is minimal. If a scroll bar is gray, there is a scroll box in it. So **if you don't see the scroll box,** there is nowhere to scroll to.

Scroll Box

Check the position of the scroll box on the scroll bar—it indicates where you are in relation to the outer edges of the entire window.

The **scroll box** shows you where you are in that list or in that window, not only at your Desktop or in dialog boxes, but within applications also. If you're typing in your word processor and your text suddenly disappears, check the scroll box—is it at the bottom of the bar? Drag it back to the top to find your text. Did you place something on the pasteboard in PageMaker and then turn the page and can't find that item on the pasteboard? Go back and check the horizontal scroll box on the other page.

You've probably already noticed that when you look at a menu, a little **checkmark** often appears to tell you what is currently selected or what is considered "on." If you pull down a font menu or a size menu and you notice there is **no checkmark** at all, it means there is more than one font or more than one size of type in the text you selected. The Mac can't tell you more than one thing at a time so it tells you nothing instead—*but that nothing is actually a valuable clue.*

Select a smaller portion of text, or just click the insertion point within the text, to find out what the actual font or size is. Maybe *you* can't see any other font or size—remember, the Mac sees blank spaces and blank lines as characters. If even one of those selected blank spaces or blank lines is formatted in a different font or size or style than the rest of the text, you won't see a checkmark in the menu.

Sometimes you may have more than one disk in the computer, or you may be connected to more than one hard disk. You can always tell **which disk is booting,** or running, the computer: its icon is the one at the top in the upper right of the screen. (You may be surprised one day when you discover you actually need to know that bit of information. Then again, you may live a long time and never have a use for it.

If you see a little **diamond shape** next to an item in the Application menu (the menu at the far right), it is an indication that the progam wants to tell you something. It's usually not good news. Choose that item from the menu—typically you will get a message from the troubled program with a suggestion of what to do about it.

Once you become aware of these visual clues, you'll start noticing more and more of them. Every program has its own little set. Cursors change to tell you what will happen if you press now; each program has a way to indicate that an item is selected; buttons sometimes give you a clue as to what will happen if you click; etc., etc., etc. Take advantage of what they are showing you!

Menu Checkmark or Lack of Checkmark

A checkmark, as you know, indicates what is selected. No checkmark in the menu indicates that there is more than one size (or font or style, etc.) within the selected text.

Boot Disk

In this example, the Hard Disk is running the computer.

Diamond in the Application Menu

Look for Clues!

Use the dialog box below to answer the following questions.

Character

Font:
New York

Size:
12

OK

Underline:
None

Color:
Black

Cancel

Apply

Style
☐ Bold
☐ Italic
☐ Outline
☐ Shadow
☐ Strikethru
☐ Small Caps
☐ All Caps
☐ Hidden

Position
◉ Normal
○ Superscript
○ Subscript

By:

Spacing
◉ Normal
○ Condensed
○ Expanded

By:

1. How many menus are in this dialog box?

2. If you were to type, where would the text go?

3. How many edit boxes (places where you can type) are in this dialog box?

4. How many Styles can you choose?

5. How many Positions can you choose?

6. How many regular buttons (not checkboxes or radio buttons) are in this dialog box?

7. If you hit the Return key, what would happen?

8. Can you move this dialog box around? How do you know that?

9. Extra Credit: In almost all dialog boxes, what will happen when you press Command Period? (This is clueless—but it is elsewhere in the book and it's good to know.)

Scarlett Jimmy Ryan

10. Of the three icons to the left, which will change its name when you type?

Answers on page 374.

PART THREE

This section contains a variety of useful informaton—a collection of all the tips in the book (this might be the only chapter you read!), some Help tips, and information about the Performa model of Macintosh.

A FEW EXTRA TIPS

This is a collection of some of the tips or important notes that are embedded in the rest of the book, as well as any other hints or fascinating bits of information or shortcuts that haven't been mentioned. Again, nothing is software-specific; it all relates to the general Mac environment.

The page number in the tip indicates where more information on that tip can be found.

Use the **Return key to activate default buttons.** p.56, 308

Press **Command Period to activate Cancel button.** p.49

Clean up the Desktop. p.44

Clean up Windows according to a particular view. p.71

Use the mouse left-handed. p.37

Use the **Shift and arrow keys to select text.** p.58

System 7.5.1: **PowerOn key is also Shut Down key.** p.59

To make a window active, click on any visible part. p.63

To move a window without making it active, hold the Command key while you press-and-drag in its title bar. p.63

System 7.5: Double-click in title bar **to roll up window.** p.65

To switch window views, click on another column header in the information bar. p.69

To view the list by name yet still see the individual icons, use the Views Control Panel. p.250

To put the application at the top of a window list so it's easy to find, view By Kind. p.70

To organize the icons according to the last list view you chose, hold the Option key down before you choose "Clean up Window." p.71

To organize the icons into the invisible grid, hold Command key as you drag them in window. p.71

To close the active window, press Command W. p.65

To close every window, press the Option key and click in the active window's close box, *or* press Command Option W. p.72

To make the previous window close instantly, hold down the Option key while opening folders. p.72

To close all the Desktop windows before you even get there, hold down the Option key while quitting. p.72

To make sure all previously left-open windows are closed when you open the disk, hold down the Option key while inserting a disk or just before the Mac gets to your Desktop when starting up. p.72

To open a window as large as possible, press Option while you click the zoom box. p.74

To view the hierarchy of a nested folder, hold the Command key down and press on the title of the window. p.73

To open documents, drag document icon on top of application icon. p.82

To put files back where they came from, press Command Y. p.84

To print the contents of the active window, choose "Print Window" from the File menu. p.76

To print the entire screen, choose "Print Desktop" from the File menu. p.76

To make the Desktop level active, press Command Shift UpArrow. p.75

To expand a folder, press Command RightArrow. p.97

To compress a folder, press Command LeftArrow. p.97

To compress all the folders that are expanded, press Command A to select all, then press Command LeftArrow. p.97

To select a file in a window, just type the first letter or several letters of the name of the file. p.106

To select items from more than one folder at a time, expand the folders. p.108

To select an icon that is alphabetically after the currently selected icon, press Tab. To select the icon that is alphabetically *before* the currently selected icon, press Shift-Tab. p.106

To force the selected file name to appear at the top of the list window, press the End key before you type the first letter of the file name. p.107

To select the name of an icon faster so you can rename it, type the first letter or two of the icon to select it, then press Return. p.95

To undo an icon name change, press Command Z. p.85

To select files in windows using arrow keys, edit keys, the Tab key, and letters. p.106

To color your icons, use the Labels menu. p.86, 237

To customize your icons, see p.87

Use Find File to find files you are too lazy to dig for. p.262 (System 7 and 7.1); p.266 (System 7.5)

To make a copy of a file on the same disk, select it and press Command D. p.103

To make a copy of a file into another folder on the same disk, hold down the Option key while moving the file. p.103

To copy from floppy to floppy with only one floppy drive, p.104

To go back to work while copying a large file, use the Application menu to choose the program you were previously working in. p.103

To make a template out of any document, called a stationery pad, use the Get Info box. p.91

To throw away a locked file, hold down the Option key. p.91

To avoid the trash warning box, hold down the Option key while trashing the item. p.84

To permanently remove the trash warning, uncheck the "Warn before emptying" box in the Get Info window. p.113

To open a document, drag the icon and drop it on top of its application icon. p.118

To open an unknown document, drag the icon over the top of all your applications or aliases of your applications. The application icon that highlights will open the document. p.82

To open any desk accessory, wherever it is stored, double-click on it. p.180

To hear a sound when you reach the Desktop on startup, place a sound into your Startup Items folder. p.181, 247

To hear a sound when you shut down, place a sound into your Shutdown Items folder. p.181, 247

To use keyboard shortcuts in Open and Save As dialog boxes, p.294

To see what applications are still running, check the Application menu. p.172, 301

A diamond symbol in the Application menu means that program needs to tell you something. p.313

Enlarge the application heap if you are always running out of memory in a particular program. p.302

To create a copy of the date and time, press Command C while the clock is the active window. Paste the date and time into your document. p.204

Use aliases to keep track of files that you keep stored on floppy disks or cartridge hard disks. p.256

To find the original of an alias in System 7, use Get Info. p.259

To find the original of an alias in System 7.5, use the "Automated Task" from the Apple menu. p.259

To put an alias into the Apple menu in System 7.5, use the "Automated Task" from the Apple menu. p.224

You can still **type numbers while Caps Lock is down.** p.54

To create your own puzzle, see p.210 (System 7 and 7.1); p.211 (System 7.5)

To organize your Apple menu, see p.221 (System 7 and 7.1), 223 (System 7.5)

To write notes on a file, use the Get Info box. p.90

To eject a floppy disk and to unmount CDs and cartridges, press Command Y. p.167

To eject a stuck disk that didn't come out when the computer was turned off, hold the mouse button down while you turn the machine back on. p.169

To eject a disk as a last resort, use a paper clip. p.169

To unfreeze the screen, try a "force quit." p.329

To restart after you crash without having to turn off the power, use the Restart button. p.336

To replace highlighted text, just type. p.308

To delete forward while typing, use the del key. p.59

While typing, the insertion point picks up the formatting of the character to its left—font, style, size, alignment, and ruler settings, so load the insertion point *before* you type. p.126

To remove all the styles attached to characters (bold, italic, shadowed, etc.), select the text and choose Plain or Normal. p.126

To place accent marks over letters, use the Option characters. p.133

To use special characters, use Key Caps. pp.131,208–209

If you change your mind about the changes you just made, close the document and don't save those changes; when you reopen it, the document will have reverted to the last-saved version. p.139

To make several versions of a document, use "Save As." p.138

To make a PostScript file of a document, see p.154

To get rid of the pesky message telling you to insert the missing disk, try typing Command Period. p.166

To replace highlighted text, just type. p.308

To avoid wasting paper and toner every time you turn on your laser printer, pull the paper tray out a bit before you turn it on. p.114   For a more permanent solution, use the LaserWriter Font Utility. p.157

Three dots (the ellipsis: ...) **after a menu item** indicates that you will get a dialog box when you choose that item. p.308

Create your own Desktop patterns, p.229 (System 7 and 7.1), 235 (System 7.5)

Listen to audio CDs through your Macintosh CD player. p.207

Create your own categories on the Launcher, p.241.

Drag-and-drop files onto the Launcher to create new buttons, p.241

To remove items from the Launcher, Option-drag them to the Desktop or trash can. p.240

To remove unnecessary "Recent Items" folders from your System 7.5 Apple menu, use the Apple Menu Options control panel and set the number of remembered items to zero. p.248

To open the Extensions Manager on startup so you can turn off certain extensions, hold down the Spacebar when you restart. p.249

To be really mean and change someone's Desktop font to Zapf Dingbats, use the Views control panel. p.250.

To connect to a shared computer quickly, make an alias of the file server icon. p.279

To have text read to you, use SimpleText and the voices. p.284

To use keyboard shortcuts while navigating dialog boxes, see p. 294.

To view a PICT graphic, open the Jigsaw Puzzle (from the Apple menu) and drag the pict icon onto the Jigsaw Puzzle. p. 211

An **Easter Egg** is a surprise hidden in a program, a surprise created by the programmers. Here is a particularly great one; unfortunately, it doesn't work on System 7.5.1.

In any of the programs or utilities that let you create a clipping file, such as the Note Pad, SimpleText, or Stickies, type these words: **secret about box**. Select that text (drag over it), then press on it and drag it off to the Desktop. If it works, you will get a great surprise. If all you get is a little icon named "text clipping," it didn't work. Darn it.

Easter Egg!
System 7.5 only

text clipping

If this is all you get, it didn't work.

Application Menu Don't forget that you can choose to "Hide Others" from the **Application menu** to hide all the windows from the other programs that are running and that are visible from the Desktop.

If you hold down the Option key as you choose an application from the Application menu, all other windows will automatically hide. Also, if you hold down the Option key when you click to get to the Desktop, all other application windows will be hidden when you arrive at the Desktop.

Tab to Select In any dialog box that contains boxes for you to fill in, press the Tab key to move the selection from box to box. If there is data already in the box, that data will be highlighted and anything you type will replace it (you don't have to delete it first). If there is no data in the box, the Tab key will set the insertion point there, ready for you to type.

Screen Savers There are several varieties of screen savers available to help avoid screen burn. A screen saver usually turns the screen black or colors and has images that constantly move, like shooting stars or geometric shapes or flying toasters. As soon as you move the mouse it disappears. Some screen savers are desk accessories that you access through your Apple menu; some you put in your System Folder and they automatically turn on after a certain period of time if the keys or mouse haven't been touched.

One Space Type only one space between sentences! p.133

Real Quotation Marks!

" and "
' and '
not " and '

Using inch and foot marks in place of real quotation marks and apostrophes is an easily made mistake. Yes, on the typewriters we grew up with we used those marks, but we are no longer using typewriters. Also, we are attempting to come close to professional type, and you never see inch and foot marks used as quotation marks in professional type. Unfortunately, they are not located in an obvious spot, so you won't know they're there unless somebody tells you. So I'll tell you:

To type this mark:	Press these keys:
"	Option [
"	Option Shift [
'	Option]
'	Option Shift]

Several paint programs allow you to create a **StartupScreen** (one word). Once you have a StartupScreen installed in your System Folder, every time you boot (start the computer), this image will show on the screen for a minute or two. This is quite fun! Simply create a paint document, or use clip art, and save the document in the PICT file format with the name "StartupScreen." It doesn't matter what letters in the name are capitalized, but it does have to be one word. Put that file *into the System Folder*. The next time you boot, you'll see it!

StartupScreen

StartupScreen

You can also make a Startup Movie in the same way. Use just about any little QuickTime movie, name it **Startup Movie** (two words) and drop it into the System Folder or the Startup Items folder. If you are in a hurry when you turn on your Mac and don't want to watch the whole movie, press the Spacebar.

Startup Movie

If you have a hard disk, you may start to notice that it slows down after a few months. This is because there is an invisible file that keeps track of all the icons that have ever been seen on your Desktop, even if you just loaded them on to see what they looked like! There is a way to **rebuild your Desktop** and remove all the unnecessarily stored information. Follow these steps:

Rebuilding Your Desktop

1. From the Special menu choose "Restart".
   Or you could do this next time you start up.

2. As it starts up, hold down the Command and Option keys.

3. Hold down those keys until you see this dialog box:

4. Click OK (*or* simply hit the Return key).

Rebuild floppy disk desktop files the same way: hold the Command and Option keys down while inserting a disk, until you see the above dialog box.

Rebuilding does destroy anything you had typed into a Get Info comments box, though! See page 90 for info on the Get Info box.

How Much RAM? Do you want to know exactly how much RAM your System or any program you are running is actually using from the amount allotted to it?

> ▼ At the Finder, choose "Show Balloons" from the Help menu (the question mark, called the Guide menu in System 7.5).
>
> ▼ From the Apple menu, choose "About this Macintosh...."
>
> ▼ Position the pointer over the bar representing the largest unused block and a balloon will appear with the information.

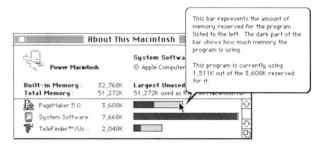

Checking Your Fonts at the Desktop To see **what fonts are in the System** while you are at your Desktop, from the Apple menu choose "Key Caps." A new menu item will appear in your menu bar: Key Caps. Press on it to see your font list.

Disable Extensions Occasionally you may find the need to **disable the system extensions** you have installed. You might need to do this because one of them is causing problems and you have to get it out but you can't take it out while it's working.

System 7.0 or 7.1: Hold the **Shift key** down when you turn on your Mac or restart, and *none* of your extensions will start up. This is an all-or-nothing deal. If you have lots of extensions, you may want to get one of the various utilities that manage these startup documents.

System 7.5: Hold down the **Spacebar** instead of the Shift key when you restart. The Extensions Manager will appear and you can turn off just the extensions you think may be causing trouble. If in doubt, choose the set, "System 7.5 Only," to allow just the extensions that enable the system to be fully functional. Close the Extension Manager to continue booting.

AAACK!! HELP!

This list doesn't pretend to be an all-inclusive reference for every sort of catastrophe that may befall; rather, it is a compilation of the most common, simple problems one may encounter when first beginning to work on a Macintosh.

Computer Doesn't Turn On

If the **computer doesn't turn on**, check *all* your switches and plugs. When a switch is labeled **I** or **O,** the **I** means **On.**

▼ If you have a floor surge-protector bar with an on-off switch, it may have been kicked to the *off* position—make sure it is *on.*

▼ If your hard disk is external, it has its own on-off switch that must be turned on *first* so it can boot up; then the Mac must still have its own switch turned on *also.*

▼ If your computer has a fan unit on top with buttons to push, those buttons still won't work unless the switch on the back of the computer is *also* on. The button on the left of the fan unit typically starts the Mac, while the button on the right will start your hard disk (but the hard disk itself should be turned on first).

▼ If you have any other devices attached to your computer, such as a scanner, hard disk, or CD-ROM player, sometimes they must be turned on first or sometimes they need to be turned on in a specific order. Try changing the order.

You see the Question Mark, the Flashing X, or the Sad Mac on Startup

The Happy Mac. We like this guy.

The disk with the flashing question mark.

The disk with the flashing X.

Ideally, when you start the computer you see the **Happy Mac.** This means all is well. Sometimes, though, you may see another icon, like a disk with a flashing **question mark.** This is a visual clue that the Mac cannot find the System Folder. The System Folder *must* contain the System file and the Finder file. If you are using an external hard disk, make sure the hard disk unit itself is turned on and is up and running, and make sure any extra switches are also on. If there are any other devices attached to the computer, they sometimes have to be turned on first. When you start attaching a lot of things to a Mac, they start getting fussy about the order they're turned on.

The disk with a **flashing X** means the Mac found the disk you thought was a startup disk, but it really isn't. There may even have been a System on it, but the Mac can't use it. Try your other startup disk (next page).

The icon you really don't want to see is the **Sad Mac.** This means there is something really wrong and you probably need your power user friend to help you figure it out. Even more serious is when the Sad Mac shows up on a black screen (rather than gray or colored or patterned) and plays the Chimes of Doom for you. On the black background, it looks like a **Dead Mac.** I, personally, have heard the Chimes of Doom six times now.

The Sad Mac, better than the Dead Mac.

Startup dsk

You should always keep a floppy disk around that holds a stripped-down System on it for those times when, for whatever reason, your computer won't boot. In your original disks for System 7, this is called "Disk Tools." Even the Performa (which makes you create your own backup System disks) comes with a startup disk called "Utilities." If you are lucky enough to have your entire system on a CD-ROM, you can boot from that.

You can usually at least boot from this emergency startup disk (if not, something is seriously wrong) and then take a look at your System Folder and perhaps find something obviously wrong, like a Finder missing. Or perhaps you know it is the extension you installed a half-hour ago—at least you can get to it now. Or you can move that corrupted font out to the Desktop finally throw it away (or at least rename it, then throw it away after you restart).

Occasionally the computer screen just up and **freezes.** The pointer may move around, but you can't click on anything and it doesn't respond to the keys. Very often this is the result of static electricity, or sometimes from running out of memory. You can try pressing Command Period, but it usually doesn't help.

Screen Freezes

What is sometimes effective, though, is a **force quit.** Press Command Option Escape (esc). You will get a dialog box asking if you really want to force the application to quit. Well, you have no choice. Usually this will just force quit that application and you won't have to turn off the computer (the only other option if this doesn't work). Anything you had not saved is lost. It's a good idea, if the force quit works, to save and quit in all other open applications and then restart.

Force quit

**Can't Find
Your Document**

In the beginning you may very often save a document dutifully, but then when you get to your Desktop you **can't find** it anywhere. This is because when you saved it you weren't paying attention into which disk and/or folder you were saving the document. Be sure to read Chapter 15 on Saving and Chapter 29 on Navigating, and carefully look at the dialog boxes pictured there so you understand how to save files where you can find them again.

Anyway, at the moment you can't find it. Use Find File (Chapter 26). When you find your document, put it in a folder you have created (page 94), just as if you were going to put it in a file folder in the filing cabinet. Press-and-drag the document icon over to the folder or disk of your choice. The folder/disk should turn *black;* when it's black, let go and the document will drop right in.

Can't Open a File

This symbol indicates the disk is locked.

Sometimes when you click on an icon you get a message that tells you the **file is locked or in use,** or maybe that **an application can't be found.**

If the **disk is locked,** you'll see a little lock symbol in the upper left of its window. When a disk is locked you can't save to it, nor can you print from a locked *System* disk (if you are one who still works from a floppy System disk which you probably aren't if you're reading this book). To unlock a floppy disk, first eject it. In one of the corners is a little black tab that covers or uncovers a hole. When the hole is open, the disk is locked (seems backwards, doesn't it?). So to unlock it, switch the tab back so the hole is closed. (More details on page 20.)

If the **file is locked,** click once on it and choose "Get Info" from the File menu. In the lower left corner there is a little box called "Locked" that may be checked. If that box is checked, then click in the box to uncheck it and thus unlock the file.

If the **file is locked** and it's a folder, click once on it and choose "Sharing..." from the File menu. If the little checkbox at the botton is checked, "Can't be moved, renamed, or deleted," then uncheck it.

If the **file is in use,** then it's in use. Usually you get this message if you try to open an icon that looks like a Macintosh; Mac icons are part of the System.

If it tells you an **application can't be found,** then one of two things is happening:

▾ The software application in which you created the document is not in the computer. Even though your document icon may *look* like SuperPaint, in order to view the document it has to go *into* the application SuperPaint to create itself.

▾ Some files cannot go straight from the Desktop to the application, even if the application is in the computer. In this case, if you know the document was created in a certain application and you know that particular application is in your machine, then go into the *application* itself (double-click on its icon) and open the file you want from inside, choosing "Open" from the File menu.

Try the tip on page 118 to find another application that may open the file besides the one that created it. Most applications can usually open several file formats.

When trying to **view clip art,** often you will get the message that "An application can't be found," even when the program it was generated in is on the disk. You need to open *the actual application itself,* then open each individual document through the File menu, choosing "Open" (such as MacPaint, or SuperPaint with the MacPaint format chosen). Also see the previous suggestion for "An application can't be found."

Running out of **RAM** is a prime cause for System crashes. RAM (random access memory) is the area in your computer where all the information is temporarily stored while you are working on it. When you Save, you send that information permanently to the disk and thus free up that much space in RAM. If you don't save very often, **RAM gets full** and the Mac just checks out (crashes). If you have a lot of extensions (page 351), remember many of those get loaded into RAM as soon as you turn the computer on. Then your application gets loaded into RAM. Then the fonts you use get loaded into RAM. If you open more than one application at a time, they all take up RAM. Then as you work, there is not a great deal of room left. You need to read Chapter 30, Very Important Information. If you run out of RAM often, buy more (in the form of SIMMs, see the Jargon chapter). Also decide whether you *really* need all those extensions and fonts and eliminate any unnecessary ones or get extension and font manager utilities.

Desktop File is full

If the invisible **Desktop File gets too large,** you may run out of memory (and your computer will work slowly). At least once a month you should *rebuild your Desktop* (it's very easy; see page 325).

Extension conflicts

If you use **extensions** (previously called INITs, page 351), keep in mind that it is not unusual for them to be buggy, unstable, corrupted, etc., especially the free ones. It's a well-known fact that they can cause problems, including System crashes. If you think one of your extensions might be a catalyst for bombs, take them all out and put them back in one at a time, using your computer for several days between adding each one. See the tip on page 326. If you are running **System 7.5,** use the control panel called Extensions Manager to help discover the source of the problem (see page 326).

Text Formatting Unexpectedly Changed

It's not uncommon to open your document on another *System* and find major **formatting changes.** If you created a document on your hard disk using the font Palatino, then gave a copy of the document on disk to a co-worker who opened it up and found it had transmogrified itself into the font Helvetica and all your formatting was thrown off, that's because Palatino was not in the co-worker's *System*. If the document can't find the font in which it was created, then it has to choose another from what is available. The solution is to make sure both Systems have the fonts from the same vendors.

Oh dear. There are a number of reasons why printing sometimes doesn't work. Here are a few of the most common.

▾ One of the most common reasons why **printing won't work** is that the appropriate printer icon wasn't chosen. Go to Chooser from the Apple menu and choose your printer (see page 144).

▾ Make sure the printer is on, that it has paper, and that the paper tray, if there is one, is firmly attached.

▾ Make sure any networking cables are connected.

▾ On an ImageWriter, make sure the Select light is on. It *must* be on in order to print.

▾ Also on an ImageWriter make sure the lever on the hand roller corresponds to the way you are feeding paper—that is, friction-feed for single sheets (that's the symbol with two rollers, towards the back); and pin-feed for pin-fed labels and paper (that's the symbol with one roller and little pins, pulled towards the front).

▾ If the hard disk that the *System Folder is on* is running out of space, Mac cannot print. It needs some free space (always leave at least 1MB free!) to send over the messages for printing. You will have to free up some space on that disk by removing a file or two.

▾ Sometimes gremlins prevent printing properly. If you have checked everything and there really seems to be no logical reason for the file not to print, go away for a while, let someone else print to that printer, shut down, come back later, try again. This sometimes works. One never knows.

▾ Unusual printing problems are a common symptom of a virus attack. See page 365 for a brief explanation of viruses.

If you want to **form-feed or line-feed the paper,** the Select light must be *off*. Be sure to turn it back on again before you try to print!

*Can't form-feed
or line-feed
the ImageWriter
paper*

Notice that the line-feed button will feed the paper through one line at a time for four lines, then it turns into a controllable form-feed; as soon as you let go it stops. Form-feed itself will roll through an entire page length (generally 11 inches).

There's Garbage Hanging Around Outside the Trash Can

If **garbage piles up around your can,** it's because you didn't put it *inside* the can, but set it down *outside,* just like the kids. When the *very tip of the pointer* touches the can and turns it black, that's the time to let go. *It doesn't matter if the icon you are throwing away is positioned over the can*—it's the **pointer tip** that opens the lid.

Gray Disk Icon is Left on the Screen

A **gray disk icon** can mean one of two things, either it is open or it is in **RAM.**

Blank disk icon indicating the disk is open.

If the disk itself is still in the floppy drive, then the blank gray shadow only means that you have already double-clicked on it and its window is open somewhere on the screen. If you can't see the disk's window because there are other windows in the way, simply double-click on the gray shadow and it will come forth as the active window.

Gray disk icon left on the screen after being ejected.

If the disk itself is not in the floppy drive, then you most likely ejected that disk by choosing "Eject Disk" from the Special menu or by pressing Command E. This procedure does eject the disk, but also leaves its information in the Mac's *memory.* Read page 166 for an explanation of what happened and how to avoid it.

Lost Your Application? Other Windows Popped Up in Front of Your Face?

You **lost your application?** Your menu suddenly changed and you can't find "Font"? Now your window is buried under other windows? You just accidentally switched applications or perhaps you clicked on the Desktop and popped back to the Finder where all your Desktop windows are. Use the Application menu to choose the application you were previously working in: when you press on the Application menu (upper right of your menu bar) you will see a list of programs that are open. Choose the one you want. Then read Chapter 30 on Very Important Information, taking special note of the Application menu. Also see the tip on page 318 regarding hiding other windows.

If your **Desktop windows open too slowly** or perhaps everything on the Desktop seems to take longer than it should, check to see if you have told your windows to calculate the folder size. In your window in a list view, under the column "Size," do you see the size of folders? That's what is slowing you down. Go back to the View control panel (found in the Control Panels folder inside the System Folder) and uncheck the box, "Calculate folder size."

Desktop Windows Open Very Slowly

Is the movement of the **mouse rather erratic?** Does your typing jerk around? Do your menus not show up right away? You are probably trying to do something in the background, like copy a large file or print. While the computer is doing something like printing, it has to spread its attention between you and the printer, which results in putting you on hold for seconds at a time.

Erratic Typing or Mouse Movement

You can't just push the button to **eject a CD or a cartridge hard disk.** You must first *unmount it*—drag its icon to the trash, *or* select the icon and press Command Y. After it has disappeared from the screen, then you can push the button to eject it.

Can't Eject a CD or Cartridge

If you get the annoying message that **the disk cannot be ejected because it is being shared,** you have to stop file sharing before the disk will unmount. On **System 7 or 7.1,** get the Sharing Setup control panel and click the "Stop" button. If you want to file share again, you will have to reconnect (which is why you should make an alias of your file server). On **System 7.5,** use the wonderful "Automated Task" in the Apple menu. Slide down to "Automated Tasks" and out to "Stop File Sharing." The Mac does it for you. When you want to reconnect, just choose "Start File Sharing" from the same menu.

In **System 7.5,** if you try to move or rename files in the System Folder or the Applications folder and you get a message telling you that something is **locked** or that you **don't have access privileges,** shoot it. No, that doesn't work. Go to the Control Panels (in the Apple menu) and choose General Controls. Uncheck the boxes that say, "Protect System Folder" or "Protect Application Folder." Quit the General Controls control panel.

You Don't Have Access Privileges, or Something is Locked

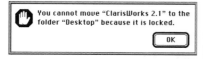

You cannot move "ClarisWorks 2.1" to the folder "Desktop" because it is locked.

OK

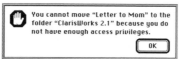

You cannot move "Letter to Mom" to the folder "ClarisWorks 2.1" because you do not have enough access privileges.

OK

Reset Switch **When you crash and must restart,** sometimes you cannot get to the Desktop to choose "Restart" from the Special menu. (The "Restart" button on the alert box that tells you have crashed almost never works.) Before you resort to actually turning off the power, try these:

▾ On some machines you can restart by holding down the Control and Command keys, then pushing the PowerOn key (the key that turns on your Mac if you have the kind of Mac that you turn on by tapping the triangle-marked key on the keyboard).

▾ If that doesn't work, press the reset button on your Mac, if you have one. It's a little button somewhere on the front, side, or back of most Macintoshes. There are usually two buttons—the reset one is the one with a tiny triangle on it.

▾ If that doesn't work, turn off the computer by pressing the little button on the back (oh, sometimes its on the front) of the computer box (not the the monitor). On some machines it isn't even a button, but a little plastic tab that presses in. It might look like this: ◑ or: ⏻

Wait at least ten seconds before you turn it back on.

THE PERFORMA 34

The **Macintosh Performa** is Apple's "home market" computer. If you don't know whether or not you have a Performa, check the front of the computer. There is an Apple logo and the name "Macintosh Performa" with a number indicating the model, such as 400 or 600 or 637CD.

The Performa models are exactly like any other Macintoshes in that they use the same software, virtually the same operating system, and have the same features and friendliness.

In this chapter I'll explain just the special features that relate to using the Performa right out of the box that are different from a Macintosh. Everything else in this book applies to a Performa as well as to a Mac, so you can't read just this one chapter and know everything there is to know about working on the machine! I suggest you read Chapters 1 through 6, then come here.

THE ONE ON THE RIGHT IS *REALLY* SMART.

Setting it Up The Performa comes out of the box with lots of software programs already loaded (installed). Just follow the directions in the manual to **set up the machine.** Basically all you need to do is plug all the plugs into their matching sockets. Make sure you plug the power cord into a surge protector (available at any hardware store), not directly into a wall outlet. And if you live in an area where there is a lot of lightning, unplug your entire system from the *wall* during a lightning storm.

Backup the Hard Disk The manuals for the software are also in the box, but what is missing in older Performas are the disks for the software that has already been installed. Now, I really must recommend that you **backup your hard disk!** If you don't back it up and you have a bad system failure or crash or some sort of damage to your hard disk, you won't have any copy of all the software that came with the computer. Complete directions for backing up are in the manual and on the screen as you do it.

But! It's very easy, but it is now *very* time-consuming and expensive. It can take over 100 disks to back everything up, and over six hours of your time as you sit there and put disks in and out. If you have one of the Performas the comes with a CD-ROM drive, then you also have a CD with all the original software **so you don't have to back it up**—the CD *is* your backup. If you don't, then the easiest thing to do is find out who in your town can *write* to a CD (ask your local user group [see page 14], or call a service bureau). Take your computer down there and let them put a copy of your hard disk on a CD-ROM. Even if you don't have a CD-ROM player, you can borrow one on the day you have an entire system crash and need to use the CD.

This is the button on the Launcher that will start the process of backing up. Click it; it will tell you how many disks you need and how long it will take.

Apple Backup

If you're not using the Launcher, the actual Backup application is stored in the Apple Extras folder.

The **Launcher,** a software program from Apple that is installed in the computer, is responsible for the unique interface of the Performa. When you turn on the Performa, you see this window:

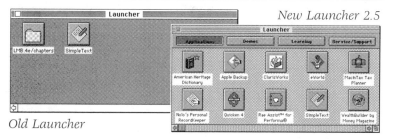

New Launcher 2.5

Old Launcher

This is the Launcher window (the exact contents may be different from yours). Its purpose is to make it easier for you to find and "launch," or start, programs. The buttons in the window represent the applications (programs) and other files that are already installed on your Performa. Click once (not twice) on any button to launch that program.

The idea is that you use the Launcher window *instead* of the hard disk window. Since the Launcher automatically opens whenever you turn on your computer, you will always have just what you need here at your fingertips with the click of a mouse.

The Launcher window acts like any other window (see Chapter 7 on All Windows) in that you can scroll with the scroll bar, scroll arrows, or scroll box to see other items. You can move the window by pressing-and-dragging in its title bar (wherever you leave the window when you shut down, that is where the window will appear next time you turn on the Performa). You can use the resize box to resize the window. You can close the Launcher by clicking in the close box. (Each of these items is explained in detail in Chapter 7 on All Windows.)

The items in the Launcher are just *buttons* that launch the real thing. The Launcher window is merely a place from which to open, or launch, applications and documents. Because that is its purpose, you may want to remove items from the Launcher window that you don't use, and you may want to add items, either documents or applications, that you use regularly. The Launcher is now a control panel in System 7.5, meaning everyone can use it, not just Performa owners. Details on how to use and customize the Launcher are in the Control Panels folder, page 238–241.

Removing and Re-installing the Launcher

Launcher

This is the Launcher control panel.

Startup Items

Double-click the Startup Items folder (above) to get the Startup Items window (below).

If you use the Launcher exclusively, a lot of this book won't make much sense. If you want your Performa to act just like anyone else's Mac, **remove the Launcher.** You can always re-install it later. On System 7.5 (see below), you can turn it on and off with just the click of a control panel button.

▾ **System 7 or 7.1:** Open the System Folder. Find and double-click on the folder called "Startup Items." (Find the folder quickly by typing "st.") Remove the alias called "Launcher." You can throw this in the trash. If you ever want a Launcher alias again, you can always make a new one (see Chapter 25).

▾ Close the Startup Items folder; close the System Folder. From the Special menu, choose "Restart." Et voilà, it's done.

▾ If you ever want to use the Launcher again, you can open it from the Control Panels menu in the Apple menu. But *if its alias is not in the Startup Items folder, Launcher will not start **automatically.*** You will have the Launcher window, but the other special features, such as hiding the other applications and windows, and defaulting to the Documents folder when you save, will not be in effect. **To re-install,** make an alias of the Launcher control panel and put it in the Startup Items folder.

▾ **System 7.5:** Click in the close box (upper left corner) of the Launcher.

▾ From the Apple menu, slide down to "Control Panels" and over to "General Controls."

▾ If there is an X in the box "Show Launcher at system startup," then click in that box once more to remove the X. Click its close box to put it away.

If there is no checkmark here, the Launcher will not start up automatically.

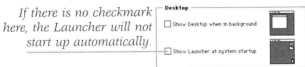

▾ If you want to use the Launcher again, just choose it from the control panels. Put the checkmark back in the General Controls control panel to have it start automatically.

On a regular Macintosh it is so easy for beginners to lose applications and documents and windows in the mess that results from having several files and applications open at once. It can be difficult to understand where you are and where files disappeared to and how to get them back. But on the Performa, you can see only one application at a time, even though several may be open. It will always be clear what is open and *active* at the moment. Now, you may not think this is such a big deal at this moment, but really, this is for your own good and it will help you control the urge to toss the machine out the window.

On the Mac (and thus the Performa, since it is really a Mac), remember, you can have more than one application open at a time. Even though you can't *see* any other application or the Desktop of the Performa, you can always switch to any application that may be open, or switch back to the Desktop/Finder at any time: just press on the Application menu (far right of the menu bar) and choose the open application you want to switch to, *or* choose "Finder" to take you back to the Desktop and the Launcher window. For details on the Application Menu, read pages 301. To stop this feature, remove the Launcher.

On **System 7.5,** you have the option of whether to allow the Desktop to be visible and available while you are in other applications. From the Apple menu, slide down to "Control Panels" and out to "General Controls"; the illustrations you see below are from that control panel.

Even if you choose *not* to show the Desktop in the background, when you go to the Desktop through the application menu, you will still see any open windows from the program you were working on. Click on any window from the program to go back to it instantly.

Desktop in Background

The Application menu shows you what is open on your computer. Just choose the application you want to go back to.

Optional: Desktop in Background

*If this box **is not** checked, you will not see the icons on the Desktop while you are in any other application. You cannot accidentally click on the pattern and "lose" your application.*

*If this box **is** checked, you will see windows from the Desktop and any other application while you are working in any program. You can click on the patterned Desktop to go back there.*

Documents Folder

See page 343 if you are running System 7.5!

One of the features of the Performa is that when you *save* a document you have created, the Performa automatically takes you to the **Documents folder.** Now, if you haven't ever tried to figure out where a document goes when you save it, this won't mean much to you. But typically, a beginner chooses "Save As..." from the Edit menu, names the document, clicks the Save button, and then can't find the document the next day because he doesn't know where it went when he saved it. This *default,* or automatic feature, of taking you to the Documents folder when you save means that every document will end up in the Documents folder on the hard disk. You will always know where to look for it.

Also, if you are working on one document and want to open another, when you choose "Open..." from the File menu you will see the Documents folder. The document you want to open is probably in there, in which case you can double-click on its name to open it.

Save into the application folder

Inside the Documents folder are folders for the software programs (applications) that are already installed on your Performa. When you choose to save, you can save the document directly into the folder that holds the software itself. For instance, if you are working in ClarisWorks, you might want to save your database into the ClarisWorks folder instead of the generic Documents folder.

> To save the document into the ClarisWorks (or other application) folder, double-click on the name ClarisWorks in the Save As dialog box list. Name the document, then click the Save button.

When you want to retrieve that document, you will need to go to the hard disk window and open the Documents folder (double-click on it), then open the folder titled with the name of the program you used (double-click on that folder).

If you are dependent on the Launcher, it becomes a minor problem that the Documents folder is not on the Launcher. If you want to depend on the Launcher for a while, have someone help you through the process of adding the Documents folder to it (details on page 238).

But you know what? You really don't *want* to store every document you ever create into the Documents folder *or* into the application folders. You need to learn how to make your own folders to organize your work; read Chapter 10 on Folders and Chapter 15 on Saving.

When you eventually start saving items into other folders you may get a little irritated with the default always popping you back to the Documents folder.

To stop the Performa from defaulting to the Documents folder, System 7 or 7.1:

▼ Rename the Documents folder. Adding a period to the end of its name is sufficient.

To stop the Performa from defaulting to the Documents folder, System 7.5:

▼ Renaming the Documents folder doesn't do anything—you can name it Dogfood and your documents will still go there. That's because the Documents folder in System 7.5 is "bless-ed." Notice the icon on its folder.

▼ Whether documents are saved into the Documents folder or not is now controlled in the General Controls control panel. When the button is checked for "Documents folder," every time you save or open a file, you will go to this folder. The Mac will *make* a special, bless-ed Documents folder on the Desktop if there isn't one already.

▼ When you grow out of this feature, go back to the General Controls control panel and change the button to the most appropriate one, "Last folder used in the application."

> **Documents**
>
> When opening or saving a document, take me to
> ○ Folder which contains the application.
> ○ Last folder used in the application.
> ● Documents folder.

Click here or click another option, depending whether you want this feature on or not.

Documents!

Add any character to the end of the name, or change it altogether.

Documents   dogfood

Notice the icon on the folder? This is not an ordinary folder—it is a bless-ed folder. Even with a different name, the Mac will know which folder to save documents into.

Wean yourself from the Documents folder

1. If you're using the Launcher, do you single-click or double-click the *buttons* on it? (Remember those are *buttons,* not *files.*)

. . . .

2. In the rest of the Mac environment, do you single-click or double-click to open documents and applications?

. . . .

3. How can you put the Launcher away temporarily?

. . . .

4. Briefly explain how to stop the Launcher from *automatically* appearing, should you choose to do so. Explain only for the system you are running (7 or 7.5).

. . . .

5. Explain how to set your Mac so you *do not* end up saving every file into the Documents folder. Explain only for the system you are running (7 or 7.5).

. . . .

6. On System 7.5, if you *want* to be able to click on the pattern of the Destkop to get back to the Finder, how can you make that happen (or not happen)? *(If you don't know what I'm talking about yet because you are very new to your Mac, never mind. Eventually it will make sense. Come back then and don't worry about it now.)*

. . . .

Answers on page 374.

PART FOUR

The computer world is full of all kinds of abstruse jargon and many of us are too embarrassed to ask what the unfamiliar terms mean. And then when somebody tells us what they mean, half the time it still doesn't make sense but we pretend it does. For years I pretended I knew what a SIMM was. I've made a list of the most common terms you may hear so you can look them up in the privacy of your own room. This isn't a complete list at all, but it should take care of most needs. **If you don't see what you want here, also look in the index.** An *italicized word* within the definition means it is also in the list.

If you do need more complete, illustrated definitions for Macintosh terms, as well as words relating to those other computers, see the book *Jargon: An Informal Dictionary of Computer Terms.* Well, yes, I did write it.

JARGON

impress your friends

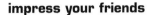

An **accelerator card** is a *board,* a plastic circuit board with chips on it, that you can buy and install or have installed into your Mac. It makes the computer work faster.

accelerator board

An **alert box** is a message that appears on the screen to warn you of some imminent disaster.

alert box

AppleTalk is how your Mac talks to your LaserWriter or to other Macs or to other sorts of machines (provided they are hooked together with cables).

AppleTalk

ASCII (pronounced *askee*) stands for American Standard Code for Information Interchange. It's a standard code that almost all computers can read that enables them all to understand how to create numbers and letters, even though they use different programs. For instance, if you are working in ClarisWorks and you need to send the file to someone else, but they use WordPerfect, you can save the document as an ASCII file (which is the same as *text-only*) and their WordPerfect will be able to open the file.

ASCII

See *ASCII.*

askee

When you use a modem to send information from one computer to another, the information goes through the phone lines at a certain rate of bits per second (a bit being one electronic unit of information). This bits-per-second rate (bps) is commonly called the **baud rate** (pronounced "bod"). Technically, though, the baud rate is not really the same as the bps, and someone someday will surely correct you. Modems most typically send at 2400, 9600, or 14.4 (14,400, pronounced "fourteen four") baud; the higher the baud rate, the faster the information flies through the phone lines and the less costly your phone bill.

baud rate

BBS stands for Bulletin Board Service, which is a service usually set up by organizations or clubs to provide or exchange information. You reach the BBS through your *modem* and special software called "tele-communications software." You call up the number for the BBS, and on your screen you see the computer equivalent of a bulletin board. You can post messages, send and receive *e-mail,* ask questions, answer questions, make new friends. BBSs are usually non-profit, as opposed to "online services" that charge you fees.

BBS

beta : When a piece of *software* or *hardware* is in the testing stage, it is said to be in **beta.** Usually beta versions are sent out to people (called beta testers) who test it and report back the things that are wrong or buggy or that need improvement.

bit : **Bit** is short for "binary digit." It's the smallest unit of information that the computer works with; it's kind of like an on/off electronic pulse. See page 18.

bitmapped : When an image or text is **bitmapped,** that means it is built out of the dots on the screen. Bitmapped graphics can be edited dot by dot. TIFF graphics are bitmapped.

Other kinds of graphics, *EPS,* for instance, or *PostScript* fonts, have two parts to them: They have a screen representation that is bitmapped so the Mac can read and produce it on the screen. Then they also have a *PostScript,* or *outline* version of the same image that is *not* bitmapped; this is the part that the printer reads to produce it on paper.

bomb : I don't think it's nice of them to use a **bomb** metaphor when the System *crashes* (has a malfunction bad enough to make the computer wish it were turned off). It's very disturbing. It lays a guilt trip on us, too; we always think it's our fault.

boot : To **boot** or **boot up** means to turn on your computer or other *hardware.* See page 17.

bug : The B word. If a piece of *software* or *hardware* has something wrong with it, making it act weird, it is said to have a **bug** or to be **buggy.** That's something *beta* testers do—they try to find and report the bugs in new products so the bugs get exterminated before we pay lots of money for the products. The term comes down to us from the real live crawling bugs that used to get into those giant-sized computers, particularly a moth at Harvard in 1945.

bulletin board : See *BBS.*

bus : A **bus** is a combination of software, hardware, and electrical wiring that creates a way for all the different parts of your computer to communicate with each other. For instance, you see the cables plugged into the back of your computer that connect it with the monitor or the printer or the hard disk or some other device—they all connect into the bus. If there was no bus, you would have an unwieldy number of wires connecting every part to every other part. It would be like having separate wiring for every light bulb and socket in your house.

byte : A **byte** is eight *bits* strung together to make a message that the computer can interpret. See page 18.

CAD : **CAD** stands for Computer Aided Design. It actually has nothing to do with the sort of desktop publishing design projects that most of us think of—it is referring to engineering and architectural tasks.

A **card** is a piece of plastic with *chips* attached to it that you put inside the computer box. You can get video cards and accelerator cards and clock cards and printer cards or whole computers on a card. They all enhance your computer in some way. Some of them you can just order through the mail and then open the computer and stick 'em in, which I find to be a very frightening but empowering experience.

card

A **chip** is that truly amazing and remarkably tiny piece of silicon that has an entire integrated electronic circuit embedded in its surface. Chips are what make the computer. Chips are the computer. A tiny chip is one of the biggest pieces of human-made magic on earth.

chip

A **cdev** is a control panel device. It's a little program (or *utility*) that usually makes life easier for you, like a screen saver. You can control some of the functions of the little program through the control panel. Many, but not all, cdevs must be stored in the Control Panels folder in the System Folder or they won't work.

cdev

CD-ROM stands for Compact Disk, Read-Only Memory. A CD-ROM actually looks just like the CDs we play music with. You can get a CD-ROM player for your Mac that will read these disks. There are disks with the entire works of Shakespeare, with dictionaries, with history, with images of the works in the Louvre, etc. etc. etc. You can only "read" from them, you cannot store information onto them. Well, if you find someone with a "CD writer," you can make your own CDs for storage.

CD-ROM

The **CPU** is the "central processing unit." It is the one tiny little *chip* in the Macintosh, often called the "microprocessor," that runs the show. Powerful magic. Sometimes people refer to the circuit board it lives on as the CPU. Since both the board it lives on and the chip itself are inside the box part of the computer, we often refer to the box itself as the CPU.

CPU

There's probably not much question about what a **crash** is. The first time it happens to you, you say, "Oh. This must be a crash. I get it now." When you see the *bomb* on the screen or when the screen freezes or when the Mac just decides to check out, that is a crash. The only thing you can do at that point is turn the computer off. Wait several minutes before you turn it back on again. Sometimes you may have a clue as to why it crashed (see pages 299, 331); sometimes you just have to accept the fact that you will never know why. Yes, everything you did not Save to your disk is gone. (Also known as "System bomb.")

crash

A **database** document is like a giant collection of 3 x 5 cards. Since they're on the computer, though, a click of a button can alphabetize those "cards," select just the names you want to invite to your party, tell you who owes how much money, etc. The term "database" can refer either to the software package you create in, or to the document itself. A database is one of the most useful tools on the Mac, and it actually is an incredible amount of fun. Everybody needs a database.

database

default   A **default** is an automatic choice already made for you. When you open a dialog box and see measurements or specifications that are already filled in for you, when a font style and size has already been chosen, these are the defaults. You can always change the actual specifications, and sometimes you can change the default itself so next time you use this dialog box or menu it has your choices as the defaults. Some defaults, though, are built in at the program level and you can't get to them. Also, when a button has a dark border around it, that is considered the default button. Press the Return or Enter key to activate the default button.

dialog box   I use the term **dialog box** loosely in this book to avoid confusing you. I refer to any of the messages you get on the screen that tell you something or ask you something as dialog boxes. Technically, some are dialog boxes and some are alert boxes and some are actually windows and there are probably a few others, but few people will argue and all will understand if you just call them all dialog boxes.

Dogcow   This little creature is the **Dogcow**. His name is Clarus. He says *Moof!* Sometimes he says !fooM.

dot matrix printer   A **dot matrix printer** is a printer that uses coarse dots to create the text and graphics on the page. An ImageWriter is a dot matrix printer.

dots per inch   **Dots per inch** is how the *resolution* of a printer or a scanner is measured.
dpi   For instance, the Apple LaserWriter prints at 300 dots per inch. This means there are 300 rows of dots in one inch. The ImageWriter II prints at 72 dots per inch. The higher the number of dots per inch, the smoother the image.

     You may hear the resolution of a monitor spoken of in terms of dots per inch. Yes, there are a certain number of dots (*pixels*) per inch, but it is not really the **number** of dots that determine the resolution of the image on the screen. How highly resolved an image on the screen appears is determined by how much information each pixel contains. Basically, the more colors or shades of gray your monitor can display, the more highly resolved your images will appear. See the example under *resolution.* The abbreviation for dots per inch is **dpi.**

download   **Download** means to take information from one source, like another computer, to your computer through a *modem.* When you send information from your computer to another one, you are *uploading* the files. Downloading also refers to sending certain fonts to the PostScript printer before they can be printed.

dpi   See *dots per inch.*

drive   The **drive** is the part of the computer that takes the disks and spins them to make them work. There are floppy disk drives, the ones with the little slots where you insert a floppy disk; hard disk drives that are sealed inside the computer or inside the box they come in; removable cartridge hard disk drives that have a large slot in which to insert a cartridge hard disk; AND CD-ROM drives that spin your CDs.

A **driver** is a piece of *software* that tells the Mac how to communicate with or operate another piece of hardware, most commonly a hard disk or a printer. Your System Folder has a printer driver in it (if not, you can't print).

driver

E-mail refers to the electronic mail that you can send or receive directly on your computer. Yes, it actually means people can write you letters and send them to your computer. You can turn on your Mac and go pick up your mail. Many a love affair has begun through e-mail. I know. It's really fun, too. And useful, of course. You do need to have a *modem* or be on a *network* to send or receive e-mail.

e-mail

EPS or **EPSF** stands for Encapsulated PostScript File. This is a graphic *file format*. Graphics that are saved as EPS are made of two parts. One part is a simple *bitmapped* image that the **computer** reads and displays on the screen. The other part is a complex *PostScript* code that the **printer** reads (if the printer reads *PostScript*). EPS files are called "device independent" or "resolution independent." This means they will print at whatever resolution the printer happens to be. The same graphic will print at 72 *dpi* on the ImageWriter, at 300 dpi on a LaserWriter, at 1270 or 2540 dpi on an imagesetter.

EPS, EPSF

An **extension,** previously called an **INIT** (accent on the second syllable) is a little program that does things like make extra sounds, pictures, bizarre cursors, clocks, etc. Some applications have extensions as adjuncts to the main program. Extensions work only if they are stored inside your blessed System Folder or in the Extensions folder within the System Folder; if you put them in any other folder, they don't work.

extension

These things were called INITs because they work upon *initialization* of your computer; that is, when you start it up. When you turn on your machine, all these little extensions get loaded into RAM and start working even before your System gets up and running. Those little icons that appear in the lower left portion of your screen as you *boot up* represent your extensions (some are also *cdevs,* which are like extensions except that you have some control over them through the Control Panel).

Most extensions from reputable sources will work invisibly and well. But many extensions, especially those written by individuals and sent out as *freeware* or *shareware* are a well-known source of trouble to the System. If things start acting weird after you install an extension, take the extension back out, restart (from the Special menu), and see if things are normal again. Never install more than one extension at a time; rather, put one in, work on your machine a few days, then put another one in. That way you will be able to pinpoint the one that causes trouble. (For instance, I've heard of an extension that inadvertently affects the column guides in PageMaker. Weird.) In System 7.5, learn to use the Extensions Manager control panel to keep track of all your extensions.

file format : A **file format** refers to the particular structure that a document (graphics, text, spreadsheet, etc.) is saved in. For instance, in text there are file formats like *ASCII* (text-only) or RTF (rich text format), in addition to the standard file format for your particular word processor, such as ClarisWorks or Nisus. In graphics there are file formats like *EPS, TIFF, PICT,* or MacPaint. Different programs can read different formats.

file server : A **file server** is used on a *network,* where several or many computers are connected with wires of some sort. Often one computer and its hard disk are dedicated to the job of being a file server. Everybody on the network (everybody who is connected with cables to this computer) can use the software and the hard disk belonging to that computer, rather than everyone having their own. There is also file server *software* that controls who gets to read and use what and how many people can do it at the same time.

Finder : The **Finder** is the software program that runs the Desktop (see Chapter 4). Because the Desktop and the Finder are so inter-related, and when you are at the Desktop level you have access to the Finder capabilities, the two terms are often interchanged.

Fkey : The terms **Fkey** and **function key** are used interchangeably, although
function key : really there are two separate meanings. Both terms refer to creating shortcuts, or *macros,* that can do a series of steps with one keystroke.

Fkey usually refers to a mini-program, or *utility,* that can be added to your Mac (kind of like a desk accessory). The little Fkey program makes things happen when you press a certain key combination, like Command Shift 7.

Function key usually refers to the 10 to 15 extra keys along the top of an extended keyboard, numbered F1 through F10 or F15, that you can program to perform certain tasks, usually with a *macro* utility.

freeware : **Freeware** refers to the *software* that nice people create and then put out into the world for the benefit of humanity, at no cost to the user and for no benefit to themselves. Freeware is often available on *bulletin board services,* through *user groups,* or from friends. See also *shareware.* People who create freeware are diametrically opposite to the evil people who create *viruses.*

function keys : See *Fkey.*

gigabyte : A **gigabyte** (G) is a unit of measure, measuring file size or hard disk
G : space, etc. It's very large. Technically, one gigabyte is 1024 *megabytes,* which is the same as one billion *bytes,* which is really 1,073,741,824 bytes. Impress your friends with this useful knowledge.

grayscale : Some Macintosh screens are **grayscale,** rather than plain ol' black-and-white, and any color monitor can be changed to show grayscale. On a black-and-white screen (or on printed material), gray tones are simulated by black and white dots that give the illusion of gray when seen from a slight distance. A grayscale image (a photograph, for instance, that has been *scanned* into the computer) on a black-and-white monitor is broken into dots to represent the gray values. On a grayscale monitor, though, the same image will display in actual gray values. It's very beautiful to see.

Hard copy refers to the printed version of what you have in the computer. For instance, this book is a PageMaker file stored on a disk. I printed up hard copy for editing and for producing the pages of the book in your hands.

hard copy

Hardware refers to the parts of the computer or of any *peripherals* you can bump into. The monitor, the external hard disk, the mouse, the keyboard, the modem, the scanner—all those things you can touch are hardware. As opposed to *software*.

hardware

The **Hierarchical File System,** or HFS, is the name applied to the Macintosh's system of keeping track of what is inside folders, and folders inside of folders.

Hierarchical File System

An **INIT** (accent on the second syllable) is now called an *extension*. Please see "extension" for details.

INIT

When you buy a new floppy disk or a hard disk, it is unformatted; that is, it is completely blank and doesn't have any of the tracks necessary in which to lay down the data you are going to give it. So you have to **initialize** it. Blank hard disks come with special software to use for initializing them.

initialize

When you insert a blank floppy disk, the Mac asks if you want to initialize it (see page 20). You have to, if you want to use it. If you re-initialize any disk, the process permanently erases anything that currently exists on that disk.

Kerning is the process of adjusting the fit between letters. You can only do it in certain programs, like the more expensive page layout or illustration applications.

kern

To **launch** simply means to start or open an application.

launch

Leading ("ledding") is the amount of space between lines of text. It is typically measured in *points*. In page layout programs and in most word processing programs you can adjust the amount of space between the lines.

leading

Lines per inch is very different from *dots per inch*. Dots per inch refers to the *resolution* of the printer, which can get up into the 2000 dots per inch range. The lines and curves of text appear to be perfectly smooth because the dots are so small our eyes can't separate them. But when a graphic that is in gray tones or in color, such as photographs or gray bars, goes to the printing press or a copy machine, the tones must be broken into dots big enough to print ink or toner. A specification of 85 lines per inch means that in an inch there are 85 lines of dots. The more lines that fit into an inch, the smaller the dots. The smaller the

lines per inch

dots, the higher quality the printing press must be in order to **hold** (print clearly) the dots.

Copy machines and newspapers need graphics at 65 to 85 lines per inch. Low-cost presses (quick printers) need 85 to 100 lines per inch. A good press can usually print 133 lines per inch. Only very high-quality art-type books are printed higher than 133 line. An Apple LaserWriter NT has a default for grayscale graphics of 53 lines per inch, which means that any gray image that comes out of the LaserWriter will have the gray values broken up into dots in lines of 53 per inch.

log on, log off — These terms refer to the process of checking in, or **logging on,** to a *bulletin board service* or a *network,* or to the process of checking out, **logging off.** Typically when you log on somewhere you have to use a password.

macro — The term **macro** sounds very arcane and intimidating, but once you use them you get hooked, they are so cool. A macro is simply a shortcut. A series of steps (menu commands, mouse clicks, keystrokes, etc.) are programmed into one key or one key combination. Once it is programmed and you press that key combination, the entire series of steps is executed at high speed.

For instance, if you're creating a database of names and addresses, you can create a macro that will type "P.O. Box " for you so you just press one key combination and that phrase will appear. Or if you regularly have to type the phrase "Robin's and Janet's Private Club for the Dissemination and Elucidation of Macintosh Magical Mysteries," make a macro for it. If at the end of each week you always gather up all the accounts entered, copy them, open another spreadsheet, drop them in, then print up a report with sums and totals and balances, create a macro for it. Anything you do repeatedly, you can lighten your life by making a macro for it.

With special software, macros are very easy to create; basically, you just choose the menu command that says Do This, show the macro what you want done by doing it, Stop when the action is finished, and the macro Does It. Some applications have macro features built right in so you don't need special software.

memory — **Memory** generally refers to RAM, which is Random Access Memory. Memory is temporary, volatile storage space, as opposed to the permanent storage space you have on a disk. You should read Chapter 30 (it's short) to get a good grasp on this important subject.

modem — A **modem** is usually a little box that sits next to your computer, although you may have a modem installed directly inside your Mac, such as inside some of the PowerBooks. The external modem has a cable that plugs into your Mac, and another cord that plugs into your phone jack. With a modem hooked up, then, your computer can call any other computer that is also hooked up to a modem. You can sit at your computer and "talk" to other people who are sitting at their computers. You type a couple lines of conversation, hit the Return key, and your conversation shows up on both of your computer screens. It's really addictive. People have been known to meet and eventually marry through meeting *online* (on the screen). And many a one-night-online-stand has happened. It's a fascinating phenomenon.

But, practically speaking, an incredible amount of business goes on through the modem. You can send any file through the phone lines. If you live out in the boonies, you can send your publication out for high-level output to a service bureau hundreds of miles away; they'll just express the finished product back to you through the mail. If your magazine column is due by 12 noon on Friday, you can finish it at 11:45 and still have it in their hands across the country by noon. You can conduct research, make plane reservations, join clubs, play long-distance chess, send faxes—oh, the possibilities are endless. Just so you know, the word modem is derived from the terms **mod**ulator and **dem**odulator.

Modifier keys are the ones that have no character attached to them, but that alter the behavior of another key. These are Macintosh modifier keys: Shift, Option, Command, Caps Lock, and Control (if your keyboard has it). Always when using modifier keys you press those keys down and *hold* them, and then just *tap* the character key that it modifies. For instance, the keyboard shortcut for Paste is Command V. So hold down the Command key and tap the letter V. If you *hold* the letter V down, you'll end up pasting in more than one of the item.

modifier key

Moof! is what the *Dogcow* says.

Moof!™

Isn't this a nice name? It's sometimes called a "logic board," but **mother-board** sounds so much more earthy and close to the heart. The motherboard contains the heart of the Mac. It's the "board," or piece of fiberglass, that contains the most important *chips* that run the computer, including the *RAM* and the *CPU* (central processing unit).

motherboard

Multimedia refers to presentations, books, proposals, etc., that are created using a variety of media, such as sound, video, graphics, and text. If the user can click buttons and do things with the presentation, it is called "interactive multimedia."

multimedia

When folders are stored inside of folders, they are said to be **nested.** If you hold the Command key down and press on the name of the window belonging to a folder, you will see all the folders that this one is nested into.

nested

When you connect computers together, either directly through cables or else through *modems* and phone lines, they are all on the same **network.** People on a network can share files, applications, e-mail, etc. Also see *file sharing.*

network

Paint programs create *bitmapped* images, where dots on the screen are either on or off and you can edit images dot by dot. Draw programs are **object-oriented** and create images as entire objects. You can't edit the objects dot by dot; you can only change the entire object as a whole. Each object is on a separate, transparent layer, and is defined by a

object-oriented

mathematical formula rather than bitmapped dots. Since they are not bitmapped, object-oriented graphics print much smoother, taking advantage of the resolution of the printer.

OCR   **OCR** stands for Optical Character Recognition. You can use a *scanner* and OCR *software* to take text on a printed page, *scan* it into the computer, and have the computer turn the text into the *characters,* not into a graphic image. That means you can take all the typed letters your lovers have sent you over the past ten years and input them into your computer *without retyping them.* This opens up incredible possibilities.

online   When you are talking through your computer to another computer or to an information service (see *bbs* or *modem*), you are **online.** Also, online in general refers to being connected and ready to work with any other *peripheral* (external) device connected to your computer. For instance, your printer is considered online when it is up and running.

online help   **Online help** is the file an application provides within itself where you can find information about the program or how to work it, without ever leaving the application or your computer. It's a manual on screen. System 7 has an online Help feature (see page 281). It's pretty wimpy. System 7.5, however, has a pretty good Macintosh Tutorial and Macintosh Guide. Get it from the Guide menu, under the question mark on the far right side of the menu, while you are at the Desktop.

output   Output refers to whatever comes out of your computer. Usually it comes out through a printer.

peripherals   Any *hardware* that is attached to the outside of the computer is considered a **peripheral.** Modems, scanners, CD-ROM players, printers, external hard drives, etc., are all peripherals.

pica   A **pica** is the unit of measure that typesetters have used for many years to measure type and line lengths. There are six picas in one inch (one pica = .167 inch), and there are 12 *points* in each pica.

PICT   A **PICT** is Apple's graphic *file format.* PICTs don't take up much disk space, and most programs can read them. They're very undependable, though, when printing to *PostScript printers.* If you must print a PICT to a PostScript printer, try to avoid including any *bitmapped* graphics within it, and don't use any *downloadable* fonts. Even then, they often decide to change their appearance without warning you.

Pict

     PICTs are more dependable if you never try to print them. For instance, they are usually fine in presentations that are meant to be presented straight from the computer. Or you can scan a photograph as a PICT (which is much smaller than a TIFF) with the intention of manipulating it and then outputting it straight to slides or Kodak film.

pirate   In computer jargon, **pirate** is a verb that describes making a copy of commercial software without permission and without paying for it. It is essentially stealing.

A **pixel** (**pic**ture **el**ement) is the smallest dot that the Macintosh can display on the screen. On a standard Mac screen, there are 72 pixels per inch, both across and down.

pixel

A **point** is the unit of measure that typesetters have used for many years to measure the size of type and the space between the lines. It is the unit of measure on the Mac to measure type and the space between the lines. There are 72 points in one inch. There are 72 *dots per inch* on the standard Macintosh screen. That was not an accident. (For type aficionados: you will be interested to know that 72 points on the Mac equals exactly one inch.)

point

Port is another name for a plug (a socket, actually) on the back of the Mac where you plug the cords and cables in. The difference between a port and a plug or socket, however, is that information flows *both ways* on a port, rather than just *out,* as in a socket.

   You can't go wrong with plugging things in to the Mac or the monitor—there is either a picture above the port giving you a clue as to what should go in the socket, or the port is shaped in such a way that only one kind of connector will fit.

   Port also refers to rewriting software so it works on another kind of computer. Mac users have a great amount of disdain for PC programs that have been sloppily ported over to the Mac and still retain PC features.

port

PostScript is a page description language, developed by Adobe Systems, that has become an industry standard. It's a language that *PostScript printers* interpret (as opposed to a language that your *computer* reads) and use to create the printed pages. It is PostScript that enables complex graphics to be printed at any resolution (whatever the resolution of the printer). Also see *PostScript printer.*

PostScript

A **PostScript printer** (or PostScript-compatible printer) is a printer that is really a high-powered computer—it has RAM, ROM, and a CPU. This printer can interpret the graphics and fonts that are written in the PostScript page description language (pages 154–155). Not all laser printers can read PostScript. Just because a printer has a high *resolution* does not mean it is PostScript. For instance, the Apple StyleWriter prints at 400 *dots per inch,* but it is not PostScript. Usually if a printer is not PostScript, it is called a *QuickDraw printer.*

PostScript printer

Once you start using keyboard commands, install a few *extensions* and *cdevs,* create a *macro* or two, and start throwing around words like RAM and *PostScript,* you can consider yourself a **power user.** Say the word SIMM, *motherboard,* or CPU in mixed company and you will really get respect.

power user

public domain   **Public domain** is an adjective describing any kind of work, not just computer *software,* for which the public has every right to copy and use in any way they see fit. The author has retained no rights nor liabilities (usually because they've been dead for a while). Public domain software is different from software that is copyrighted to the author yet distributed publicly. See *freeware* and *shareware.*

QuickDraw   **QuickDraw** is the part of the Macintosh operating system that is used for creating the screen display, supporting the windows, drawing lines, handling the color, and basically taking care of all the graphics and drawing functions.

QuickDraw printer   A **QuickDraw printer** is generally any printer that can't read *PostScript.* If a printer cannot read PostScript, then it has to recreate what it sees on the screen. That's the big deal about ATM (Adobe Type Manager) and TrueType (Chapter 21 on Fonts). These two things make type clean and smooth on the screen, and also make your QuickDraw printer print the text clean and smooth.

QuickTime   **QuickTime** is the equivalent (and beyond) of *QuickDraw* for video, images, and animation. You don't create anything with the QuickTime *extension* itself, just like you don't create anything with QuickDraw itself. QuickTime is the "architecture," the software, that allows the Mac to display, compress, edit, create, and store video. You don't need any special hardware to run QuickTime movies on your Mac.

    QuickTime is going to change how we use computers. It won't be long before any application, including your word processor and your *e-mail,* will be able to hold a picture that, when you double-click on it, will play a movie. You can cut, copy, and paste these movie clips, or even parts of these movie clips. And these movies are not just video— you can animate a slide presentation, spreadsheet charts, architectural plans. QuickTime brings us closer to the paperless office stage in history.

read-only   When a file or a disk is **read-only,** that means you can look at and print the file or disk, but you cannot save changes onto it. Often you think you can, because the file lets you select and edit text, but when you go to Save it, you won't be allowed. Locking a disk (page 20) or a file (page 91) will make it read-only. *CD-ROMS* are read-only. A certain part of the Mac's inner workings are read-only.

ReadMe   You will usually see a **ReadMe** file on a disk when you get a new software package. It's a good idea to read them (how can you resist?) because they describe the product and often give you the details on any last-minute changes, additions, or *bugs.*

redraw   When you move an object across the screen, when you scroll, change windows, etc., all or part of the screen has to be **redrawn.** The Mac has to figure out where everything has moved to and redraw them in their new places.

The computer is constantly renewing the screen, making sure it is bright, something like 65 to 75 times a second. How fast it does this is called the **refresh rate.** Faster is better, of course. It's called "refresh" because the electron beam inside the computer is re-energizing (refreshing) the phosphors on the screen.

The **resolution of a printer** is measured in *dots per inch.* The greater the number of dots per inch, the higher the resolution. The higher the resolution, the smoother the graphics and text can print. The Apple LaserWriter has a resolution of 300 dots per inch. The Apple StyleWriter has a resolution of 360 dots per inch. The Apple LaserWriter Select has a resolution of 600 dots per inch.

The **resolution of a monitor** is not actually perceived through the number of *pixels per inch.* How clearly an image is "resolved" on the screen is determined by how easily the computer can fool our eyes. Our eyes get fooled when there are so many colors or shades of gray that we can't easily differentiate where one color blends into another. When there are only two colors on the screen, black and white, an image is not resolved very well because our eye can clearly see the two separate parts. When there are shades of gray, an image appears to be more resolved because our eyes can't tell as easily where one gray shade blends into the next. When there are 16 million colors, our eyes perceive that the image is in high resolution. So the same monitor with the same number of pixels per inch can actually show varying "resolutions," depending on how many shades of gray or color are displayed. The number of colors or grays available to you depends on how much memory you have, what kind of video *card* you use, and whether or not your computer uses *32-bit Color QuickDraw.*

resolution

These two screen shots are exactly the same image on the same monitor. The image on the left has only 4 shades of gray to trick my eyes into thinking this object has some sort of dimension. The one on the right appears to be in higher resolution because there are more shades of gray (16). You an imagine if the monitor had 16 million colors to fool me with.

The initials **ROM** stand for Read-Only Memory. Certain system information is built into the ROM *chips* inside the computer, the information that gets the System up and running. If it's in the ROM chips, you can't do anything with it. RAM, random access memory, is the memory that you, as a user, have some control over. The initials in CD-ROM also stands for read-only memory—at this point in time, you cannot put a CD-ROM into your computer and save documents onto it; you can only get information off of it. Also see *read-only.*

ROM

RTF is Rich Text Format, another *file format* in which you can save text. It holds onto a little more formatting, such as bold and italic, than does an *ascii* file, and is usually capable of storing graphics. Most programs can open a file saved as RTF.

RTF

A **scanner** is a piece of *hardware.* What it does is **scan** an image: You put a photograph or a piece of drawn art or sometimes a three-dimensional object on the scanner. You close the lid and push a button, the machine views (scans) the image, and sends a copy of it to the computer. It's sort of like making a xerox copy, but instead of coming out the other end, the copy comes out in the computer. (Not all scanners work like I described here; some are hand-held and you roll the little

**scan,
scanner**

This was a photo-graph. I scanned it as a grayscale TIFF at 210 dpi.

machine over the top of the image. There are also video scanners that can input live stuff, and slide scanners that input directly from color slides.) The image to the left was scanned in.

When you scan images, the scanning software usually offers you several *file format* options. Unless you have a clear idea and a good reason as to why you would save it in any other format, always save scanned images as TIFFs.* TIFFs were invented for scans.

▼ If the image is straight black-and-white with no gray areas, save it as a line art TIFF.

▼ If the image has gray tones, such as a photograph or pencil or charcoal drawing, save it as a grayscale or con-tone TIFF.

Halftones: Halftones only apply to gray or color areas. A halftone breaks the gray area into dots that a printer can print. You can see the dots in any newspaper photo, and if you look closely you can see them in the halftoned photograph in the upper left of this page. If the image is solid black-and-white, no gray areas, you don't need any sort of halftone.

▼ If your scanning software can create special effect halftones that you want to use (or if your printer is not *PostScript*), save the image as a halftone TIFF.

▼ If there is no special effect halftone you need, then don't bother saving it as a halftone—let the PostScript printer halftone it on the way out. (Yes, all PostScript printers will do that; they take any gray or color image and break it into *lines per inch.* The number of lines per inch varies depending on the printer. An Apple LaserWriter halftones at 53 lines per inch; a Linotronic 300 halftones at 105 to 150 lines per inch, or just about any number of specify.)

* If the image you scan in will never see a printed page, then sometimes it is best to scan it as a PICT. For instance, if you are scanning a slide into the computer where you will manipulate it and then output it back to a slide, you will find a PICT image is much smaller in disk size. But PICTs are unpredictable when you go to print them.

screen saver If you leave an image on the screen for an extended period of time, it will eventually burn in and leave a permanent shadow. A **screen saver** is a little program (a *utility*) that prevents burn-in by creating interesting animated effects when you are not working. Effects range from simple fireworks to moving patterns to flying toasters with wings that you can hear beating if you listen closely. Some screen savers activate automatically if the keyboard or mouse haven't been touched in a certain number of minutes (those bug me; I hate to be interrupted while I'm thinking). Others you must turn on yourself. A good one lets you choose either.

SCSI (pronounced "scuzzy"), stands for Small Computer Systems Interface. SCSI is a connecting system, an interface, that allows computers and their *peripheral* devices (machines outside the computer, such as scanners, printers, etc.) to exchange information. Those big cables with the little pins in them (usually 50 pins or 25 pins) are SCSI connectors and they plug into SCSI *ports* (outlets) on the back of the Macintosh.

See *SCSI.*

Shareware is copyrighted software that somebody went to the trouble to create and then distributed through *user groups, bulletin board services,* and friends. You can try the software for free, but if you like it you should pay for it. Shareware is generally pretty cheap ($5 to $20) and you really should pay it to encourage other people to create nice things for us.

Ha. Now I know what a **SIMM** is. It's a Single Inline Memory Module. Well, that's what dictionaries say it is. I say it is a little piece of plastic, usually about as long as your finger, with tiny *chips* on it. These particular chips are *memory* chips. When you want to add more memory, more *RAM,* to your computer you buy SIMMs. Then somebody installs the SIMMs into your computer. They just pop into the little holders that are made for them.

Hardware is the stuff you can knock on. **Software** is the invisible stuff, the programming, the information coursing through the *chips* that makes the computer work. Software is in the form of *applications,* or *programs,* in the *memory* stored inside the Mac, it's on the disks, it's in the *System* that runs the machine. It's the big magic.

A **spooler** is *software* (or sometimes a combination of software and *hardware*) that allows you to work on your screen while your printer is printing. Typically what happens when you print **without** a spooler is that the computer sends the pages to the printer. The computer can send the information much faster than the printer can deal with it. So the computer has to hang around and wait while the printer processes all the information. Then it sends a little more info and waits. Sends a little more and waits. Meanwhile, you are also waiting because the computer is busy and won't let you have your screen back.

But when you use a spooler, the computer sends the information to the spooler instead of to the printer. The spooler takes it all, says thank you very much, and then funnels the information to the printer. Since the computer did its job of sending off the info, you get your screen back and you can work merrily along while the spooler finishes telling the printer what to do.

Sometimes while using a spooler your screen may get interrupted for a minute here and there while the computer takes care of details. But in general, it's painless.

SCSI

scuzzy

shareware

SIMM

software

spooler

spreadsheet

Spreadsheet is another one of those terms that intimidates us at first. A *database* is for making a list of items that you can then manipulate; a *spreadsheet* is generally used for number-crunching. You can do your home budget on a simple spreadsheet (I hire my teenager to do it), create invoices for your small business, project your mortgage payments, etc. etc. etc. They are so cool. It's quite a feeling of power to set one up, plug in some numbers, and watch it work.

Most spreadsheets also have a method for applying borders (lines) on the page, which means it is so incredibly easy to make great, instant forms: As you widen the page, the lines get longer; if you delete a row or a column, the lines will also be deleted; as you make the point size bigger, the space between the lines gets bigger. It's terrific, even if you don't use a single number on the page. There are always reasons to make forms.

startup volume, startup disk, boot disk

Some people have more than one hard disk attached to their computer. Sometimes more than one of those hard disks has a System Folder (be careful—don't do that unless you know why and how to deal with two System Folders). The hard disk that is running the machine at the moment is the **startup volume.** Or you could call it the **startup disk** or sometimes the **boot disk.** The startup volume *boots* the computer. The startup volume will always put its icon in the top right corner.

suitcase

FuturaFamily

Desk Accessories

*Suitcase icons hold fonts and Fkeys, although they no longer **have** to be stored in suitcases— it's just handy.*

Suitcase™

This is the icon for Suitcase, the font management utility.

The term **suitcase** gets confusing because two very important, closely related, but not connected items both refer to it: *suitcase icons* and the font management program called *Suitcase™*.

Suitcase icons represent *screen fonts* or *desk accessories*. If you double-click on a suitcase it opens up to a window with an icon for each font size and you can double-click each one to take a look at it; see page 199. *Just because you have icons that look like suitcases does not mean you have the font management program called Suitcase™!*

The wonderful program called **Suitcase™** helps you manage a large number of fonts. It also resolves font conflicts, or identity crises, which happens regularly when a lot of fonts get together. If you're a font freak (meaning you like and collect them), it is absolutely indispensable to use a program like Suitcase or Master Juggler to manage your fonts (even with System 7, no matter what they tell ya). A font management utility allows you to store and access your fonts without having all of them in the System all the time, which can take up a lot of your memory.

But the confusion between the two items occurs because people banter around the word *suitcase* referring to either the screen font icon *or* to the font management program, and a beginner doesn't see the difference yet.

You'll know a **system crash,** or bomb, when you see one. Either you get a very polite yet disturbing notice on your screen with a picture of a bomb about to explode (cute, very cute), or things will just stop working. Your keys won't work, the mouse won't work. There are a couple of things you can try before turning the computer off, but no matter what you do you will have lost whatever you did not save to disk. See pages 331–332 for a couple of reasons why you might crash, how to avoid crashing, and what to do about it when it does happen (which it will).

system crash

TeachText is a tiny little word processing program (it takes up less than 50K of disk space). Often when you get new software you will see an icon called *ReadMe.* This file has the latest info on the software, or maybe some tricks you should know about. To make sure you can read the file, since the software company has no idea what word processing program you use or even if you have one, they write the ReadMe file in TeachText, and then also send along the TeachText application on the disk so you can open ReadMe.

TeachText

TeachText

I bet you have about a dozen copies of Teach-Text on your Mac!

The term **telecommunications** refers to communicating over the phone lines through a *modem* as opposed to using your voice. It's even faster than overnight mail.

telecommunications

A document that is formatted (saved) as **text-only** is able to be read by almost any word processing or page layout program. It has no formatting, such as font size or style or columns, etc. Text-only is synonymous with ASCII, so you should take a quick moment to look up that term.

text-only

TIFF stands for Tagged Image File Format. It is a format used for saving or creating certain kinds of graphics. Graphics in TIFF are always *bitmapped,* but the bitmap *resolution* can be very high, depending on the program you are working in. TIFFs can be black-and-white line art, or they can be *grayscale* images. They were invented for *scanning,* so you might want to also read the scanning information (pages 359–360).

TIFF

Some menu commands and keyboard shortcuts are **toggle** switches. This means if you choose it once, the command is turned on; if you choose the same command again, it is turned off. Sometimes a command that can be toggled shows up with a checkmark next to it (although a checkmark does not mean it is necessarily a toggle switch!). Sometimes a command that can be toggled changes the name of the command when you choose it (e.g., "Show Clipboard" becomes "Hide Clipboard"). See "Changing Styles Mid-Sentence" on page 127.

toggle

Type 1 font — There are two distinct formats for *PostScript* type, **Type 1** and *Type 3* (there is no *Type 2* format). The corporation Adobe Systems, Inc., had a monopoly on Type 1 fonts; they used a secret formula to produce them and wouldn't let anybody else have the formula. So everybody else had to make Type 3 fonts.

Type 1 fonts are *PostScript,* and they are especially designed to print well at "low" resolutions (like 300 *dpi*). They print fast and clean on PostScript printers, and they can be scaled with *Adobe Type Manager (atm)* to appear very smooth on your screen and even when output to non-PostScript printers. In 1990 Adobe decided to publicize the secret formula so everyone could create Type 1 fonts.

Type 2 font — **Type 2 fonts** was a proposed font technology that never made it, so there are no Type 2 fonts.

Type 3 font — **Type 3 fonts** are the typefaces that are made without Adobe System's proprietary font technology. They tend to be less expensive, and they often don't print as clean and smooth, nor as fast, as *Type 1* fonts. They also tend to be more graphic in nature; that is, many Type 3 fonts are very decorative, with gray shades and elaborate fills and fancy shadows.

upgrade — When a company improves their software or hardware, that improvement is called an **upgrade.** The upgrades are indicated by the *version number;* e.g., PageMaker 5.0 (pronounced "five point oh" or sometimes "five oh") is in its fifth major upgrade since it was invented. Minor little fix-its are noted by points. For instance, usually within a couple of months of releasing a new upgrade, say 4.0, a software company will release the fix-it, called 4.01 ("four point oh one") which fixes the bugs they couldn't get to in time for shipping. If you are a registered owner of the software, you can usually purchase an upgrade at a significantly reduced cost, and sometimes you even get the upgrade free.

If your *hardware* goes through an upgrade, however, you just have to buy the new piece. You can buy new parts for your existing computer which would upgrade your "system," your collection of hardware that you work on.

upload — When you use your *modem* to copy information off of another computer and put it on yours, you are *downloading* (taking it down from the other computer). When you use your modem to put information onto another computer, you are **uploading** (loading it up onto the other computer).

utility — A **utility** is an application, generally a very small application, that has a very limited function. Utilities don't create documents; they just make things work better or add a bit of sparkle or convenience to your computer. Adobe Type Manager and Disk First Aid are utilities.

vaporware — When a company announces that their software is about to appear on the market and then it doesn't appear when it is supposed to, that software is considered **vaporware.** The term even gets loosely applied to books that don't appear on time, or to blind dates.

A **video card** is the *card* (the piece of plastic with *chips* attached to it) that controls the display on your screen. You can get different kinds of video cards for different kinds of monitors that allow the monitor to display different levels of *grayscale* or colors.

Viruses are very interesting things. A **virus** is a program that a very intelligent, very skilled, and very evil, sick person writes. It is written to do such things as destroy the data on your computer, corrupt your System, lock you out of your own machine, eat your programs. They can wipe out an entire hard disk. Viruses travel from computer to computer through floppy disks, networks, and even modems. You don't always know you have a virus; they often have a delayed reaction time, so you use the sick program for a while until one day it eats you. It seems that a person who can write a program to do so much evil is certainly bright enough to get a real job and direct that energy into making people happy instead.

This is a virus scenario: You have a disk that is infected. You put it into your Mac. As you use an application on that disk, the virus gets into your System. You take that disk out and insert another one. The virus jumps from your System onto an application on the floppy disk. You take that disk out, go to another computer in the office and insert it. The virus jumps from that disk onto the other person's System. Ad infinitum. The WDEF virus that was floating around for a while was so contagious that simply inserting an infected disk into a computer infected the computer. It's sort of comparable to somebody with a social disease getting on a bus and everybody on the bus automatically getting the disease. Then everybody on the bus gets off the bus and goes into the stores and everybody in the stores gets the disease. Fortunately WDEF was not a terribly devastating virus, just very irritating. (System 7 is immune to WDEF and to CDEF).

How do you know when you have a virus? Things start acting funny on your computer. Windows may not function properly, printing might not work right, files may be changed, programs may be "damaged." If anything starts acting weird, you can suspect a virus. (Actually, first you should suspect any *extensions* or *cdevs* you may have in your System Folder, since they are a much more likely cause of little troubles. Take out any that you may have installed right before your problems, and put them back in again, one at a time, over a period of a couple of days. That way you can pinpoint the offensive creature and remove it.) If you think the problem really is a virus, then get virus-protection software and disinfect your hard disk *and every single disk in your entire house and office.* And never again let anyone put a disk in your computer without checking it first.

Everyone should own virus-protection software as a normal part of computer life. One of the best packages is **Disinfectant.** It has an application that will locate and kill any virus, and it comes with an *extension* that will quietly check any disk you put in your machine. If an infected disk is inserted, Disinfectant sets off bells and whistles (literally). It is *freeware,* written by a wonderful man named

John Norstad at Northwestern University. He takes the time to write this program and is constantly updating it to catch new viruses. Can you believe that? He does this out of the kindness of his heart, an intrepid soul battling the forces of evil. Write him a nice thank-you letter and tell him how wonderful he is.

Disinfectant is available on several of the *bulletin board services,* from *user groups,* or from friends. You do need to be on the lookout at all times for the latest version of it, since those evil minds are constantly striving to outsmart the current virus-protection software.

Viruses have the potential to cause catastrophic damage; however, most Macintosh viruses have been held in check by virus-protection software, and with a little knowledge you can easily protect yourself and your loved ones.

wizziwig See WYSIWYG, just below.

WYSIWYG **WYSIWYG** stands for What You See Is What You Get, which means that what you see on the screen is what will print out on paper. If you are just beginning to use a Mac and you have never used any other computer, you may wonder what the big deal is about WYSIWYG because of course that's the way it is and that's the way it should be. But it is actually a relatively new concept, and one where the Mac excels over those other machines.

32-bit addressing This term, **32-bit addressing,** would take several pages to satisfactorily explain. I am going to give you just a very brief, simplified explanation here. See, your computer has a hard disk, right? It stores all the information on the hard disk. But when it wants to actually work, it has to take the information out of the hard disk and put it into memory (read Chapter 30 on Very Important Information). Memory is like all these little cubby holes, or mailboxes. Each megabyte has millions of mailboxes, but each mailbox can only hold a certain amount of information. When the computer puts stuff in a box, it remembers that particular address of that particular mailbox.

Now let's say you have a Mac with 8 megabytes of memory. Have you ever had the computer complain that you were out of memory, or maybe an application "unexpectedly quit"? That's because all the mailboxes were full. So you decide you need to buy more memory, and you install 8 more megabytes, for a total of 16 megs of RAM (random access memory). This is fine, but you know what? The computer naturally runs on 24-bit addressing. What? Well, let's pretend there is a bus inside the computer that drives the mail carriers around to the mailboxes. This bus only has seats for 24 mail carriers (24-bit addressing). With only 24 mail carriers, they can only get to the mailboxes for those first 8 megs of memory. With 32-bit addressing, though, it's like using a bigger bus and putting 32 super-mail-carriers on it. The 32-bit addressing lets the Mac "address" (or "get to") the information in more memory than just 8 megabytes.

So, if you install more than 8 megs of memory, you must go to your Memory control panel and turn 32-bit addressing on if you want to *use* that extra memory.

These numbers designate different *chips* (designed by Motorola). These particular chips run the computers, and the higher the number the faster and more powerful the machine. For instance, the **68000** chip is the one in the older Macs, like the 128, the 512, the Plus, and the SE. The Mac II has a **68020** and runs about five times faster than the 68000. The **68030** was a big deal and was installed in the SE/30, IIx, and IIcx. And the **68040** is of course even faster and does more tricks. (Although, the speed of the computer is dependent on more factors than simply the chip.)

68000
68020
68030
68040
etc.

Other important chips have these other numbers and do things like increase the floating point mathematics speed by about 100 times, which speeds up not only math functions but complex graphic rendering as well.

68551
68882
etc.

TYPES OF NEW MAC USERS (4 OF MANY)

THE DETERMINED LEARNER

THE PERPETUAL BEGINNER

THE LUDDITE (ANTI-TECH)

MS. MACRO

13. Opening Files

1. Application; you can tell because of the version number in its name, plus there is no turned-down corner.
2. It will open the application ClarisWorks, giving you a blank, new document or a choice of what kind of blank new document you want.
3. A document—it has a corner turned down.
4. It will open the application it was created in and put itself on the screen.
5. Click on the header, "Kind," in information bar.
6. "New" opens a new, blank page to create a document; "Open" opens a document you previously created and saved.
7. a: The directory, or list, is the box full of file names.
   b: "About angels" or "Birthday plans" can be opened.
   c: Scarlett.
   d: Under Scarlett.

14. Typing

1. Select first, then do it to it.
2. I-beam: ⌶
   Insertion point: |
   Pointer: ➤
3. I-beam.
4. Insertion point.
5. Either the character to its left, or the specifications you choose from the menu while the insertion point is flashing.
6. Usually Command B for Bold, Command I for Italic, Command U for Underline. Some applications also use a Shift key in combination (for instance, Command Shift B to change to Bold).
7. Press Command B (or whatever the command is), type the bold word(s), then press Command B again to toggle off the command.
8. 1) Select the paragraph (press-and-drag over it with the text tool, or try triple-clicking on it). 2) Cut the paragraph (from the Edit menu, choose "Cut," or press Command X). 3) Position the I-beam where you want to insert the paragraph, then click to set the insertion point at that spot. 4) Paste (from the Edit menu, choose "Paste," or press Command V).
9. *Cut:* Command X.
   Copy: Command C.
   Paste: Command V.
10. "Cut" removes the item and places it on the Clipboard. "Clear" removes the item and does *not* place it on the Clipboard—it's just gone.

15. Saving Documents

1. A (There is a border around the directory/list.)
2. B (There is an insertion point flashing in the edit box.)
3. You would select (highlight) the folder named "Books/Library" because it starts with the letter B.
4. It would open the folder "April Newsletter" and the files in that folder would be listed in the directory.
5. Tab.
6. Press on the "SFMUG" label at the top.
7. You would view the files stored on the hard disk named "Macintosh HD."
8. If the File menu has a command to "Revert," use it. Or close the document and when you are asked if you want to save changes, click "No."
9. In RAM, also known as "memory."
10. "Save as..."

16. Printing Documents

1. D/E: Open the document or turn on the printer.
   D/E: Turn on the printer or open the document.
   I: From the File menu, choose "Chooser."
   F: Choose the printer driver.
   B: Choose name of printer.
   J: Click the Setup button, if there is one, choose "Auto Setup," click OK.
   H: Close the Chooser.
   A: Choose "Page Setup," click OK.
   G: From File menu, choose "Print."
   C: Customize specs; click OK.
2. Because the computer is trying to do two things at once.
3. PostScript printer is a computer.
4. 11 x 13 inches.

5. The active window.

6. Click anywhere.

7. The icon in the upper right will flash, and if you pull down the Application menu, PrintMonitor will have a diamond next to its name.

17. Closing and Quitting

1. Close.

2. Quit.

3. Close.

4. Quit.

5. Close.

6. Quit.

7. Application menu, far right of menu bar.

8. Three (ClarisWorks, DeskPaint, and PageMaker).

9. PageMaker—you can tell by the checkmark.

10. Choose ClarisWorks from the Application menu. Press Command Q to quit (or choose "Quit" from the File menu).

18. Ejecting Disks

1. The disk ejects, but leaves a gray icon of itself on the screen.

2. The computer remembers the disk and may ask for it.

3. Drag the disk to the trash can, or select it and press Command Y.

4. Command Y (after you select the icon of the disk).

5. From the Application menu, choose "TeachText" or "SimpleText," or whichever word processing program opened the ReadMe file. Then press

Command Q to quit that program.

6. Either from Save As or Open dialog boxes, or press Command Shift 1.

7. *First:* Insert the disk again. *Then:* If you don't have the disk, drag the icon to the trash. *Then:* Press Command Period (perhaps several times). *Then:* Restart the Mac.

19. Shut Down

1. Three (ClarisWorks, DeskPaint, PageMaker).

2. Choose the application from the menu, then press Command Q. Go back to the Application menu and choose another open application, then press Command Q. Continue until nothing is left in Application menu except Finder.

3. The Mac will ask if you want to save any open documents and quit any open applications before it shuts down the computer.

4. Command Option W.

5. You can Shut Down even if you are not at the Finder.

20. System Folder

1. Nothing.

2. Nothing.

3. No.

4. System and Finder.

5. No.

6. Drop the files onto the closed System Folder.

7. Apple Menu Items, Startup Items, Shut Down Items.

8. Startup Items folder.

9. Apple Menu Items folder.

10. Of course not.

21. Fonts

1. PostScript.

2. Both PostScript and TrueType.

3. No. The screen fonts can hang around anywhere.

4. ATM (Adobe Type Manager).

5. *Linos:* PostScript printer font. *Linoscript 12:* bitmapped screen fonts *Times (italic):* TrueType

6. PostScript.

7. Drop the files (or a folder containing the files) onto the icon of the System Folder.

8. ATM cannot find the printer font for Avant Garde because its printer font lies in the PostScript printer's ROMs.

9/10. *Times, Times (italic), Times (bold),* and *Times (bold italic)* are one group because they are all members of one TrueType font family. *Machine 24* is the screen font for *Machi* printer font, and *Machine Bold 24* is the screen font for *MachiBold* printer font— they are all part of one font family.

22. Desk Accessories

1. Alarm Clock, or Date & Time control panel.

2. CD Player.

3. Key Caps.

4. Scrapbook.

5. Stickies.
6. Chooser.
7. Calculator.
8. Key Caps.
9. Note Pad.
10. Puzzle or Jigsaw Puzzle.

23. Apple Menu

1. Aliases (unless it is a true desk accessory).
2. A substitute for the real thing.
3. Into the Apple Menu Items folder, which is in the System Folder.
4. All of the items listed.
5. Type a blank space before each of their names.
6. Use the "Automated Task" in the Apple menu to "Add Alias to Apple Menu."
7. Go to the Apple Menu Options control panel and type a 0 (zero) for the number of recent servers you want the Mac to remember.
8. No.
9. Its name is in italic.
10. This is up to you!

24. Control Panels

1. Mouse control panel; set to fastest speed.
2. *System 7 or 7.1:* General Controls; your choice or edit one.
   System 7.5: Desktop Patterns; your choice or make a new one.
3. Sharing Setup; set File Sharing to Start.
4. Views; set to 10 to 14 point (use a city-named font).
5. Labels control panel; colors of your choice.

6. Date & Time; set to correct time.
7. General Controls; **un**check "Show Desktop when in background."
8. Monitors control panel; choose 256 or 16.
9. Sound control panel; click "Add" to record.
10. Apple Menu Options; type 0 (zero) in "Servers" edit box.

25. Aliases

1. A representation of the real file. It goes and gets the real file.
2. 2 to 3 K.
3. 1) Select the file.
   2) From the File menu, choose "Make Alias."
   In System 7.5, you can press Command M.
4. Select the original file, from the Apple menu, slide down to "Automated Tasks" and choose "Put Alias in Apple Menu."
5. Nothing.
6. Nothing; they stay, now useless, right where you left them.
7. Click once on the alias. From the File menu, choose "Get Info" (or press Command I). Click the button "Find Original."
8. In the Startup Items folder found in the System folder.
9. The file is actually put into the **real** folder.
10. Nothing. The alias can still find it.

26. Find File

1. No. The more characters you give the computer, however, the faster it can find your file.
2. No. It is "case independent," meaning it does not check for caps and lowercase letters.
3. Yes. A space is a character to the computer.
4. Press the menu bar next to "Find Items" and choose where you want it to look.
5. *System 7 or 7.1:* Click the "More Choices" button. Search for files where "name contains budget." Click the "all at once" button. While those found files are still selected, search for "date created is after 3/1/95."
   System 7.5: Search for "name contains budget." Click the "More Choices" button. Also search for "date created is within 2 weeks of 3/15/95."
6. Choose "Find File" from the Apple menu.
7. Double-click on the tiny icon right there in the Find File box.
8. Command O (select it first!).
9. Drag its icon right out of the Find File box and into the trash can.
10. Click on the header name (Name, Size, Kind, Date) of the view you want them sorted (organized) by. Or choose a view from the View menu while the Find File window is active.

29. Navigating

1. "Navigating" refers to finding your way around dialog boxes such as Open, Save As, import, export, etc.
2. The filing cabinet.
3. The folders on the hard disk or floppy. Or you could say it is another way of looking at the Desktop.
4. The disk name is displayed in the upper right corner of the dialog box.
5. The folder name is displayed right above the list, or directory.
6. On the Desktop, right under the hard disk icon on the right (well, the Mac will put it in the next available spot under the hard disk icon).
7. On the Desktop, open that folder. If you forgot which folder you saved it into, you can always use Find File.
8. This is a "Save as" dialog box. You see the names of all the other files that are also saved into this folder so you don't name the new one the same as an old one—these are just gray because their only purpose is to let you know they are there. The folder names are black because you can open one of them to store a file within.
9. You will select the folder, "Font designs," because the directory is selected—it has a border around it.
10. Tab.

30. Very Important Information

1. Hard disk (storage, like your filing cabinet).
2. RAM (temporary, like your work on your desk).
3. RAM (System is stored on the hard disk, but goes into RAM to run).
4. Hard disk (System is stored on the hard disk, but goes into RAM to run).
5. RAM (memory is full and the computer can't work on that file anymore).
6. Hard disk (no more room left on your hard disk).
7. Hard disk (permanent, that is, until your hard disk dies).
8. Hard disk (document is permanently stored onto hard disk when you save).
9. RAM (document is stored in RAM until you save it to the disk).
10. RAM (analogy to your office—where you work and where the computer works).
11. RAM (which applications are still open in memory).
12. RAM (how much memory is allocated to the application).
13. Hard disk (how much storage space it takes up on your disk).
14. Both (using hard disk as memory).

31. Visual Clues

1. Four (Font, Size, Underline, Color).
2. Into the Size edit box.
3. Three (Size, Position by, Spacing by).

4. None to eight (checkboxes indicate you can choose any, all, or none of them).
5. One (you can only choose one radio button).
6. Three (OK, Cancel, Apply).
7. It would activate the OK button, as indicated by the dark border around it.
8. Yes, you can move it. You can tell by the lines in the title bar.
9. Command Period activates the Cancel button.
10. Ryan, as indicated by the border around the name.

34. The Performa

1. Single-click on *buttons*. What you see on the Launcher are buttons that go and get the real thing.
2. Double-click on *icons* for documents and applications.
3. Click in its close box, the tiny box in the upper left corner of the Launcher.
4. *System 7 or 7.1:* Remove the *alias* from the Startup Items folder in the System Folder.
   System 7.5: In the General Controls panel, *uncheck* "Show Launcher at startup."
5. *System 7 or 7.1:* Change name of Documents folder.
   System 7.5: In the General Controls panel, choose "Last folder used in the application" instead of "Documents folders."
6. In the General Controls panel, check "Show Desktop when in background" so you *can* click to the Finder.

INDEX

Typeface examples

Avant Garde	Doch Bep, flink sexy qua vorm, zwijgt.
Bookman	Doch Bep, flink sexy qua vorm, zwijgt.
Courier	Doch Bep, flink sexy qua vorm, zwijgt.
Helvetica	Doch Bep, flink sexy qua vorm, zwijgt.
New Century Schoolbook	Doch Bep, flink sexy qua vorm, zwijgt.
Palatino	Doch Bep, flink sexy qua vorm, zwijgt.
Symbol	Δοχη Βεπ, φλινκ σεξψ θυα ϖορμ, ζωιφγτ.
Times	Doch Bep, flink sexy qua vorm, zwijgt.
Zapf Chancery	Doch Bep, flink sexy qua vorm, zwijgt.
Zapf Dingbats	❖□✳✻ ✚✳□❧ ✺●✷■✳ ▲✳❘ □◆❀ ❖□□○❧
Garamond	Doch Bep, flink sexy qua vorm, zwijgt.

All of these fonts on this page are PostScript, Type 1.
The fonts displayed above are commonly found on most Macintoshes.
The fonts displayed below are the ones I used in this book.

Veljovic Book	Doch Bep, flink sexy qua vorm, zwijgt.
Eurostile Bold	**Doch Bep, flink sexy qua vorm, zwijgt.**

I have no idea what this sentence means, but I love it.
It is from the Dutch translation of The Little Mac Book.

Special Characters

Here is a handy chart for finding some of the special characters available that will make your work look more professional

"	Option [	Opening double quote
"	Option Shift [	Closing double quote
'	Option]	Opening single quote
'	Option Shift]	Closing single quote; Apostrophe
-	Hyphen	Hyphen
–	Option Hyphen	En dash
—	Option Shift Hyphen	Em dash
…	Option ;	Ellipsis *(this character cannot be separated at the end of a line as the three periods can)*
•	Option 8	Bullet
❏	o	(in font Zapf Dingbats)
■	n	(in font Zapf Dingbats)
☐	n (outlined)	(in font Zapf Dingbats)
©	Option g	Copyright symbol
™	Option 2	Trademark symbol
®	Option r	Registration symbol
°	Option Shift 8	Degree symbol: 105° F
¢	Option $	Cents symbol
/	Option Shift !	Fraction bar *(doesn't allow fractions to break; doesn't descend below the baseline as the slash does)*
fi	Option Shift 5	Ligature for **f** and **i**
fl	Option Shift 6	Ligature for **f** and **l**
£	Option 3	English pound sign
¿	Option Shift ?	Spanish symbol
ç	Option c	Cedilla, lowercase
C	Option Shift c	Cedilla, capital
⌘	Control Q	(only in the Chicago font)

Accent Marks

Refer to page 133 to learn how to type these in; this page is merely a quick reference

´	Option e
`	Option ~
¨	Option u
~	Option n
^	Option i

Text	Zapf	Shift	Option	Shift & Option
1	☞	✂	②	➚
2	☜	✄	♥	➛
3	✓	✀	♦	➜
4	✔	✂	♣	→
5	✕	☎	∞	➔
6	✖	❀	♥	⇒
7	✗	©	❧	▥
8	✘	☛	❦	○
9	✚	✈	➏	➡
0	✐	⌧	➐	➢
-	✎	❁	➐	➑
=	†	☞	≠	±
q	❑	✱	➏	➎
w	◗	✲	Σ	➤
e	❄	✛	♠	♠
r	❐	❅	♣	➤
t	▼	✳		➧
y	❘	✸	⑨	❥
u	◆	✴	①	①
i	❂	☆	①	⇨
o	❏	✵	⑩	④
p	❒	✩	π	∏
[	✻	‘	➒	⑩
]	✼	“	→	→
a	❀	✡	❴	❵
s	▲	✱	⟿	⇨
d	❉	❖	∂	⇝
f	❈	◆	⑤	⟾
g	❋	◇	◆	⟱
h	❊	★	➙	⇨
j	✽	✪	Δ	⇨
k	✾	☆	❯	⇨
l	●	✫	③	⇨
;	✢	✚	⑩	⟲
'	⊛	✂	⑨	③
z	■	✶	Ω	⟿
x	❙	✴	≈	⇛
c	✣	✛	❱	❨
v	❖	✱	√	◇
b	⊛	✢	∫	⟿
n	◼	✯	“	⟿
m	○	✵	μ	➡
,	✌	❖	≤	⟿
.	✑	✝	≥	➹
/	☯	✞	÷	①
`	❀	“	❀	❀
space-bar	✽	’	❶	❶
\			⑧	⑨

In the chart to the left, find the **Zapf Dingbat** you wish to type. Hold down the Shift, the Option, or the Shift-and-Option keys while pressing the text character. The dingbat in the Zapf column needs no extra keys.

Sh]	“		n (outlined)	□
Sh `	”		l (outlined)	○
Sh [	‘		t (outlined)	▽
Sh \	’		s (outlined)	△
			u (outlined)	◇
			Opt 6 (outlined)	♡

Opt Sh /	①		Opt u space	①
Opt 1	②		Opt =	≠
Opt l	③		Opt Sh '	③
Opt v	√		Opt Sh o	④
Opt f	⑤		Opt 5	∞
Opt x	≈		Opt Sh =	±
Opt j	Δ		Opt ,	≤
Opt \	⑧		Opt .	≥
Opt Sh \	⑨		Opt y	⑨
Opt ;	⑩		Opt m	μ

Opt d	∂		Opt Spcbar	❶
Opt w	Σ		Opt ` then Sh a	❷
Opt Sh p	∏		Opt n then Sh a	❸
Opt p	π		Opt n then Sh o	❹
Opt b	∫		Opt Sh q	❺
Opt q	❻		Opt q	❻
Opt 0	❼		Opt -	❼
Opt z	Ω			
Opt '	❾			
Opt o	❿			

ORDER FORM

qty.	title	price	total
	The Little Mac Book,* fourth edition	16.00	
	The Mac is not a typewriter*	9.95	
	The PC is not a typewriter*	9.95	
	Peachpit's PageMaker 5 Companion*	34.95	
	Tabs and Indents on the Macintosh (includes disk)	12.00	
	Jargon, An Informal Dictionary of Computer Terms*	22.00	
	How to Boss Your Fonts Around	12.95	
	The Non-Designer's Design Book*	14.95	
	A Blip in the continuum, a celebration of fringe typography (includes disk of weird fonts)	22.95	
	Beyond the Mac is not a typewriter	16.95	

All Peachpit Press books have an unconditional money-back guarantee. If you don't like a book for any reason, just send it back and we will cheerfully refund your money.

		Subtotal	
		8.25% Tax (CA only)	

Shipping Charges:	UPS Ground	UPS Blue	Canada	Overseas	Shipping	
First Book:	$4	$8	$6	$14		
Each Additional:	$1	$2	$4	$14	**TOTAL ($U.S.)**	

UPS Ground orders arrive within ten days on the West Coast and within three weeks on the East Coast. UPS Blue orders arrive within two working days anywhere in the US, provided we receive a fax or phone call by 11 A.M. Pacific Time.

*indicates award-winning book

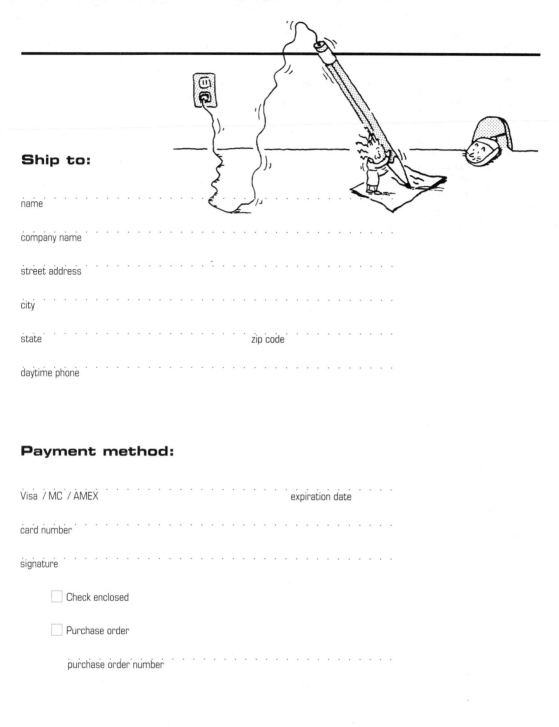

Ship to:

name ....

company name ....

street address ....

city ....

state .... zip code ....

daytime phone ....

Payment method:

Visa / MC / AMEX .... expiration date ....

card number ....

signature ....

☐ Check enclosed

☐ Purchase order

purchase order number ....

Mail your order: Peachpit Press, 2414 Sixth Street, Berkeley, CA 94710 (mail both pages!)

Phone your order: 800-283-9444 or 510-548-4393

Fax your order: 510-548-5991 (don't forget to fax both pages!)

Just in case you wanna know

I live on 2.5 acres of high desert just south of Santa Fe, New Mexico, with my three kids and various animals. I helped start and continue to help run the Santa Fe Mac User Group. I have columns in several magazines and a bunch of other books relating to the Mac and design and typography. I run around the country teaching and doing workshops, and I hang around online. I quite enjoy my life. But then, my sister says I can have fun in a paper bag.

And about that illustrator

Freelance illustrator John Grimes draws cartoons and conclusions in his studio overlooking Ocean Beach in San Francisco. His whimsy is found in these other Peachpit publications: *The Little Online Book, Little PC Book, Little Quicken Book, Little Internet Book, Jargon, Little Windows '95* cover, *Macintosh Bible* series covers and CD-ROM, and Peachpit's World Wide Web site. *Reality Check,* a collection of topical "GRIMES" cartoons, was published by Ten Speed Press.

Colophon

I created this book entirely within PageMaker 5—the writing, editing, page layout, table of contents, and indexing. PageMaker's table of contents and indexing features are incredible. I now work on a Power Mac 8100/100 with a 20-inch multisync color monitor. I used Capture to create the screen shots and cleaned them up when necessary in DeskPaint. I always use Suitcase to manage my fonts. I proofed pages on a LaserWriter Select 360.

The main fonts I used are ITC Veljovic from Adobe, Eurostile Bold from Linotype-Hell, and Comic Strip from Swifte International.

The beautiful cover design (which I love even though it is a man and I am not) is by Ted Mader and Associates.

Final output was on a Linotronic 330 at Indian Rock Imagesetting in Berkeley, California.

Photo-illustration by John Tollett, based on original photo by Alan Bartl.